The Houghton Mifflin
Brief
Accounting
Dictionary

As part of Houghton Mifflin's ongoing commitment to the environment, this text has been printed on recycled paper.

The Houghton Mifflin
Brief Accounting Dictionary

Houghton Mifflin Company
Boston • New York

Director of ESL Programs: Susan Maguire
Senior Associate Editor: Kathy Sands Boehmer
Editorial Associate: Kevin M. Evans
Development Editor: Angela Castro
Lexical Reviewers: Julia Penelope, Linda Butler
Accuracy Reviewer: Gail A. Mestas
Pronunciation Reviewer: Rima McKinzey
Project Editor: Tracy Patruno
Director of Manufacturing: Michael O'Dea
Associate Marketing Manager: Tina Crowley Desprez

Cover design: Rebecca Fagan
Cover image: EyeWire

www.hmco.com/college

Copyright © 2000 by Houghton Mifflin Company. All rights reserved.

No part of this work may be reproduced or transmitted in any form
or by any means, electronic or mechanical, including photocopying
and recording, or by any information storage or retrieval system
without the prior written permission of Houghton Mifflin Company
unless such copying is expressly permitted by federal copyright law.
Address inquiries to College Permissions, Houghton Mifflin
Company, 222 Berkeley Street, Boston, MA 02116-3764.

Printed in the U.S.A.

Library of Congress Catalog Card Number: 98-72041

ISBN: 0-395-93706-X

123456789-CS-03 02 01 00 99

Contents

Preface	vii
Introduction	ix
Elements of the Dictionary	xi
Pronunciation Key	xii
Dictionary	1–125
Accounting Abbreviations	126

Preface

The Houghton Mifflin Brief Accounting Dictionary is the first accounting dictionary published by an American publisher. Business and accounting students in the United States and around the world have told us that they need help understanding the terms used in the field of accounting. We have listened to your concerns and have published a Dictionary that gives you comprehensible definitions for the words, phrases, abbreviations, and acronyms that you find in accounting work whether in the classroom or on the job. *The Houghton Mifflin Brief Accounting Dictionary* was written to address the needs of native and non-native speakers alike.

I would like to thank Bonnie Binkert, the Editor-in-Chief for Business, and Margaret Monahan, Associate Sponsoring Editor, for working with us on this project. I am also grateful to Angela Castro, Julia Penelope, and Rima McKinzey for their expert work in the writing and development of this Dictionary. Lastly, a debt of gratitude goes to Kevin Evans, Charline Lake, and Tracy Patruno for their good work in turning this manuscript into a Dictionary.

The Houghton Mifflin Brief Accounting Dictionary joins the family of fine Dictionaries that the College Division is publishing, namely *The American Heritage® ESL Dictionary* and *The American Heritage® Idioms Dictionary for ESL Students*. If you like this Dictionary, visit the Houghton Mifflin Web site at www.hmco.com for information on more great dictionary products.

Susan Maguire

Introduction

The Houghton Mifflin Brief Accounting Dictionary is designed specifically for students who are enrolled in introductory college accounting courses.

The words and phrases that are included in the *Brief Accounting Dictionary* were compiled from the glossaries and distilled from the chapters and chapter reviews in Houghton Mifflin's broad range of introductory college accounting textbooks by the teams of Needles, Anderson, and Caldwell, and McQuaig and Bille.

Following the approach in Houghton Mifflin's college accounting textbooks, the words and terms in the *Brief Accounting Dictionary* have been selected not only for their relevance to accounting students but also to business students in general.

Because of the nature of specialized language used in specific fields of study such as accounting, maintaining the integrity of the original definition is important. A definition that is overly simplified might not be precise enough when used in an actual accounting classroom. Therefore, the definitions that appear in the *Brief Accounting Dictionary* have been revised to make them more readily comprehensible for students whose first language is not English, but the integrity of the definitions themselves remains intact.

The *Brief Accounting Dictionary* connects the specialized language of accounting to everyday English. The Dictionary includes many definitions that have a broader business sense as well.

The Dictionary also includes many separate entries for words that appear as part of specialized accounting terms. These separate entries enable students to analyze and understand the words that comprise many of the more complex terms. The Dictionary lists **parts of speech** and shows **inflected forms** of verbs and irregular plurals as well as **related word forms.**

The **pronunciation** for each entry, whether a word or a phrase, appears in parentheses immediately following the entry. A full pronunciation key appears on pages xii–xiii. Another key, which compares the pronunciation system used in the *Brief Accounting Dictionary* with the International Phonetic Alphabet (IPA), appears on the inside front cover.

The **definitions** in the Dictionary draw from the most up-to-date sources, cover a range of topics including international business, provide illustrative examples and explanations, and refer users to alternate and related terms.

The Dictionary includes entries for key **abbreviations** in the field of accounting. A complete list of these abbreviations and what they represent appears at the end of the Dictionary.

Elements of the Dictionary

- entry word
- sense number
- definition
- inflected forms
- abbreviation entry
- cross-reference
- pronunciation
- run-on entry
- example
- part-of-speech label
- usage label

deposit (dĭ pŏz′ĭt) *tr.v.* To put (money) in a bank or other financial account: *I deposited my paycheck this morning.* —*n. Abbr.* **dep. 1.** Something, such as money, put in a place for safekeeping: *The bank deposit won't be credited until tomorrow.* **2.a.** A partial payment of a cost or debt: *make a deposit on a house.* **b.** An amount of money given to sbdy. as assurance on sthg.: *a security deposit for the apartment.*

depreciate (dĭ prē′shē āt′) *tr. & intr.v.* **depreciated, depreciating, depreciates.** To go down in or lessen the value or price of (sthg.): *A new car begins to depreciate as soon as you drive it off the lot. I plan to depreciate my computer over the next five years.*

dept. *Abbr.* An abbreviation of department.

detailed income statement (dĭ tāld′ ĭn′kəm stāt′mənt) *n.* A complete and explicit statement of an economic entity's financial activities and holdings. See also **condensed financial statement, multistep form, single-step form.**

dilute (dī lōōt′ *or* dĭ lōōt′) *tr.v.* **diluted, diluting, dilutes. 1.** To weaken the force, intensity, purity, or condition of (sthg.): *Those bonds may dilute profits.* **2.** To make (a substance) thinner by adding a liquid to it: *We can dilute the paint by adding turpentine.* —**dilution** *n.*

direct expense (dĭ rĕkt′ ĭk spĕns′) *n.* An operating (or overhead) expense that can be assigned to a specific department and is under the control of the department head. *The usual way to identify a direct expense is: If the department did not exist, the expense would not exist.* See also **indirect expense.**

direct labor costs (dĭ rĕkt′ lā′bər kôsts′) *pl.n.* The labor cost is for specific work that can be easily and economically traced to an end product.

direct material (dĭ rĕkt′ mə tîr′ē əl) *n. (usually plural).* A material that will become part of a finished product and can be easily and economically traced to specific product units, for example, sthg. used to manufacture an automobile or a washing machine.

xi

Pronunciation Key

A list of the pronunciation symbols used in this Dictionary is given opposite in the column headed **Symbol.** The column headed **Example** contains words that show how the symbols are pronounced. The letters that correspond in sound to the symbols are shown in boldface.

The symbol (ə) is called *schwa*. It is used to represent a reduced vowel, a vowel that receives the weakest level of stress within a word. The schwa sound varies, sometimes according to the vowel it is representing and often according to the sounds around it.

> **a•bun•dant** (ə **bŭn′**dənt)
> **mo•ment** (**mō′**mənt)
> **civ•il** (**sĭv′**əl)
> **pro•pose** (prə **pōz′**)
> **grate•ful** (**grāt′**fəl)

Note that the consonants *l* and *n* in English can be complete syllables by themselves. Some examples of words in which syllabic *l* and *n* occur are **needle** (**nēd′**l), **rattle** (**răt′**l), **sudden** (**sŭd′**n), and **rotten** (**rŏt′**n).

Stress

Stress, the relative emphasis on each syllable in a word or phrase, is marked in three different ways. A syllable with no marking has the weakest stress. The syllable with the strongest stress (primary stress) is marked with a bold mark (**′**). The syllable that receives the primary stress is also set in boldface type. Syllables with intermediate stress are marked with a lighter mark (′).

Symbol	Example
ă	cat
ā	pay
âr	care
ä	father
b	bib
ch	church
d	dead, filled
ĕ	get
ē	be, see
f	fife, phase, cough
g	gag
h	hat
hw	when
ĭ	sit
ī	nice, by
îr	dear, deer, pier, here
j	judge
k	kick, cat, unique
l	lid, needle
m	mum
n	no, sudden
ng	thing
ŏ	got
ō	go
ô	caught, saw, for
oi	noise, boy
oŏ	took

Symbol	Example
oō	boot
ou	out
p	pop
r	roar
s	sauce
sh	ship, dish
t	tight, stopped
th	thin
th	this
ŭ	cut
ûr	urge, term, firm, word, heard
v	valve
w	with
y	yes
z	zebra, xylophone
zh	vision, pleasure, garage
ə	about, item, legible, gallop, circus
ər	butter

Foreign Symbols

Symbol	Example
œ	*French* feu
ü	*French* tu
KH	*French* loch
N	*French* bon

Aa

ABA *Abbr.* An abbreviation of American Bankers Association.

ABA number (ā′bē ā′ nŭm′bər) *n.* A number that the American Bankers Association assigns to each bank, for example, 88-2258/1113. The first part of the **numerator** (88), the upper or left-hand number, represents the city or state in which the bank is located; the second part of the upper number (2258) shows the bank on which the check is drawn. The lower or right-hand number, the **denominator** (1113), indicates the Federal Reserve District in which the check is cleared and the routing number used by the Federal Reserve Bank.

ABC *Abbr.* An abbreviation of activity-based costing.

absorb (əb sôrb′ *or* əb zôrb′) *tr.v.* **1.** To take over (the cost of sthg.): *The company has absorbed the cost of retraining workers.* **2.** To take in or soak up (a liquid): *A sponge will absorb the spilled coffee.* **3.** To occupy (the complete attention or interest of sbdy.): *I was so absorbed in my work that I didn't hear you knock.* **4.** To take in (sthg.) and make it a part of another thing: *This conglomerate has absorbed many smaller business entities.* **5.** To receive or withstand (sthg.) without an effect or a reaction: *The car's bumper absorbed the shock of the accident.*

absorption (əb sôrp′shən *or* əb zôrp′shən) *n.* **1.** The act or process of taking over the cost of sthg.: *My client's absorption of incidental costs helped me stay within budget.* **2.** The act or process of taking in or soaking up sthg.: *Living things sustain themselves by absorption of food.* **3.** A state of complete attention or interest: *Your absorption in your studies causes you to miss a lot of fun.*

absorption costing (əb sôrp′shən kôs′tĭng) *n.* An approach to product costing that assigns a representative portion of all types of manufacturing costs—**direct material, direct labor, variable factory overhead,** and **fixed factory overhead**—to individual products: *Absorption costing enables the accountant to assign the cost of something, such as electricity, that is otherwise hard to assign to a particular product.* See also **variable costing**.

a/c *Abbr.* An abbreviation of account.

A/C *Abbr.* An abbreviation of account.

accelerate (ăk sĕl′ə rāt′) *tr. & intr.v.* **accelerated, accelerating, accelerates.** To speed up or cause (sthg.) to go or happen faster: *The car accelerated as it went down the hill. Can you accelerate payment of your bill?*

accelerated (ăk sĕl′ə rā′tĭd) *adj.* Happening at a faster pace or in an earlier period: *Businesses try to depreciate machinery at an accelerated rate.*

Accelerated Cost Recovery System (ăk sĕl′ə rā′tĭd kôst′ rĭ kŭv′ə rē sĭs′təm) *n. Abbr.* **ACRS** A method of depreciating certain kinds of assets for federal income tax purposes that took effect in 1981. It was modified in 1986 to the **Modified Accelerated Cost Recovery System** *Abbr.* **MACRS.**

accelerated depreciation (ăk sĕl′ə rā′tĭd dĭ prē′shē ā′shən) *n.* A way of gradually depreciating tangible assets over time. During the early years of an asset's use, relatively larger amounts of depreciation are recorded, and decreasing amounts are claimed in later years: *Accelerated depreciation allows a company to get back more of an asset's cost early in its useful life.*

accelerated method

accelerated method (ăk sĕl′ə rā′tĭd mĕth′əd) *n.* A method of depreciation that spreads relatively large amounts of the **depreciable cost** of an asset over its early years of use and a reduced amount to its later years: *An accelerated method of depreciation is one way of recognizing that an asset, such as a machine, is most valuable in its early years of use.*

account (ə kount′) *n. Abbr.* **A/C, a/c, acct. 1.** A precise list of financial transactions, the basic storage unit for accounting (or bookkeeping) data, used to accumulate amounts from similar transactions. An accounting system has a separate account for each asset, liability, and component of owner's equity: *The company's liabilities should be entered in a separate account from assets.* **2.** The category to which an account belongs, under the main headings of Assets, Liabilities, and Owner's Equity. **3.** The unique label assigned to these categories, used by accountants to identify the amounts that result from similar financial transactions. **4.** A business arrangement with a bank, store, or company in which money can be kept, exchanged, or owed: *a bank account; a charge account.* **5.** A client or customer of a store or company: *He landed a big corporate account this morning.* See also **general ledger. 6.** A written or spoken description of events: *Your account of the accident wasn't accurate.*

accountant (ə koun′tənt) *n.* **1.** A person licensed by the state in which she or he lives who sets up the system that a company, an organization, or an individual will use to enter and maintain financial records. **2.** A person who audits the financial records of a business or other organization. **3.** A person who keeps the records of a company's or organization's financial records.

account balance (ə kount′ băl′əns) *n.* Another term for **balance.**

account for (ə kount′ fôr) *tr.v.* **1.** To explain or give a reason for sthg.: *The manager was unable to account for the missing inventory.* **2.** To be the reason for sthg.: *Fog closed the airports, which accounted for the late shipment.*

account format (ə kount′ fôr′măt) *n.* The form of the balance sheet in which assets are placed to the left and liabilities and owner's equity are placed to the right. See also **report format.**

accounting (ə koun′tĭng) *n.* **1.** The process of keeping a record of financial transactions and preparing statements that list the assets, liabilities, and owner's equity of a business or other organization: *Where did you learn accounting?* **2.** The system used to measure, process, and provide information to decision makers about the assets, liabilities, and owner's equity of a business or other organization: *management accounting.* **3.** The profession of keeping such accounts and preparing statements of them for a business or other organization: *Why did you decide to major in accounting?*

accounting clerk (ə koun′tĭng klûrk′) *n.* A person who records the routine financial information of a business or an organization, either by hand or electronically. The duties vary, and depend on the size of the organization.

accounting cycle (ə koun′tĭng sī′kəl) *n.* The sequence of steps followed in the accounting process to measure business transactions and transform the measurements into financial statements for a specific period. There are six steps in a typical accounting cycle: (1) analyzing financial transactions; (2) recording entries in the **journal**; (3) posting the entries to the ledger and preparing a **trial balance**; (4) adjusting the accounts

accounts receivable ledger

and preparing an adjusted trial balance; (5) closing the accounts and preparing a **post-closing trial balance;** (6) preparing **financial statements:** *Have all the expenses been recorded for this accounting cycle?*

accounting equation (ə koun′tĭng ĭ kwā′zhən) *n.* An equation that expresses the relationship among assets, liabilities, and owner's equity, Assets = Liabilities + Owner's Equity. Also called **fundamental accounting equation.**

accounting firm (ə koun′tĭng fûrm′) *n.* A business that employs **Certified Public Accountants** to prepare financial information for businesses and organizations.

accounting information (ə koun′tĭng ĭn′fər mā′shən) *n.* The actual numbers used to provide financial information to decision makers. The two most important **qualitative characteristics** of such information are **understandability** and **usefulness.**

accounting period (ə koun′tĭng pĭr′ē əd) *n.* A specific length of time, such as a month, quarter, or year, during which the financial results of business transactions are recorded and measured. See also **interim period.**

accounting period issue (ə koun′tĭng pĭr′ē əd ĭsh′o͞o) *n.* The difficulty of finding the best way to assign revenues and expenses to a short period of time.

accounting rate-of-return method (ə koun′tĭng rāt′ əv rĭ-tûrn′ mĕth′əd) *n.* A way of evaluating **capital investments** that measures the benefit of a potential **capital project.** The potential rate of return is calculated by dividing the project's average **annual after-tax net income** by the average cost of the investment.

accounting system (ə koun′tĭng sĭs′təm) *n.* A way of gathering data, putting it into a useful form, and communicating the results to management, including the analysis and recording of financial transactions, posting entries, adjusting and closing accounts, and preparing statements.

account number (ə kount′ nŭm′bər) *n.* The unique number assigned to an account according to the **chart of accounts.** Each **digit** in the account number indicates classifications of accounts, for example, 1 represents assets.

accounts payable (ə kounts′ pā′ə bəl) *pl.n. Abbr.* **A/P** *(used with a plural verb).* A liability account used for short-term liabilities or charge accounts, usually due within thirty days. Also called **expense, liability.**

accounts payable ledger (ə kounts′ pā′ə bəl lĕj′ər) *n.* A secondary ledger that lists the individual accounts of creditors in alphabetical order.

accounts payable subsidiary ledger (ə kounts′ pā′ə bəl səb-sĭd′ē ĕr′ē lĕj′ər) *n.* A financial record of an individual account payable in which entries can be made daily.

accounts receivable (ə kounts′ rĭ sē′və bəl) *pl.n. Abbr.* **A/R** *(used with a plural verb).* An account that records short-term liquid assets that arise from sales on credit at the wholesale or retail level.

accounts receivable aging method (ə kounts′ rĭ sē′və bəl ā′jĭng mĕth′əd) *n.* A way of estimating how much **uncollectible accounts** of a business will amount to, based on the assumption that a predictable proportion of each dollar of **accounts receivable** still owed will not be collected. Also called **aging of accounts receivable.**

accounts receivable ledger (ə kounts′ rĭ sē′və bəl lĕj′ər) *n.* A secondary ledger that lists the individual accounts of charge customers in alphabetical order.

accounts receivable subsidiary ledger

accounts receivable subsidiary ledger (ə kounts′ rĭ sē′və bəl səb sĭd′ē ĕr′ē lĕj′ər) *n.* A financial record of an individual account receivable, for example, a customer's credit account, in which entries can be made daily.

accounts receivable turnover (ə kounts′ rĭ sē′və bəl tûrn′-ō′vər) *n.* Used to measure a company's ability to collect cash from credit customers. Found by dividing net sales by average net accounts receivable. See also **turnover** (sense 2).

accrual (ə krōō′əl) *n.* The **recognition** of an expense or revenue that has occurred but has not yet been recorded.

accrual accounting (ə krōō′əl ə koun′tĭng) *n.* The attempt to record the financial effects of transactions and other events in the periods in which those transactions or events occur rather than only in the periods in which cash is received or paid by the business, using all the techniques developed by accountants to apply the **matching rule.**

accrual basis (ə krōō′əl bā′sĭs) *n.* Another term for **accrual accounting.**

accrue (ə krōō′) *v.* **accrued, accruing, accrues.** —*intr.* **1.** To come to sbdy. as a gain, an addition, or an increase: *As the interest accrues in our savings account, our savings will increase.* **2.** To increase in size or amount as a result of growth: *Praise continues to accrue to her first novel.* —*tr.* To increase (sthg.) over time: *The money in my savings account accrues interest.*

accrued expense (ə krōōd′ ĭk spĕns′) *n.* An expense that has occurred but is not recognized in the accounts. To record an accrued expense, an expense account is debited and a payable account is credited. Also called **unrecorded expense.**

accrued interest income (ə krōōd′ ĭn′trĭst ĭn′kŭm) *n.* The interest income that is earned but has not yet been received from a note receivable that begins in one fiscal period and matures in the following one, for example, from the date of the note until the last day of the fiscal period.

accrued interest on notes payable (ə krōōd′ ĭn′trĭst ŏn nōts′ pā′ə bəl) *n.* For **notes payable** beginning in one fiscal period and maturing in the following fiscal period, the unpaid interest expense from the date of issue of the note until the last day of the **fiscal period.**

accrued revenue (ə krōōd′ rĕv′ə nōō′) *n.* Revenue for which a service has been performed or goods delivered but for which no entry has been recorded. To record an accrued revenue a receivable account is debited and a revenue account is credited. Also called **unrecorded revenue.**

accrued wage (ə krōōd′ wāj′) *n.* The amount of money owed to employees for the time between the end of the last pay period and the end of the **fiscal period.**

acct. *Abbr.* An abbreviation of account.

accumulated depreciation (ə kyōōm′yə lā′tĭd dĭ prē′shē-ā′shən) *n.* The total depreciation expense of a specific **long-term asset.**

accumulated depreciation account (ə kyōōm′yə lā′tĭd dĭ-prē′shē ā′shən ə kount′) *n.* An account used to record the depreciation expense of a specific long-term asset. The balance appears on the financial statement as a deduction from the related account. See also **contra account.**

acid-test ratio (ăs′ĭd tĕst rā′shō) *n.* The relationship of a company's current assets that can be converted into cash to its current liabilities. It is determined by dividing **quick assets** by current liabilities. Also called **quick ratio.**

adjusted balance

acquire (ə kwīr′) *tr.v.* **1.** To gain possession of (sthg.): *Our company has just acquired another subsidiary.* **2.** To get (sthg.) by one's own efforts: *acquire a second language.*

acquisition (ăk′wĭ zĭsh′ən) *n.* **1.** The act or an instance of gaining possession of sthg.: *The vice president needs to approve the acquisition.* **2.** Something that comes into sbdy.'s possession: *Where should we put the new acquisition?*

acquisition costs (ăk′wĭ zĭsh′ən kôsts′) *pl.n. (used with a plural verb).* The amount it costs for a business to buy property, plant, and equipment, including the expenses of readying the acquisition for use.

ACRS *Abbr.* An abbreviation of Accelerated Cost Recovery System.

activity (ăk tĭv′ĭ tē) *n., pl.* **activities. 1.** An action needed to accomplish the purpose or objective of a function: *accounting activities.* **2.** A specific pursuit in which sbdy. participates: *She enjoys all kinds of sports activities.*

activity-based costing (ăk tĭv′ĭ tē bāst kôs′tĭng) *n. Abbr.* **ABC** A way of assigning cost that identifies all of a company's major operating activities (both production and nonproduction), traces costs to those activities, reduces or eliminates **non-value-adding** activities, and then determines which products use the resources and services supplied by those activities.

activity-based management (ăk tĭv′ĭ tē bāst măn′ĭj mənt) *n.* A way of managing a business that identifies all its major operating activities, determines what resources are used in each activity, identifies what causes use of these resources for each activity, and categorizes the activities as either adding value to a product or being nonvalue-adding. This approach to financial management emphasizes the reduction or elimination of nonvalue-adding activities.

activity level (ăk tĭv′ĭ tē lĕv′əl) *n.* The use of a specific activity to identify and allocate factory overhead costs to the work unit that produces the cost.

actual cost (ăk′chōō əl kôst′) *n.* A cost that has already been incurred and can be shown to be accurate.

add (ăd) *v.* —*tr.* **1.** To join or unite (one thing to another) in order to increase the size, quantity, quality, or scope of sthg.: *They've added a new department to the division.* **2.** To combine (two or more numbers, such as a column of figures), and arrive at their total: *Would you please add our bill?* —*intr.* **1.** To find the sum of two or more numbers: *What figure did you get when you added the day's receipts?* **2.** To build or create sthg. joined or united to a larger physical structure: *We've already added to this factory three times.*

addition (ə dĭsh′ən) *n.* **1.** An enlargement added on to an existing physical asset, such as an addition to a building: *When will the new addition be ready to open?* See also **betterment.** **2.** The process of combining two or more numbers in order to find their sum: *Children learn addition after they learn to count.*

adj. *Abbr.* An abbreviation of adjustment.

adjust (ə jŭst′) *tr.v.* **1.** To change, set, or regulate (sthg.) in order to improve it: *My boss says I need to adjust my attitude.* **2.** To bring the various parts or elements of (sthg.) into a more effective arrangement: *The manager adjusted the production schedule.*

adjusted balance (ə jŭs′tĭd băl′əns) *n.* The amount of money in a bank account and a ledger after they have been reconciled. Also called **true balance.**

5

adjusted gross income

adjusted gross income (ə jŭs′tĭd grōs ĭn′kŭm) *n.* Income less certain adjustments to income, such as deductions for amounts invested in IRAs and alimony paid. Calculated on the U.S. individual income tax return.

adjusted trial balance (ə jŭs′tĭd trī′əl băl′əns) *n.* A **trial balance** prepared after all adjusting entries have been recorded and posted to the accounts. If the adjusting entries have been posted to the accounts correctly, the adjusted trial balance should have equal credit and debit totals.

adjusting entry (ə jŭs′tĭng ĕn′trē) *n., pl.* **adjusting entries.** An entry made to record the financial effects of transactions and events that cover more than one accounting period. Adjusting entries have at least one balance sheet (or permanent) account entry and at least one income statement (or temporary) account entry, and are used to record **accruals** and **deferrals.**

adjustment (ə jŭst′mənt) *n. Abbr.* **adj. 1.** Internal financial transactions that bring ledger accounts up to date, as a planned part of the accounting procedure. They are first recorded in the Adjustments columns of the work sheet. **2.** A change, alteration, or correction of sthg. in order to make it accurate: *an adjustment to property taxes.*

advance (ăd văns′) *n.* **1.** A portion of a worker's salary paid by a company before it is normally due: *My manager has offered to give me an advance so I can make a down payment on a car.* **2.** An amount of money that sbdy., such as a lawyer, has paid out on behalf of a client and that must be repaid: *Her attorney has been quite generous with advances to cover the cost of filing various documents.*

after closing account (ăf′tər klō′zĭng ə kount′) *n.* The stage after all accounts have been closed, when temporary accounts have zero balances, and the ledger is set up for the next accounting period.

age (āj) *tr.v.* **aged, aging, ages. 1.** To analyze the accounts receivable by classifying the remaining balance of each charge customer's account according to the length of time it has been outstanding (sense 2). Multiply the total accounts receivable for each time period by a percentage regarded as uncollectible and add the totals to determine the balance of **Allowance for Uncollectible Accounts. 2.** To cause (sbdy./sthg.) to grow old: *Their hard life has aged many workers.*

aging of accounts receivable (ā′jĭng ŭv ə kounts′ rĭ sē′və-bəl) *n.* The process of listing each customer who owes money according to the due date of the account. Also called **accounts receivable aging method.**

AICPA *Abbr.* An abbreviation of American Institute of Certified Public Accountants.

allocate (ăl′ə kāt′) *tr.v.* **allocated, allocating, allocates.** To set aside (a part or portion) for a specific reason: *allocate funds for new construction.* —**allocation** *n.*

allow (ə lou′) *v.* —*intr.* To consider sthg. that might happen: *Restaurants must allow for the cost of food that spoils.* —*tr.* **1.** To let (sbdy.) do sthg: *How many sick days does your employer allow you to take?* **2.** To provide (sthg.) in case of sthg. unexpected or potential: *Allow an extra five minutes for your trip to the airport.*

allowance (ə lou′əns) *n.* **1.** An amount that is given or granted: *a generous trade-in allowance.* **2.** Something, such as money, that is given at regular times for a specific purpose: *That company provides generous travel allowances.*

6

appoint

3. Something, such as money, set aside to cover an event that might or might not happen: *a breakage allowance.*

Allowance for Doubtful Accounts account (ə lou′əns fôr dout′fəl ə kounts′ ə kount′) *n.* Another term for **Allowance for Uncollectible Accounts account.**

Allowance for Uncollectible Accounts account (ə lou′əns fôr ŭn′kə lĕk′tə bəl ə kounts′ ə kount′) *n.* A contra-asset account used to reduce accounts receivable to the amount that is expected to be collected in cash. Also called **Allowance for Bad Debts account, Allowance for Doubtful Accounts account,** or **Reserve for Bad Debts account.**

allowance method (ə lou′əns mĕth′əd) *n.* A way of accounting for uncollectible accounts by writing off an estimated amount in the period in which the related sales take place.

American Bankers Association (ə mĕr′ĭ kən băng′kərz ə sō′sē ā′shən) *n. Abbr.* **ABA** The professional organization for people in the banking industry.

American Institute of Certified Public Accountants (ə mĕr′ĭ kən ĭn′stĭ tōōt əv sûr′tə fīd pŭb′lĭk ə koun′tənts) *n. Abbr.* **AICPA** The professional association of certified public accountants.

AMHS *Abbr.* An abbreviation of automated material handling system.

amortization (ăm′ər tĭ zā′shən *or* ə môr′tĭ zā′shən) *n.* The periodic distribution of the cost of an intangible asset, such as goodwill, patents, or trademarks, over the accounting periods it benefits.

amortize (ăm′ər tīz′ *or* ə môr′tīz) *tr.v.* **amortized, amortizing, amortizes. 1.** To pay off (a debt, such as a mortgage) by making small regular payments or by making payments into a special account called a **sinking fund:** *How soon can we amortize that loan?* **2.** To write off (an expense, such as goodwill) by spreading the expense over a specific period: *We should amortize the new patent over the next seventeen years.*

annual after-tax net income (ăn′yōō əl ăf′tər tăks nĕt′ ĭn′kŭm) *n.* The net income of a business after local, state, and federal taxes have been paid.

annual percentage rate (ăn′yōō əl pər sĕn′tĭj rāt′) *n. Abbr.* **APR** Another term for **effective interest rate.**

annual report (ăn′yōō əl rĭ pôrt′) *n.* A once-a-year publication in which the general-purpose external financial statements of a business are presented to stockholders and other interested individuals.

annuity (ə nōō′ĭ tē) *n., pl.* **annuities. 1.** The payment of income or an allowance of equal cash flows to sbdy. on an annual basis: *She's retired and lives off an annuity.* **2.** The right of sbdy. to receive such income or the responsibility of paying it: *Annuity is one way of providing for retirement income.* **3.** A financial investment that pays sbdy. a fixed income for a lifetime or a specific number of years. Compound interest is included in the payments: *Our firm has invested in several annuities.* Also called **ordinary annuity** or **annuity due.**

annuity due (ə nōō′ĭ tē dōō′) *n.* A series of equal cash flows for specified time periods, with the first payment being made immediately.

A/P *Abbr.* An abbreviation of accounts payable.

appoint (ə point′) *tr.v.* To select or designate (sbdy.) for an office, a position, or a duty: *The CEO will appoint a new manager when the present one retires.*

7

appointment

appointment (ə point′mənt) *n. Abbr.* **appt.** **1.** An arrangement for a meeting at a specific time or place: *I have an appointment with a new client in an hour.* **2.a.** The act of selecting sbdy. for a specific office or position: *The appointment of a new chief financial officer is an important decision.* **b.** The office or position to which sbdy. has been appointed: *The firm's president made several important appointments last week.*

appointment record (ə point′mənt rĕk′ərd) *n.* A record of appointments kept by sbdy. in a **professional enterprise**, such as medicine or law.

apportion (ə pôr′shən) *tr.v.* To divide and allot (sthg.) according to a specific plan: *We apportion our investments on the basis of current strengths in the stock market.*

apportionment (ə pôr′shən mənt) *n.* **1.** The act of dividing and allotting sthg. according to a plan: *determine the correct apportionment of company assets.* **2.** The condition of having been divided on the basis of a plan: *We can review our apportionment of the firm's assets at this time next year.*

apportionment of expenses (ə pôr′shən mənt əv ĭk spĕn′sĭz) *n.* The distribution of operating expenses to the appropriate operating department.

appraisal (ə prā′zəl) *n.* **1.** The act or an instance of judging sbdy./sthg., especially in order to estimate quality or value: *Your appraisal of her job performance isn't fair.* **2.** An expert or official estimate of the value of sthg., especially for purposes of taxation: *The appraisal indicated that the property was worth more than we thought.*

appraisal cost (ə prā′zəl kôst′) *n.* The cost of an activity that measures, judges, or audits products, processes, or services to ensure that they conform to quality standards and performance requirements. Also called **cost of conformance**.

appraise (ə prāz′) *tr.v.* **appraised, appraising, appraises.** **1.** To estimate (the value of sthg.), especially in an official capacity: *appraise a diamond.* **2.** To estimate (the quality, size, or other features of sthg.); judge: *An engineer appraised the quality of our safety precautions.*

appropriation of retained earnings (ə prō′prē ā′shən əv rĭ tānd′ ûr′nĭngz) *n.* A portion of **retained earnings** set aside for a specific purpose; the amount appropriated may not be used for cash or stock dividends.

appt. *Abbr.* An abbreviation of appointment.

APR *Abbr.* An abbreviation of annual percentage rate.

A/R *Abbr.* An abbreviation of accounts receivable.

articles of incorporation (är′tĭ kəlz ŭv ĭn kôr′pə rā′shən) *pl.n. (used with a plural verb).* A contract between the state and the incorporators giving a corporation the authority to do business. Also called **charter, corporate charter.**

asset (ăs′ĕt) *n.* An economic resource, such as cash, property, or other item of value owned by a business, that is expected to benefit future operations.

asset account (ăs′ĕt ə kount′) *n.* An account in which the economic resources owned by a corporation are entered, for example, cash and money owed to the company by customers (called **accounts receivable**) and tangible assets such as inventory, buildings, property, and equipment.

asset turnover (ăs′ĕt tûrn′ō′vər) *n.* A way of measuring how profitably and efficiently assets are being used to produce sales. This is determined by dividing net sales by average total assets.

ATM *Abbr.* An abbreviation of automated teller machine.

8

automated material handling system

ATM card (ā′tē ĕm′ kärd) *n.* A coded plastic card that sbdy. with an account at a bank can use at an automated teller machine to perform financial activities using a personal identification number (**PIN**). Also called **debit card**.

at retail (ăt rē′tāl) *adv.* At the marked selling price: *We should use at retail to estimate the value of our inventory.*

audit (ô′dĭt) *n.* An independent examination of a company's financial statement by a professional accountant or group to determine that the statement has been presented fairly and prepared using generally accepted principles. —*tr.v.* **1.** To examine (financial records or accounts) to verify their accuracy: *The IRS rarely audits big corporations.* **2.** To attend (a college class) without getting credit for it: *She audited Accounting last semester.*

audit committee (ô′dĭt kə mĭt′ē) *n.* A committee of the board of directors of a corporation, usually made up of outside directors, whose responsibility is to ensure that the board is objective in its evaluation of management's performance.

audit trail (ô′dĭt trāl′) *n.* The documents created by key people that show written proof of approval as each person routinely reviews and verifies transactions as they are processed from the beginning to final posting.

authority (ə thôr′ĭ tē *or* ə thŏr′ĭ tē) *n.*, *pl.* **authorities**. **1.** Power assigned to sbdy. else; authorization: *Do you have the authority to make such a change?* **2.** A person or a group that has the legal right to do or oversee sthg.: *She's applying to the proper authorities for a license.*

authorization (ô′thər ĭ zā′shən) *n.* **1.** An act of granting authority or power to sbdy./sthg.: *We have all the required authorizations to proceed.* **2.** Something, such as a written contract, that allows sbdy. to do sthg.: *Do you have authorization for this plan?*

authorize (ô′thə rīz′) *tr.v.* **authorized, authorizing, authorizes**. **1.** To give permission for or approve (sthg.): *The board of directors will probably authorize the purchase of additional property.* **2.** To grant (sbdy.) the power or authority to do sthg.: *My client authorized me to act on her behalf.*

authorized (ô′thə rīzd′) *adj.* Having been officially approved: *My lawyer is my authorized representative.*

authorized capital (ô′thə rīzd′ kăp′ĭ tl) *n.* The maximum number of shares defined by a firm's corporate charter that can be issued for each class of stock (**common** and **preferred**). Another term for **authorized shares** and **authorized stock**.

authorized shares (ô′thə rīzd′ shârz′) *n.* See **authorized capital**.

authorized stock (ô′thə rīzd′ stŏk′) *n.* See **authorized capital**.

auto. *Abbr.* An abbreviation of automatic.

automate (ô′tə māt′) *v.* **automated, automating, automates**. —*tr.* **1.** To begin (to do sthg.) using automatic machinery or processes: *automate an assembly line.* —*intr.* **2.** To use automated machinery or processes: *We're going to automate in order to cut costs.*

automated (ô′tə mā′tĭd) *adj.* Functioning or using machinery, such as robots, to do sthg.: *an automated factory.*

automated material handling system (ô′tə mā′tĭd mə tîr′-ē əl hănd′lĭng sĭs′təm) *n. Abbr.* **AMHS** A necessary part of a computer-integrated manufacturing system in which the handling of raw materials and partially completed product is automatic. This provides continuous movement of the product through an entirely automated process.

automated teller machine

automated teller machine (ô′tə mā′tĭd tĕl′ər mə shēn′) *n. Abbr.* **ATM** A machine that bank customers can use to perform financial transactions, such as deposits, withdrawals, and transfers, using a coded plastic card.

automatic (ô′tə măt′ĭk) *adj. Abbr.* **auto.** Performing an action or a process without being controlled by a human: *an automatic washing machine.*

automation (ô′tə mā′shən) *n.* The control or operation of a process, machine, or system by electronic devices, such as robots or computers: *Automation of a factory process can be expensive in the short term.*

av. *Abbr.* An abbreviation of average.

available-for-sale securities (ə vā′lə bəl fər sāl′ sĭ kyōōr′ĭ-tēz) *pl.n. (used with a plural verb).* Debt and equity securities that do not meet the criteria for either **held-to-maturity** or **trading securities.**

ave. *Abbr.* An abbreviation of average.

average (ăv′ər ĭj *or* ăv′rĭj) *n. Abbr.* **av., ave., avg.** A number that is derived from and considered to be typical or representative of the set of numbers it belongs to: *We should figure out the average for hours lost to illness this year.* —*adj.* Relating to or being a number that represents the set of numbers that it belongs to: *What was your average test score in that class?* —*v.* **averaged, averaging, averages.** —*tr.* **1.** To calculate the average of (a set of numbers): *You can average the number of miles you travel daily.* **2.** To have or reach (a number) as an average: *averaging five miles a day jogging.* —*intr.* To be or amount to an average: *His expenses average about $10 a day.* —*adj.* **1.** Calculated or identified as an average: *The average cost of the trip was $50 a day.* **2.a.** Typical, usual, or ordinary: *an average day at the office.* **b.** Not special; undistinguished; mediocre: *an average student.*

average costing approach (ăv′ər ĭj kôs′tĭng ə prōch′) *n.* A method of costing products, in which the cost to produce each unit is computed with the assumption that the items in beginning **work-in-process inventory** were started and completed during the current period.

average-cost method (ăv′ər ĭj kôst′ mĕth′əd) *n.* A way of arriving at the cost of inventory that computes the average cost of all goods available for sale during a fixed period in order to determine the value of inventory. See also **weighted-average-cost-method** and **moving average method.**

average cost of capital (ăv′ər ĭj kôst′ əv kăp′ĭ tl) *n.* A minimum desired rate of return on invested capital. It is computed by taking an average of the cost of debt, the cost of preferred stock, the cost of equity capital, and the cost of retained earnings.

average days′ inventory on hand (ăv′ər ĭj dāz ĭn′vən tôr′ē ŏn hănd′) *n.* The average number of days required to sell the current inventory of products available for sale. It is found by dividing the number of days in a year by **inventory turnover.**

average days′ sales uncollected (ăv′ər ĭj dāz sālz′ ŭn′-kə lĕk′tĭd) *pl.n. (used with a plural verb).* A ratio that shows the average length of time it takes a company to receive payment for credit sales. It is found by dividing 365 days by **receivable turnover.**

avg. *Abbr.* An abbreviation of average.

avoidable cost

avoid (ə void′) *tr.v.* **1.** To stay away from (sbdy/sthg.): *I try to avoid him at the office.* **2.** To keep (sthg.) from happening: *I'd like to avoid paying a lot of interest on my loan.*

avoidable (ə voi′də bəl) *adj.* Able to be avoided; unnecessary: *That was an avoidable accident.*

avoidable cost (ə voi′də bəl kôst′) *n.* An expense that will be eliminated if a particular product, service, or operating segment is discontinued.

Bb

b. *Abbr.* An abbreviation of base.

B. *Abbr.* An abbreviation of base.

bad debt (băd' dĕt') *n.* An amount of money owed to a person or a company, such as a bank or department store, that is unlikely to be paid: *That fellow left a trail of bad debts behind him.* Another term for **uncollectible accounts.**

balance (băl'əns) *n.* **1.** A state of equality in amount, status, value, or price: *We need to have a balance between work and play.* **2.** The equality of totals on the debit and credit sides of a ledger. **3.** The difference in dollars between the working totals of the debit and credit columns of an account. Also called **account balance.** —*v.* **balanced, balancing, balances.** —*tr.* **1.a.** To figure (the difference) between the debit and credit sides of an account: *balance the books.* **b.** To equalize (the sums of) the debits and credits of an account. **c.** To settle (sthg.), for example, an account, by paying the amount owed. **2.** To bring (sthg.) into a state of equality: *Somehow we have to balance the good of the company with the good of our workers.* —*intr.* To come into a state of equality: *Our books balanced this year.*

balance sheet (băl'əns shēt') *n.* The financial statement that lists the balances of the asset, liability, and owner's equity accounts of a business or other economic unit on a given date, such as June 30 or December 31. Also called **statement of financial position.**

bank (băngk) *n.* **1.** A business that handles financial transactions, such as receiving and holding money or making loans: *The bank approved our loan.* **2.** The offices or a building in which such a business is located: *Turn left at the bank.* —*v.* —*tr.* To deposit (money) in a bank: *She'll bank the money this afternoon.* —*intr.* **1.** To do business with a bank or have an account in one: *I bank at the local branch.* **2.** To run a bank: *He banked before becoming an artist.*

bank account (băngk' ə kount') *n.* A financial account at a banking institution, such as a savings or checking account, into which individuals, groups, and businesses can deposit or withdraw money.

bank balance (băngk' băl'əns) *n.* The amount of money remaining in a checking account after all deposits and withdrawals have been entered.

bank charge (băngk' chärj') *n.* An amount of money that a bank charges for its services, such as maintaining a checking account.

bank charge card (băngk' chärj' kärd') *n.* A bank credit card, like the credit cards used by millions of private citizens. The cardholder pays what she or he owes directly to the issuing bank. The business firm deposits the credit card receipts. The amount of the deposit equals the total of the receipts, less a discount deducted by the bank.

bank deposit (băngk' dĭ pŏz'ĭt) *n.* Cash or checks put in a checking or savings account at a bank: *Have you made the bank deposit?*

banking (băng'kĭng) *n.* **1.** The occupation or business of handling other people's money: *She was in banking for more than 30 years.* **2.** The performance of a financial transaction, such as a deposit or withdrawal: *I can do my banking tomorrow.*

benefit

bank loan (băngk′ lōn′) *n.* A loan made by a bank to a customer for a specified interest charge.

bank memoranda (băngk′ měm′ə răn′də) *pl.n.* Notices about credits and debits to an account that a bank sends to its customers.

bank reconciliation (băngk′ rěk′ən sĭl′ē ā′shən) *n.* A process by which an accountant determines whether and why there is a difference between the balance shown on the bank statement and the balance of the Cash account in the firm's general ledger. The object is to determine the adjusted (or true) balance of the Cash account.

bankrupt (băngk′rŭpt′) *adj.* **1.** Financially ruined: *That company was declared bankrupt last week.* **2.** Lacking valuable qualities or resources: *a morally bankrupt nation.* —*tr.v.* To cause (sbdy./sthg.) to become bankrupt: *His expensive tastes bankrupted him.*

bankruptcy (băngk′rəpt sē *or* băngk′rəp sē) *n., pl.* **bankruptcies.** A condition governed by federal law in which a debtor is excused from paying certain debts.

bank statement (băngk′ stāt′mənt) *n.* A periodic statement, usually monthly, that a bank sends to the holder of a checking account showing the balance in the account at the beginning of the month, the deposits, the checks paid, other debits and credits during the month, and the balance at the end of the month.

bar code (bär′ kōd′) *n.* Another term for **universal product code.**

bar-code (bär′kod′) *tr.v.* **bar-coded, bar-coding, bar-codes.** To print a universal product code on an item for sale: *Many products are now bar-coded.*

bargain (bär′gən) *n.* **1.** An arrangement, often one that involves payment or trade: *Do we have a bargain?* **2.** Something for sale or bought at a low price: *That property is a bargain!* —*intr.v.* To discuss or argue about the terms of an agreement, especially a price to be paid: *We can't afford to bargain at this late date.*

base (bās) *n. Abbr.* **b., B. 1.** A starting point: *base year.* **2.** The lowest or bottom part of sthg.: *the base of a lamp; the base of a mountain.* **3.** A supporting part or layer; a foundation: *built on a solid base of granite.* **4.** A basic or underlying element: *the base of the matter.*

base year (bās′ yîr′) *n.* In financial analysis, the first year to be considered in any set of data.

batch (băch) *n.* **1.** A set of data or jobs to be processed in a single program run: *How long will it take to run this batch?* **2.** A group of people or things: *a batch of applicants; a batch of problems.*

batch processing (băch′ prŏs′ĕs ĭng) *n.* The form of data processing in which processing tasks are scheduled sequentially.

bd. *Abbr.* An abbreviation of bond.

BE *Abbr.* An abbreviation of break-even.

B/E *Abbr.* An abbreviation of bill of exchange or bills of exchange.

beginning inventory (bĭ gĭn′ĭng ĭn′vən tôr′ē) *n.* The quantity of merchandise available for sale at the beginning of an accounting period.

benchmark (běnch′märk′) *n.* A reference point for making decisions.

benefit (běn′ə fĭt) *n.* **1.** *(usually plural)* A payment made according to a wage agreement, an insurance policy, or a

betterment

public assistance program: *This job has great benefits.* **2.** An advantage: *Having her on the team is a great benefit for us.* —*v.* —*tr.* To be useful or helpful to (sbdy./sthg.): *His sloppiness benefits our competitors.* —*intr.* To get or receive an advantage from sthg.: *Who benefits from these taxes?*

betterment (bĕt′ər mənt) *n.* An improvement that does not add to the physical layout of a plant asset, for example, installing a new air-conditioning system.

bill of exchange (bĭl′ əv ĭks chānj′) *n.*, *pl.* **bills of exchange.** *Abbr.* **B/E** A written document, such as a **check**, ordering that a specific amount of money be paid to a specified individual.

bind (bīnd) *v.* **bound** (bound), **binding, binds.** —*tr.v.* **1.** To place (sbdy.) under legal obligation: *This contract binds us to complete the project by September.* **2.** To fasten or secure (sthg.).: *Bind the pages with a paper clip.*

binding contract (bīn′dĭng kŏn′trăkt) *n.* A contract intended to impose a firm commitment: *Let's be sure we have a binding contract.*

blank (blăngk) *adj.* **1.** Lacking writing, images, or marks: *a blank sheet of paper.* **2.** Containing no information: *a blank tape.* —*n.* **1.** An empty space on a document to be filled in with an answer or a comment: *Write your name in the blank.* **2.** A document or form that contains empty spaces to be filled in: *Find the entry blanks.*

blank endorsement (blăngk′ ĕn dôrs′mənt) *n.* An endorsement in which the holder (**payee**) of a check simply signs her or his name on the back of the check. There are no restrictions attached.

bond (bŏnd) *n. Abbr.* **bd. 1.** A security, usually long-term, that represents money borrowed from investors by a corporation guaranteeing that the money borrowed will be repaid in full, plus interest, by a specific date. **2.** An insurance contract that guarantees payment when an employee causes financial loss. Also called **bonding.** —*tr.v.* **1.** To mortgage or guarantee payment. **2.** To place (an employee) under bond or guarantee for potential financial loss: *If we hire you, you will have to be bonded.* **3.** To supply a guarantee for (sbdy./sthg.). —**bondable** *adj.*

bond certificate (bŏnd′ sər tĭf′ĭ kĭt) *n.* Evidence of a company's debt to sbdy. who has loaned it money.

bond discount (bŏnd′ dĭs′kount) *n.* The amount below par value that a bond sells for. See also **discount** (sense 1).

bondholder (bŏnd′hōl′dər) *n.* A person who owns a bond certificate issued by a government or corporation.

bond indenture (bŏnd′ ĭn dĕn′chər) *n.* An additional agreement to a **bond issue** that defines the rights, privileges, and limitations of bondholders.

bonding (bŏn′dĭng) *n.* **1.** The process of carefully checking an employee's background and insuring the company against theft by that person. **2.** The process of insuring the offering party of a contract against losses suffered due to a contractor's poor performance or lack of performance.

bond issue (bŏnd′ ĭsh′o͞o) *n.* The total value of bonds issued by a government or corporation at the same time. Issuing bonds is one way a business can borrow money to finance, for example, expansion or improvements.

bonus (bō′nəs) *n.*, *pl.* **bonuses. 1.** An amount that accrues to the original partners when a new partner pays more to the partnership than the interest received or that accrues to the new

budget

partner when the amount paid to the partnership is less than the interest received. **2.** An extra sum of money, in addition to regular salary or wages, that an employer pays to its workers: *an incentive bonus.* **3.** Financial assistance provided by a government to a business. **4.** A stock premium given by a corporation to another party, for example, sbdy. who has purchased its securities. **5.** A sum of money, more than the royalties or interest, that a corporation pays for a granted privilege or loan.

bookkeeper (book′kē′pər) *n.* A person whose job is to record the financial transactions of a business or an organization systematically on a daily basis.

bookkeeping (book′kē′pĭng) *n.* The process of recording financial transactions and keeping financial records.

book of original entry (book′ ŭv ə rĭj′ə nəl ĕn′trē) *n.* Another term for **general journal.**

book value (book′ văl′yoō) *n.* **1.** The total assets of a company less its liabilities; stockholders' equity. Also called **carrying value. 2.** The undepreciated portion of the original cost of a long-term asset. **3.** The monetary value of sthg., such as a used vehicle, not necessarily the same amount that the object might bring on the open market: *I traded in my old car at book value.*

book value of accounts receivable (book′ văl′yoō əv ə-kounts′ rĭ sē′və bəl) *n.* Another term for **net realizable value of accounts receivable.**

bottom line (bŏt′əm līn′) *n.* **1.** The line in a financial statement that shows net income or loss: *His only concern is the bottom line.* **2.** The final result of a series of events: *The bottom line here is that the business will lose money this year.* **3.** The most important point of sthg.: *The bottom line is our ability to pay our taxes.* —**bottom-line** *adj.*

branch accounting (brănch′ ə koun′tĭng) *n.* Maintaining the financial accounts of a firm or an organization's branch operations.

branch operation (brănch′ ŏp′ə rā′shən) *n.* A business location maintained somewhere other than the central office of a company.

brand (brănd) *n.* **1.** A trademark or recognizable name that identifies a product or a company. **2.** A product line that carries such an identifying name: *a popular brand of shampoo.*

brand name (brănd′ nām′) *n.* A registered name that can be used only by its owner to identify a product or service: *The marketing people came up with a good brand name for our new soap.* See also **trademark.** —**brand-name** *adj.*

break even (brāk′ ē′vən) *intr.v.* **broke even, broken even, breaking even, breaks even.** To earn an amount of money equal to the sum invested, especially in a business: *We broke even our first year in business.*

break-even point (brāk′ē′vən point′) *n.* The point at which total revenues equal total costs: *They hope to reach their break-even point within two years.*

break-even units (brāk′ē′vən yoō′nĭts) *pl.n.* The number of units of a product that must be sold before a company makes enough money to pay for direct and indirect costs of making the product. This is found by dividing fixed costs by **contribution margin** per unit.

budget (bŭj′ĭt) *n.* **1.** A detailed planning document that summarizes estimated or intended expenses during a specific time, including proposals for how these expenses are to be met. **2.** A systematic plan that describes how a specific resource, such as

budgetary control

money, should be spent during a given time. **3.** The total sum of money put aside or designated for a particular purpose or period of time. —*v.* —*tr.* To plan in advance which expenses will be paid and how they will be paid: *I budgeted $500 for the trip.* —*intr.* To make or use a budget: *He's just no good at budgeting.*

budgetary control (bŭj′ĭ těr′ē kən trōl′) *n.* The process of developing plans for a company's expected operations and controlling operations in order to carry out those plans.

budgeted cost (bŭj′ĭ tĭd kôst′) *n.* An expected or projected cost for a future period.

bus. *Abbr.* An abbreviation for business.

business (bĭz′nĭs) *n., pl.* **businesses.** *Abbr.* **bus. 1.** *(usually singular).* **a.** The work, trade, or profession in which sbdy. makes a living: *the restaurant business.* **b.** A specific trade, profession, or occupation: *How did you get into the business of consulting?* **2.** Commercial, industrial, or professional organizations, spoken of collectively: *Business has a responsibility to society and to the environment.* **3.** An economic unit that tries to sell goods and services to customers at prices that will provide an adequate return to its owners: *They want to find a business with high profits and low operating costs.* Also called **business entity, company, economic entity, firm. 4.** The volume or amount of sales during a specific period of time: *Business is usually good during Christmas.* **5.a.** A person's rightful concern or proper interest: *The primary business of most people is survival.* **b.** A matter, concern, or issue that affects sbdy. personally: *How I spend my time is none of your business.* **6.** Serious work: *He wasted no time and got right down to business.* **7.** A matter, concern, or issue: *What's this business about wanting a raise?*

business entity (bĭz′nĭs ěn′tĭ tē) *n., pl.* **entities.** A business enterprise, separate and distinct from the people who supply the assets it uses. Property acquired by a business is an asset of the business. The owner is separate from the business and in fact has claims on it and a responsibility for its debts. Also called **business, company, economic entity, firm.**

business transaction (bĭz′nĭs trăn săk′shən) *n.* An economic event that affects the financial position of a business entity.

Cc

CAD (kăd) *Abbr.* An abbreviation of computer-aided design.

CAD/CAM (kăd'kăm') *Abbr.* An abbreviation of computer-aided design/computer-aided manufacturing.

calendar quarter (kăl'ən dər kwôr'tər) *n.* Another term for **quarter**.

calendar year (kăl'ən dər yîr') *n.* A twelve-month period beginning on January 1 and ending on December 31 of the same year. See also **fiscal year**.

call (kôl) *tr.v.* **1.a.** To demand payment for (sthg.): *The bank called our loan.* **b.** To require that (a bond) be presented for payment before its maturity date. **2.** To say (sthg.) in a loud voice; announce: *Did you call my name?* **3.** To label or identify (sbdy.) in a specific way: *What did you call me?* **4.** To consider (sbdy./sthg.) as being of a particular kind: *You call this doing a good job?* —*n.* **1.a.** A demand for payment of a debt. **b.** A demand for bondholders to submit their bonds for payment before the date of maturity. **2.** A loud cry: *I thought I heard a call for help.* **3.** A telephone communication: *Do I have any calls?* **4.** Demand: *There's little call these days for typewriters.* **5.** A short visit to sbdy.: *I have several calls to make in your neighborhood.*

callable (kô'lə bəl) *adj.* Able to be redeemed or retired by sbdy.

callable bond (kô'lə bəl bŏnd') *n.* A bond that a corporation can buy back and retire at a **call price** before maturity.

callable preferred stock (kô'lə bəl prĭ fûrd' stŏk') *n.* **Preferred stock** that can be redeemed or retired at a price stated at the option of the corporation.

call price (kôl' prīs') *n.* A specified price, usually above face value, at which a corporation may, at its option, buy back and retire bonds before maturity.

cancel (kăn'səl) *tr.v.* **canceled, canceling, cancels** or **cancelled, cancelling, cancels. 1.** To mark or perforate (sthg.), such as a stamp or check) to indicate that it cannot be used again: *Your canceled check is proof of payment.* **2.** To erase or remove (sthg.) by drawing lines through it. **3.** To make (sthg.) invalid: *I canceled my doctor's appointment.*

canceled or **cancelled** (kăn'səld) *adj.* **1.** Called off: *The canceled meeting has been rescheduled for Monday.* **2.** Marked in order to prevent sthg. from being used again.

canceled check (kăn'səld chĕk') *n.* A check issued by the depositor that has been paid (**cleared**) by the bank and listed on the depositor's bank statement. It is called a canceled check because it is canceled by a stamp or perforation, indicating that it has been paid: *The customer brought in a canceled check as proof that he had paid his bill.*

capacity (kə păs'ĭ tē) *n., pl.* **capacities. 1.** The ability to hold, receive, or contain: *a theater with little seating capacity.* **2.** The maximum amount that can be held or contained: *boxes filled to capacity.* **3.** The maximum amount that can be produced: *a factory working at full capacity.*

capital (kăp'ĭ tl) *n.* **1.a.** Money or property held by a person, business, or partnership. **b.** Such assets used or available for use to produce more wealth. **2.** The remaining assets of a business after all liabilities have been paid. **3.** Another term for **capital stock**. **4.** The owner's investment, or equity, in an

17

capital account

enterprise. **5.** The long-term components of a company or an organization used to raise money.

capital account (kăp′ĭ tl ə kount′) *n.* **1.** An account stating the amount of funds and assets invested in a business by the owners or stockholders, including retained earnings. **2.** A statement of the net worth of a business at a specific time.

capital assets (kăp′ĭ tl ăs′ĕts) *n.* Long-term assets that are expected to increase a company's or organization's profitability. See also **capital facility**.

capital budgeting (kăp′ĭ tl bŭj′ĭ tĭng) *n.* The process of making decisions about **capital expenditures**. It includes identifying the need for a capital facility, analyzing different courses of action to meet that need, preparing the reports for management, choosing the best alternative, and rationing funds among competing capital projects. Also called **capital expenditure decision analysis**.

capital expenditure (kăp′ĭ tl ĭk spĕn′də chər) *n.* An expense for the purchase or expansion of a long-term asset, recorded in the **asset accounts**.

capital expenditure decision (kăp′ĭ tl ĭk spĕn′də chər dĭ sĭzh′ən) *n.* A management decision about when and how much money to spend on **capital facilities**.

capital expenditure decision analysis (kăp′ĭ tl ĭk spĕn′də chər dĭ sĭzh′ən ə năl′ĭ sĭs) *n.* Another term for **capital budgeting**.

capital expenditures budget (kăp′ĭ tl ĭk spĕn′də chərz bŭj′ĭt) *n.* A detailed plan outlining the amount and timing of expected capital expenses for a specific future period that must be integrated into the **master budget**.

capital facility (kăp′ĭ tl fə sĭl′ĭ tē) *n., pl.* **facilities.** A long-term tangible asset, such as a building, plant, or equipment.

capital investment (kăp′ĭ tl ĭn vĕst′mənt) *n.* An amount of a company's or an organization's capital invested in capital assets, such as a new plant, in order to increase profitability.

capitalization (kăp′ĭ tl ĭ zā′shən) *n.* **1.a.** The practice or act of using as capital. **b.** The amount that results from capitalizing. **2.a.** The amounts and kinds of long-term financing used by a company, including common stock, preferred stock, retained earnings, and long-term debt. **b.** The total **par value** or stated value of no-par capital stock issues.

capitalize (kăp′ĭ tl īz′) *v.* **capitalized, capitalizing, capitalizes.** —*tr.* **1.** To use or convert (sthg.) into capital. **2.** To supply (sbdy./sthg.) with financial support or investment funds: *capitalize a new business venture.* **3.** To authorize (the issue) of a specific amount of capital stock of a company: *capitalize a corporation.* **4.** To convert (debt) into capital stock or shares. **5.** To calculate the current value of (future earnings or cash flows). **6.** To include (costs) in business accounts as assets instead of as expenses. —*intr.* To turn sthg. to one's own advantage: *Can we capitalize on their mistake?*

capital lease (kăp′ĭ tl lēs′) *n.* A long-term lease in which the risk of ownership lies with the lessee and whose terms resemble a purchase or sale on installment.

capital project (kăp′ĭ tl prŏj′ĕkt) *n.* A specific project in which a business or an organization invests its money in a capital asset, such as a new headquarters.

capital projects funds (kăp′ĭ tl prŏj′ĕkts fŭndz′) *pl.n.* An account in which the funds for capital construction projects, such as a bridge or school, are recorded and maintained.

capital stock (kăp'ĭ tl stŏk') *n.* Shares of ownership in a corporation, usually divided into **common stock** and **preferred stock**.

capital structure (kăp'ĭ tl strŭk'chər) *n.* The sources and amounts of capital used for financing the capital assets of a business. Sources of capital include long-term debt, preferred and common stock, and retained earnings. See also **simple capital structure** and **complex capital structure**.

carrying value (kăr'ē ĭng văl'yōō) *n.* The portion of the cost of an asset that has not yet expired. Also called **book value**, **declining balance**.

cash (kăsh) *n.* **1.** In the statement of cash flows, both cash and cash equivalents, including coins and currency on hand, checks and money orders from customers, and deposits in bank checking accounts. **2.** Money in the form of coins and bills: *I use cash to buy groceries.* Also called **currency**. **2.** Payment for a product or service made with money or a check: *She paid cash for her new car.* —*tr.v.* To exchange (sthg.) for money or convert to money: *cash a check*.

cash basis of accounting (kăsh bā'sĭs əv ə koun'tĭng) *n.* A way of accounting for revenues and expenses on a cash received and cash paid basis.

cash budget (kăsh' bŭj'ĭt) *n.* A projection of the cash receipts and cash payments for a future period. Also called **cash flow forecast**.

cash disbursements journal (kăsh' dĭs bŭrs'mənts jûr'nəl) *n.* Another term for **cash payments journal**.

cash discount (kăsh' dĭs'kount) *n.* The amount a customer can deduct for paying a bill within a specified period of time. This is used to encourage prompt payment. Not all sellers offer cash discounts.

cash dividend (kăsh' dĭv'ĭ dĕnd') *n.* Distribution of a corporation's earnings to stockholders in the form of cash.

cash equivalent (kăsh' ĭ kwĭv'ə lənt) *n.* Short-term, highly liquid investments, including money market accounts, commercial paper, and U.S. Treasury bills, that will revert to cash in less than 90 days from the date of purchase.

cash flow or **cash flows** (kăsh' flō' *or* kăsh' flōz') *n.* The receipts and payments of cash into and out of a business.

cash flow forecast (kăsh' flō' fôr'kăst') *n.* Another term for **cash budget**.

cash flow management (kăsh' flō' măn'ĭj mənt) *n.* The planning of a company's receipts and payments of cash.

cash flows to assets (kăsh' flōz' tōō ăs'ĕts) *pl.n.* Used to measure the ability of assets to generate operating cash flows. This is found by dividing the net cash flows from operating activities by the average total assets.

cash flows to sales (kăsh' flōz' tōō sālz') *pl.n.* A way of measuring the ability of sales to generate operating cash flows. This is found by dividing the net cash flows from operating activities by the net sales.

cash flow to yield (kăsh' flō' tōō yēld') *n.* The ratio of net cash flows from operating activities to net income.

cash flow yield (kăsh' flō' yēld') *n.* Used to measure the ability of a company to generate operating cash flows in relation to **net income**. This is found by dividing net cash flows from operating activities by net income.

cash fund (kăsh' fŭnd') *n.* Separately held amounts of cash set aside for specific purposes.

cash-generating efficiency

cash-generating efficiency (kăsh′ jĕn′ə rā′tĭng ĭ fĭsh′ən sē) *n.* The ability of a company to generate cash from its current or continuing operations.

cash payments journal (kăsh′ pā′mənts jûr′nəl) *n.* A multicolumn journal used to record sums of cash paid out for expenses. Also called **cash disbursements journal**. Another term for **check register**.

cash receipts journal (kăsh′ rĭ sēts′ jûr′nəl) *n.* A multicolumn journal used to record business transactions involving the receipt of cash from other individuals or businesses.

category buster (kăt′ĭ gôr′ē bŭs′tər) *n.* A retail business that maintains high inventories for sale at low prices. This is achieved by minimizing handling and overhead costs.

certified management accountant (sûr′tə fīd′ măn′ĭj mənt ə koun′tənt) *n. Abbr.* **CMA** A management accountant who has met the stringent licensing requirements set by each state.

certified public accountant (sûr′tə fīd′ pŭb′lĭk ə koun′tənt) *n. Abbr.* **CPA** A public accountant who has met the stringent licensing requirements set by each state.

c.h. *Abbr.* An abbreviation of clearing-house.

C.H. *Abbr.* An abbreviation of clearing-house.

change (chānj) *v.* **changed, changing, changes.** *Abbr.* **chg.** —*tr.* **1.** To give or receive (lower denominations) for a sum of money paid or exchanged in larger denominations: *Can you change a twenty?* **2.** To exchange (one nation's currency) for that of another: *We can change our francs to dollars at the airport.* **3.** To give a new form or shape to (sthg.): *change a company's image.* **4.** To give and receive (one thing for another): *The two vice presidents have changed offices.* —*intr.* **1.** To become different: *This company has changed since I started working here.* **2.** To exchange sthg.: *This seat is too small; do you mind if we change?* **3.** To put on different clothing: *I need to change into my work clothes.* **4.** To transfer from one vehicle to another: *It's not a direct flight; we change in Chicago.* —*n.* **1.** Money of smaller denominations given or received in exchange for money of larger denominations: *The cashier gave me change for a twenty.* **2.** The amount of money returned when the sum paid is more than what is owed: *We can't leave until we get our change.* **3.** Coins, such as pennies, nickels, dimes, and quarters: *I think I have enough change for the parking meter.* Also called **cash**. **4.** The act or result of making sthg. different: *You've made a lot of changes since I last saw your office.* **5.** Something different from one's usual routine: *Let's have a picnic for a change.* **6.** Different clothing: *I brought several changes with me because the weather is unpredictable at this time of the year.*

change fund (chānj′ fŭnd′) *n.* A cash fund used by a firm to make change for customers who pay cash for goods or services.

charge (chärj) *v.* **charged, charging, charges.** —*tr.* **1.a.** To ask (an amount) as a price: *They're charging $25 apiece for the concert tickets.* **b.** To require payment from (sbdy.): *The store will charge you for delivery.* **2.** To buy (sthg.) on credit and pay for it later: *I charged my new coat because I was short on cash.* **3.** To attack (sbdy./sthg.) forcefully: *The lion charged the hunters.* **4.** To accuse or blame (sbdy.): *He's been charged with reckless driving.* **5.** To fill or saturate (sthg.); permeate: *The air was charged with excitement.* **6.** To fill (sthg.) with an amount of electricity: *We need to charge the battery again.* —*intr.* **1.** To ask or require payment: *They didn't charge for*

20

classified financial statement

fixing my flat tire. **2.** To rush quickly, as if with great force: *The president charged through his announcement to the press.* —*n. Abbr.* **chg. 1.** An amount of money asked as payment: *There'll be no charge for the service.* **2.** Care; supervision: *My supervisor has charge of petty cash.* **3.** A person or sthg. for which one is responsible: *The baby sitter put her charges to bed.* **4.** A formal accusation, especially in a legal case: *The judge read the charges to the defendant.* **5.** A rushing, forceful attack: *the charge of an angry elephant.* **6.** A feeling of excitement; thrill: *You'll get a charge out of this story.*

charge account (chärj′ ə kount′) *n.* A credit arrangement that allows a customer to buy goods or services without paying the total cost of the purchase at the time, and to pay the amount in regular, periodic installments.

charge off (chärj′ ôf′) *tr.v.* **charged off, charging off, charges off.** Another term for **write off.**

charge-off method (chärj′ ôf′ mĕth′əd) *n.* Another term for **direct charge-off method.**

charter (chär′tər) *n.* **1.** The written right, issued by a state government, for a corporation to exist. **2.** The approved **articles of incorporation.**

chart of accounts (chärt′ əv ə kounts′) *n.* **1.** An accounting system that assigns a unique number to each account to make it easier to find the account in the ledger. **2.** The list of account numbers and titles.

check (chĕk) *n.* A written order to a bank authorizing it to pay the amount specified to the **payee** named on the order from funds on deposit.

check authorization (chĕk′ ô′thər ĭ zā′shən) *n.* A form prepared by an accounting department after it has compared the **receiving report** for goods or services received with the **purchase order** and the **invoice.**

check register (chĕk′ rĕj′ĭ stər) *n.* **1.** A journal in which checks are listed as they are written. A check register replaces a **cash payments journal. 2.** In a voucher system, the journal in which voucher checks are listed as they are written.

check writer (chĕk′ rī′tər) *n.* A machine used to imprint the amount in figures and words on a check.

chg. *Abbr.* An abbreviation of: **1.** Change. **2.** Charge.

CIM *Abbr.* An abbreviation of computer-integrated manufacturing (system).

cl. *Abbr.* An abbreviation of: **1.** Classification. **2.** Clearance.

claim (klām) *tr.v.* To assert one's right to (sthg.): *Have you claimed your luggage?* —*n.* **1.** A demand for sthg. as a right: *Your claim for payment has been rejected.* **2.** *(usually plural).* The value of a right or claim to or a financial interest in an asset or group of assets. Also called **equity.**

class. *Abbr.* An abbreviation of: **1.** Classification. **2.** Classified.

classification (klăs′ə fĭ kā′shən) *n. Abbr.* **cl., class. 1.** The act or result of organizing things: *Classification of the accounts took two weeks.* **2.** A category or class used to organize items: *Our classifications seem pretty narrow.* **3.** The process of assigning transactions to the appropriate accounts.

classified (klăs′ə fīd′) *adj. Abbr.* **class.** Arranged by classes or categories.

classified financial statement (klăs′ə fīd′ fə năn′shəl stăt′-mənt) *n.* A general-purpose external financial statement divided into useful subcategories.

21

classify (klăs'ə fī') *tr.v.* **classified, classifying, classifies.** To arrange or organize (sthg.) on the basis of its class or category: *Classify the assets as short-term or long-term before entering them in the ledger.*

clear (klîr) *v.* — *tr.* **1.** To earn (a specific amount) as net profit: *The company cleared $2 million last quarter.* **2.** To pass (a bill of exchange, such as a check) through a clearing-house: *The bank cleared your check yesterday.* **3.** To settle (a debt): *I cleared my account with the dentist.* **4.** To remove (sbdy./sthg.): *The workers are going to clear the road of fallen trees.* — *intr.* **1.** To exchange checks and bills or settle accounts through a clearing-house. **2.** To pass through the banking system and be deducted or added to the relevant accounts: *Has my checked cleared yet?*

clearance (klîr'əns) *n. Abbr.* **cl. 1.** The passage of checks and other **bills of exchange** through a **clearing-house. 2.** The sale of old merchandise at a reduced price: *Stores often have a clearance after the holidays.* **3.** The distance or amount of space provided for a moving object, such as a truck, to pass or clear an obstruction: *How much clearance does this truck require?* **4.** Permission for an airplane, ship, or other vehicle to proceed: *We have clearance for landing.* **5.** Official certification of trustworthiness or fitness: *You need clearance to enter this facility.*

clearing account (klîr'ĭng ə kount') *n.* Another term for **income summary.**

clearing-house or **clearinghouse** (klîr'ĭng hous') *n. Abbr.* **c.h., C.H.** A central office where banks exchange checks and drafts and settle accounts.

clearing the accounts (klîr'ĭng *thē* ə kounts') *n.* Another term for **closing entries.**

close (klōz) *v.* **closed, closing, closes.** — *tr.* To clear the balances of temporary accounts in order to be ready for the next accounting period. This is done by transferring their balances to a clearing account: *Some companies close their books in mid-December.* — *tr.* & *intr.* **1.** To move or cause to move (a door, for example) so that an opening is blocked: *The door closed suddenly. Please close the door after you.* **2.** To end or bring to an end: *close a bank account. The store closed after 110 years in business.*

closely held corporation (klōs'lē hĕld' kôr'pə rā'shən) *n.* A corporation that has a relatively small group of owners.

closing (klō'zĭng) *n.* **1.** The process of clearing the balances of temporary accounts from one accounting period. This is done in order to prepare for the next accounting period. **2.** Completion of the final details or negotiations for a business transaction: *When is the closing on the purchase of the house?* **3.** An end of sthg., such as a theater production or business: *The store's closing was a surprise.*

closing entry (klō'zĭng ĕn'trē) *n., pl.* **entries.** A journal entry made at the end of an accounting period in order to prepare for the next accounting period by clearing the balances of temporary accounts and summarizing the period's revenues and expenses. Also called **clearing the accounts.**

CMA *Abbr.* An abbreviation of certified management accountant.

CMS *Abbr.* An abbreviation of cost management system.

CNC *Abbr.* An abbreviation of computer numerically controlled.

company

CNC machine (sē′ĕn sē′ mə shēn′) *n.* A computer numerically controlled machine that is self-contained and usually operates independently. A robot is a CNC machine.

co *Abbr.* An abbreviation of company.

co. *Abbr.* An abbreviation of company.

Co. *Abbr.* An abbreviation of Company.

collect (kə lĕkt′) *v.* —*tr.* **1.** To bring (sthg.) together into a group: *collect the applications.* **2.** To take in or obtain (money) for sthg.: *collect a license fee.* —*intr.* **1.** To come together; gather: *A crowd collected at the accident scene.* **2.** To build up; accumulate: *Dust has collected on the shelves.* **3.** To take in payments or donations: *I'm collecting for the office football pool.*

collection (kə lĕk′shən) *n.* **1. collections.** Payments collected by the bank, such as checks drawn on foreign banks, and added to the customer's bank account, in the form of a credit memorandum. **2.** *(usually singular).* The attempt to make sbdy. pay a bad debt after milder efforts have failed: *These accounts must be sent out for collection.* **3.** The act or process of gathering into a group: *garbage collection.* **4.** A group of things brought or kept together: *a stamp collection.* **5.** A pile of sthg.; an accumulation: *a collection of dust on the shelves.* **6.** Money received as a payment or donation: *take up a collection for flowers.*

commercial (kə mûr′shəl) *adj.* **1.** Relating to commerce: *a commercial loan.* **2.** Done or created to make a profit: *commercial photography.* **3.** Paid for by an advertiser or supported by advertising: *commercial radio.* —*n.* An advertisement that is heard on radio or seen on television: *30-second commercials.*

commercial paper (kə mûr′shəl pā′pər) *n.* A way of borrowing money by using unsecured short-term loans sold directly to the public, usually through professionally managed investment firms.

commission (kə mĭsh′ən) *n.* **1.** The act of granting authority to sbdy. to perform a certain job or duty: *The manager gave her the commission of checking the payroll.* **2.** A specified percentage of sthg., such as sales made, paid to an employee in addition to regular wages or salary: *Salespeople receive a standard commission of 10 percent on every car they sell.*

common (kŏm′ən) *adj.* **1.** Belonging to, done by, shared by, or relating to most of the members of a community: *common interests; common fears.* **2.** Found often and in many places; usual: *Fast-food restaurants are common along interstate highways.* —**commonly** *adv.*

common cost (kŏm′ən kôst′) *n.* Another term for **joint cost.**

common-size statement (kŏm′ən sīz′ stāt′mənt) *n.* A financial statement in which the elements of a total amount are stated as percentages of that total.

common stock (kŏm′ən stŏk′) *n.* Shares of stock that carry voting rights but that rank below preferred stock in dividends and distribution of assets.

common stock equivalents (kŏm′ən stŏk′ ĭ kwĭv′ə lənts) *pl.n.* **Convertible stocks** or **bonds** that appeal to investors because they are more likely to pay regular dividends and can be exchanged for shares of a company's common stock. Their convertibility is important in determining their original issue price.

comp. *Abbr.* An abbreviation of compound.

company (kŭm′pə nē) *n., pl.* **companies.** *Abbr.* **co, co., Co.** Another term for **business** (sense 3), **business entity, corporation, economic entity, firm.**

23

comparability (kŏm′pər ə bĭl′ĭ tē) *n.* **1.** The accounting convention of presenting information in a way that enables decision makers to recognize similarities, differences, and trends over different time periods or between different companies. **2.** The quality of allowing one thing to be compared to another: *The comparability of the two plans isn't clear.*

comparative financial statements (kəm păr′ə tĭv fə năn′shəl stāt′mənts) *pl.n.* Financial statements in which data for two or more years are presented in adjacent columns.

compatibility (kəm păt′ə bĭl′ĭ tē) *n.* The quality of being able to live, work, or operate without disagreements or problems.

compatibility principle (kəm păt′ə bĭl′ĭ tē prĭn′sə pəl) *n.* The accounting principle that holds that the design of a system must be in harmony with the organizational and human factors of the business.

compatible (kəm păt′ə bəl) *adj.* **1.** Able to exist or perform in harmony: *compatible coworkers.* **2.** Able to integrate and operate with other elements of a system in an orderly and efficient way, without requiring change or modification: *compatible computers.*

compensate (kŏm′pən săt′) *tr.v.* compensated, compensating, compensates. **1.** To pay (sbdy.) or make payment for sthg.: *Have you been compensated for your time?* **2.** To offset or counterbalance (sthg.): *The long vacations compensate for the long hours.* —**compensation** *n.*

compensating balance (kŏm′pən sā′tĭng băl′əns) *n.* A minimum amount that a bank requires a company to keep in its account as part of a credit-granting arrangement.

complex (kəm plĕks′ *or* kŏm′plĕks′) *adj.* **1.** Made up of parts that are interconnected: *a complex sound system.* **2.** Involved or intricate in structure; complicated: *a complex issue.*

complex capital structure (kəm plĕks′ kăp′ĭ tl strŭk′chər) *n.* A capital structure of a company that includes preferred stocks, bonds, or other stock equivalents that can be converted into common stock. See also **simple capital structure.**

compound (kəm pound′ *or* kŏm′pound′) *tr.v. Abbr.* comp., cpd. **1.** To compute (interest) on the principal and accumulated interest: *Interest on my savings account is compounded daily.* **2.** To combine (two or more things) to make sthg. else. **3.** To make (sthg.) worse: *Haste compounded the problem.* —*n.* (kŏm′pound′) **1.** A combination of two or more things: *Water is a compound of hydrogen and oxygen.* **2.** A word usually made up of two or more elements that have meanings of their own. *Loudspeaker* is a compound of *loud* and *speaker.*

compound entry (kŏm′pound ĕn′trē) *n.* A financial transaction that requires more than one debit or more than one credit to be recorded in the journal.

compound interest (kŏm′pound ĭn′trĭst) *n.* The interest cost for two or more periods, under the assumption that after each period the interest of that period is added to the amount on which interest is computed in future periods. See also **simple interest.**

comprehensive (kŏm′prĭ hĕn′sĭv) *adj.* So great in scope or content as to include almost everything one would expect to find in a given thing: *a comprehensive history of South Africa.* —*n.* **comprehensives.** College examinations that cover an entire field of major study given in the final undergraduate or graduate year.

comprehensive income (kŏm′prĭ hĕn′sĭv ĭn′kŭm) *n.* The concept of income or loss for a period that includes all revenues, expenses, gains, and losses, but excludes prior period adjustments.

consignor

computer-aided design (kəm pyōō′tər ā′dĭd dĭ zīn′) *n. Abbr.* **CAD** A computer-based engineering system with a built-in program to detect product design flaws.

computer-aided design/computer-aided manufacturing (kəm pyōō′tər ā′dĭd dĭ zīn′ kəm pyōō′tər ā′dĭd măn′yə făk′chə rĭng) *n. Abbr.* **CAD/CAM** The use of computers in product design work, in planning and controlling production, and in linking **CNC machines** and flexible manufacturing systems to the engineering design function.

computer integrated manufacturing system (kəm pyōō′tər ĭn′tĭ grā′tĭd măn′yə făk′chə rĭng sĭs′təm) *n. Abbr.* **CIM** A fully computerized, plantwide manufacturing facility in which all parts of the manufacturing process are programmed and performed automatically.

computer numerically controlled machine (kəm pyōō′tər nōō mĕr′ĭk lē kən trōld′ mə shēn′) *n. Abbr.* **CNC** Pieces of computer-driven equipment that can operate independently, including operating machines, computer-aided design hardware and software, and robots.

condense (kən dĕns′) *tr. & intr.v.* **condensed, condensing, condenses. 1.** To reduce the volume or mass of (sthg.) or to become more compact: *Can we condense this mixture?* **2.** To shorten (a piece of writing) to make it more concise: *You'll have to condense your last report because it's too long.*

condensed financial statement (kən dĕnst′ fə năn′shəl stāt′mənt) *n.* A financial statement for external reporting that presents only the major categories of information. Another term for **detailed income statement, multistep form,** and **single-step form.**

confidential (kŏn′fĭ dĕn′shəl) *adj.* **1.** Entrusted with ensuring that sensitive information about clients and customers is restricted to those who are authorized to have it: *a confidential secretary.* **2.** Told as a secret: *Please keep this information confidential.* **3.** Showing secrecy or intimacy: *a confidential tone of voice.* —**confidentiality** *n.*

conglomerate (kən glŏm′ər ĭt) *n.* A business corporation made up of a number of separate companies that do different types of work. Another term for **diversified company.**

conservatism (kən sûr′və tĭz′əm) *n.* The convention that requires that, when faced with equally acceptable alternatives, accountants must choose the one least likely to overstate assets and income.

conservative (kən sûr′və tĭv) *adj.* **1.** Tending to oppose change and favoring traditional views: *the conservative vote.* **2.** Cautious in one's approach to actions and events: *fiscally conservative.* —*n.* A person who favors traditional views and opposes change: *a fiscal conservative.*

consign (kən sīn′) *tr.v.* **1.** To deliver (merchandise) to sbdy. for sale: *I consigned my paintings to the art gallery.* **2.** To give (sthg.) to sbdy. else's care: *We consigned our dog to the veterinary clinic.* —**consignable** *adj.* —**consignation** *n.*

consignee (kŏn′sī nē′ *or* kən sī′nē′) *n.* A person who accepts goods or merchandise for sale.

consignment (kən sīn′mənt) *n.* Merchandise placed by its owner (the **consignor**) on the premises of another company (the **consignee**) with the understanding that payment is expected only when the merchandise is sold; the unsold merchandise may be returned to the consignor.

consignor or **consigner** (kən sī′nər) *n.* A person who supplies goods or merchandise for sale or custody.

25

consistency

consistency (kən sĭs′tən sē) *n.* **1.** The convention that requires that an accounting procedure, once adopted, not be changed from one period to another unless users are informed of the change. **2.** The degree of thickness or firmness of a liquid substance: *The consistency of the paint is too thin.*

consistency principle (kən sĭs′tən sē prĭn′sə pəl) *n.* The accounting principle that requires that a particular accounting procedure, once adopted, not be changed from one fiscal period to another.

consistent (kən sĭs′tənt) *adj.* **1.** In agreement with, or matching, sthg. else: *Scientific interpretations must be consistent with the known facts.* **2.** Reliable or producing uniform results or effects: *a consistent method of handling accounts.* —**consistently** *adv.*

consolidate (kən sŏl′ĭ dāt′) *v.* **consolidated, consolidating, consolidates.** —*tr.* To combine (sthg.): *He obtained a loan to consolidate his debts.* —*intr.* To join or merge with sthg. else: *Those companies have consolidated under a new name.*

consolidated financial statements (kən sŏl′ĭ dā′tĭd fə năn′-shəl stāt′mənts) *pl.n.* The combined financial statements of a parent company and its subsidiaries.

consolidation (kən sŏl′ĭ dā′shən) *n.* The merging of two or more commercial interests or companies.

cont. *Abbr.* An abbreviation of **1.** Continued. **2.** Continue.

contact (kŏn′tăkt) *n.* **1.** The physical touching of persons or things: *Do not allow the chemicals to come in contact with your skin.* **2.** The condition of being in communication with sbdy.: *I lost contact with my friends at my former job.* **3.** A person who is in a position to be of help: *She got her new job through a contact in upper management.* **4.** A contact lens: *He wears contacts.* —*v.* (kŏn′tăkt *or* kən tăkt′) —*tr.* **1.** To bring (sthg.) into contact with sthg. else; touch: *The back of the microwave shouldn't contact the wall.* **2.** To communicate with (sbdy.): *How can I contact you in case of an emergency?* —*intr.* To be or come in contact: *Bare wires that contact may cause a fire.*

contact producers (kŏn′tăkt prə dōō′sərz) *pl.n.* A company that produces the goods of other companies.

contingency (kən tĭn′jən sē) *n., pl.* **contingencies. 1.** An event that might happen but that is not likely or planned: *Numerous contingencies may cause the plan to fail.* **2.** A possible future emergency that must be dealt with before it happens: *We should prepare for any contingency.* —**contingency** *adj.*

contingent (kən tĭn′jənt) *adj.* **1.** Possible but not certain to happen; uncertain: *The weather has made our trip contingent.* **2.** [*on; upon*] Depending on conditions or events not yet known; conditional: *trade treaties contingent on the approval of Congress.*

contingent liability (kən tĭn′jənt lī′ə bĭl′ĭ tē) *n., pl.* **liabilities.** A potential liability that can develop into a real liability if an expected event happens.

continue (kən tĭn′yōō) *v.* **continued, continuing, continues.** *Abbr.* **cont.** —*intr.* **1.** To go on or persist in a particular action or condition: *She continues to call on me for advice.* **2.** To last over a long period of time: *The contract negotiations continued for most of the week.* —*tr.* **1.** To go on doing (sthg.): *I'd like to continue this discussion later.* **2.** To carry (sthg.) forward in time, space, or development: *My contract has been continued through next year.* —**continuable** *adj.* —**continuation** *n.*

control environment

continuity (kŏn′tə nōō′ĭ tē) *n., pl.* **continuities.** A coherent whole that has no breaks or interruptions: *This proposal lacks continuity.*

continuity issue (kŏn′tə nōō′ĭ tē ĭsh′ōō) *n.* The issue that arises when it is difficult to know how long a business entity will survive.

continuous (kən tĭn′yōō əs) *adj.* Not interrupted in time, process, or extent: *the continuous drone of the machinery.* —**continuously** *adv.* —**continuousness** *n.*

continuous improvement (kən tĭn′yōō əs im prōōv′mənt) *n.* The management concept that one should never be satisfied with things as they are; one should always seek a better method, product, process, or resource.

contra- (kŏn′trə) *prefix.* A prefix that means against or opposite to.

contra account (kŏn′trə ə kount′) *n.* An account that is contrary to, or a deduction from, another account. For example, Accumulated Depreciation entered as a deduction from Equipment is a contra account. Also called **contra-asset account.**

contra-liability account (kŏn′trə lī′ə bĭl′ĭ tē ə kount′) *n.* A deduction from a liability, such as Discounts on Notes Payable, which is a deduction from the balance of Notes Payable.

contrib. *Abbr.* An abbreviation of contribution.

contribute (kən trĭb′yōōt) *v.* **contributed, contributing, contributes.** —*tr.* To give (sthg.) to a fund, an activity, or a purpose: *She contributes her spare time to the local hospital.* —*intr.* To give time, money, or support to a fund, an activity, or a purpose: *He's agreed to contribute if he can remain anonymous.* —**contributor** *n.*

contributed capital (kən trĭb′yōō tĭd kăp′ĭ tl) *n.* The stockholders' investment in a corporation. It is made up of the **par value (face value)** of issued shares of stock and the amounts paid in excess of par value per share (**paid-in capital**). See also **paid-in capital.**

contribution (kŏn′trĭ byōō′shən) *n. Abbr.* **contrib. 1.** The act of giving or supplying sthg. for a fund, an activity, or a purpose: *How many contributions do we need now?* **2.** What is given or supplied: *Your contribution is appreciated.*

contribution margin (kŏn′trĭ byōō′shən mär′jĭn) *n.* The excess of revenues over all variable costs related to a particular sales volume.

control (kən trōl′) *tr.v.* **controlled, controlling, controls. 1.** To be able to decide the operating financial policies of another company through ownership of more than 50 percent of that company's voting stock (said of an investing company): *They're buying up shares so they can control the company.* **2.** To exercise authoritative or dominating influence over (sbdy./sthg.): *You can't allow her to control your life.* **3.** To restrain or limit (sthg.) in range or effect: *Try to control your temper.* —*n.* **1.** Authority or influence over sbdy./sthg.: *He's fully in control of the situation.* **2.** A device, measure, or limit: *price controls.*

control account (kən trōl′ ə kount′) *n.* Another term for **controlling account.**

control environment (kən trōl′ ĕn vī′rən mənt) *n.* The overall attitude, awareness, and actions of the owners and management of a business, as reflected in philosophy and operating style, organizational structure, methods of assigning authority and responsibility, and personnel policies and practices.

27

controllable costs

controllable costs (kən trō′lə bəl kôsts′) *pl.n.* Operating costs that result from a particular manager's actions, influence, and decisions and that are, therefore, able to be controlled.

controllable overhead variance (kən trō′lə bəl ō′vər hĕd′ vâr′ē əns) *n.* The difference between actual overhead costs incurred and the factory overhead costs budgeted for the level of production reached.

controlling account (kən trō′lĭng ə kount′) *n.* An account in the general ledger that summarizes the total balance of a group of related accounts in a subsidiary ledger. Also called a **control account**.

controlling interest (kən trō′lĭng ĭn′trĭst) *n.* Ownership of more than 50 percent of a company's stock. Also called **controlling investment**.

controlling investment (kən trō′lĭng ĭn vĕst′mənt) *n.* Ownership of a sufficient number of shares of stock in a company to control company policy. Also called **controlling interest**.

control principle (kən trōl′ prĭn′sə pəl) *n.* The principle that holds that an accounting system must provide all the features of internal control needed to protect a firm's assets and ensure that data are reliable.

control procedure (kən trōl′ prə sē′jər) *n.* A procedure and related policies established by management to ensure that the objectives of internal control are met.

convention (kən vĕn′shən) *n.* **1.** *(usually singular).* A usual or customary way of recording transactions or preparing financial statements: *Which convention did your accountant use to set up the books?* **2.** General agreement on or acceptance of certain practices or methods: *Spelling conventions in the United States differ from those in Great Britain.* **3.** A formal assembly: *She will attend the CPA convention next month.*

conversion (kən vûr′zhən or kən vûr′shən) *n.* **1.** The exchange of one kind of security or currency for another: *We'll lose money on the conversion to yen.* **2.** The process of changing one thing, use, or purpose into another: *The conversion to the new computer system is complete.*

conversion costs (kən vûr′zhən kôsts′) *pl.n.* The total of direct labor and factory overhead costs incurred by a production department, **JIT/FMS** work cell, or other work center.

convert (kən vûrt′) *tr.v.* **1.** To exchange (sthg.) for sthg. of equal value: *convert bonds into cash.* **2.** To change (sthg.) from one use, function, or purpose to a new or different one: *We could convert the garage into a workshop.*

convertible (kən vûr′tə bəl) *adj.* Able to be changed in some way: *a convertible sofa; convertible assets.*

convertible bond (kən vûr′tə bəl bŏnd′) *n.* A bond that can be exchanged for other securities of the corporation, usually its common stock.

convertible preferred stock (kən vûr′tə bəl prĭ fûrd′ stŏk′) *n.* Preferred stock that can be exchanged for common stock at the option of the stockholder.

co-ownership (kō ō′nər shĭp′) *n.* A situation in which each party owns a fractional share of all the assets of a business entity.

copyright (kŏp′ē rīt′) *n.* An exclusive right granted by the federal government to the possessor to publish and sell literary, musical, or other artistic materials for a period of the author's life plus fifty years, including computer programs.

corp. *Abbr.* An abbreviation of corporation.

cost center

corporate charter (kôr′pər ĭt chär′tər) *n.* Another term for **articles of incorporation**.

corporate income tax (kôr′pər ĭt ĭn′kəm tăks′) *n., pl.* **taxes.** The tax that an incorporated business must pay to the federal government and, often, to state and city governments as well. Such taxes must be estimated for the coming year and then paid in quarterly installments. Each entry is a debit to Income Tax Expense and a credit to Cash.

corporate work sheet (kôr′pər ĭt wûrk′ shēt′) *n.* A working paper used by accountants to record necessary adjustments and prepare up-to-date account balances in order to prepare financial statements for a corporation.

corporation (kôr′pə rā′shən) *n. Abbr.* **corp.** A business unit granted a state charter and recognized as a separate legal entity having its own rights, privileges, and liabilities distinct from those of its owners. Another term for **business** (sense 3), **business entity, company, economic entity, firm.**

correcting entry (kə rĕk′tĭng ĕn′trē) *n.* An entry made in the ledger when amounts have been posted to the wrong account. It should always include an explanation for the change.

correcting entry method (kə rĕk′tĭng ĕn′trē mĕth′əd) *n.* A way of correcting accounting entries. Another term for **ruling method.**

cost (kôst) *n.* **1.** A financial gain or loss that occurs between the date of a business transaction and the time when it is entered in the ledger. **2.** A price or payment required to buy sthg.: *What is the cost of this car?* **3.** An expense that is necessary in order to achieve a goal: *The cost of becoming successful may be too high.* —*v.* **cost, costing, costs.** —*intr.* To require a specified payment, effort, or loss: *Cars cost too much these days.* —*tr.* **1.** To require (sbdy.) to pay as a price : *That car will cost you $35,000.* **2.** To cause to lose or suffer (sthg.): *That job is costing you your health.*

cost adjusted to market method (kôst′ ə jŭs′tĭd tōō mär′kĭt mĕth′əd) *n.* A way of accounting for available-for-sale securities in which the original cost of the securities is adjusted for changes in their market value.

cost allocation (kôst′ ăl′ə kā′shən) *n.* The process of assigning a specific cost to a specific objective. Also called **cost assignment.**

cost-based pricing (kôst′bāst′ prī′sĭng) *n.* One of several ways a manager develops a price for a product or service based on how much it costs to produce, including **gross margin pricing, profit margin pricing,** and **return on assets pricing.** See also **target-costing.**

cost behavior (kôst′ bĭ hāv′yər) *n.* The way costs respond to changes in volume or activity.

cost–benefit convention (kôst′ bĕn′ə fĭt kən vĕn′shən) *n.* The convention that holds that benefits gained from providing accounting information should be greater than the cost of providing that information.

cost–benefit principle (kôst′ bĕn′ə fĭt prĭn′sə pəl) *n.* The principle that holds that the benefits derived from an accounting system and the information it generates should equal or exceed its cost.

cost center (kôst′ sĕn′tər) *n.* Any part of an organization or area of activity, such as a specific division or department, for which there is a reason to record, calculate, and allocate costs. Another term for **expense center.**

cost curve

cost curve (kôst′ kûrv′) *n.* A line on a graph representing changes in cost in relation to changes in volume or output. It is used in cost-volume-profit analysis.

cost driver (kôst′ drī′vər) *n.* In **activity-based costing**, any activity that causes a cost to be incurred.

cost effective (kôst′ ĭ fĕk′tĭv) *adj.* Purchased at an economical rate in terms of the money spent for goods or services received.

cost flow (kôst′ flō′) *n.* The association of costs with their assumed flow in the operations of a company. See also **goods flow**.

costing (kôs′tĭng) *n.* A way of finding out how much it costs to manufacture, produce, or build sthg.: *Costing will help us establish a budget.*

cost management (kôst′ măn′ĭj mənt) *n.* The management and control of activities to determine product cost accurately, improve business processes, eliminate waste, identify cost drivers, plan operations, and set business strategies.

cost management system (kôst′ măn′ĭj mənt sĭs′təm) *n. Abbr.* **CMS** A management accounting and reporting system that identifies, monitors, and maintains continuous, detailed analyses of a company's activities and provides managers with timely measures of operating results.

cost object (kôst′ ŏb′jĕkt′) *n.* Anything to which costs attach or are related. It can be a product, department, division, or sales territory.

cost objective (kôst′ əb jĕk′tĭv) *n.* The destination of an assigned or allocated cost. A division or department of a business, a specific product or order, or an entire contract can be a cost objective.

cost of capital (kôst′ əv kăp′ĭ tl) *n.* A rate that reflects the cost of funds used to finance a company's activities.

cost of conformance (kôst′ əv kən fôr′məns) *n.* The costs involved to produce a product or service that is high in quality. See also **appraisal cost** and **prevention costs**.

cost of debt (kôst′ əv dĕt′) *n.* The cost of raising long-term funds through borrowing. It is computed as the ratio of loan charges to net proceeds of the loan.

cost of doing business (kôst′ əv do͞o′ĭng bĭz′nĭs) *n.* Another term for **expense**.

cost of equity capital (kôst′ əv ĕk′wĭ tē kăp′ĭ tl) *n.* The cost of raising long-term funds by issuing new common stock. It is the rate at which investors discount the expected dividends of the firm to determine its share value.

cost of goods manufactured (kôst′ əv goodz′ măn′yə făk′chərd) *n.* The total manufacturing costs attached to units of a production completed during an accounting period.

cost of goods sold (kôst′ əv goodz′ sōld′) *n.* The amount a merchant paid for the merchandise sold during an accounting period. Also called **cost of sales**.

cost of nonconformance (kôst′ əv nŏn′kən fôr′məns) *n.* The cost required to correct the defects in a product or service. See also **external failure costs** and **internal failure costs**.

cost of preferred stock (kôst′ əv prĭ fûrd′ stŏk′) *n.* The cost of raising long-term funds by issuing new preferred stock. It is computed by dividing the annual dividend by the net proceeds from the sale of the stock.

cost of quality (kôst′ əv kwŏl′ĭ tē) *n.* All of the costs specifically associated with the achievement or nonachievement of product or service quality.

credit

cost of retained earnings (kôst′ əv rĭ tānd′ ûr′nĭngz) *n.* The cost of financing long-term projects with retained earnings. It is equal to the opportunity cost or the dividends given up by the common stockholders.

cost of sales (kôst′ əv sālz′) *n.* Another term for **cost of goods sold**.

cost-plus transfer price (kôst′ plŭs′ trăns′fər prīs′) *n.* A transfer price computed as the sum of costs incurred by the producing division plus an agreed-on percentage markup for profit.

cost principle (kôst′ prĭn′sə pəl) *n.* The principle that a purchased asset should be recorded at its actual cost (the agreed amount of a transaction) until the asset, liability, or component of owner's equity is sold, expires, is consumed, is satisfied, or is otherwise disposed of.

cost summary schedule (kôst′ sŭm′ə rē skĕj′ōol) *n.* A costing schedule that makes it simpler to distribute all the production costs during a specific period among the units produced, either those completed and transferred out of the department or those still in production at the end of the period.

cost variance (kôst′ vâr′ē əns) *n.* The difference in amount between the actual cost and the standard cost of sthg.

cost-volume-profit analysis (kôst′ vŏl′yōom prŏf′ĭt ə nal′-ĭ sĭs) *n.* *Abbr.* **C-V-P** An analysis of the cost behavior patterns that underlie the relationships among cost, volume of output, and profit.

coupon (kōo′pŏn′ *or* kyōo′pŏn′) *n.* *Abbr.* **cp. 1.** A negotiable certificate attached to a bond that represents an amount of interest due: *Present your coupon at the bank each month for payment.* **2.** A certificate that a customer can use to buy a product or service at a cash discount, sometimes attached to the product itself: *She uses food coupons at the supermarket.*

coupon bond (kōo′pŏn bŏnd′) *n.* A bond that is usually not registered with the issuing corporation but instead bears interest coupons stating the amount of interest due and the payment date.

cp. *Abbr.* An abbreviation of coupon.

CPA *Abbr.* An abbreviation of certified public accountant.

cpd. *Abbr.* An abbreviation of compound.

credit (krĕd′ĭt) *n. Abbr.* **cr. 1.a.** The deduction of a payment made by a debtor for an amount owed: *I haven't received credit for my last payment.* **b.** The right-hand side of a **T account** in which such amounts are recorded. Credits represent increases in liability, capital, and revenue accounts, and decreases in asset, drawing, and expense accounts. **c.** A single entry or the entries on this side of an account. **d.** The amount remaining or the positive balance in an account. **e.** A credit line. **2.a.** A way of paying for a loan or purchase over a period of time: *He bought his computer on credit.* **b.** The terms of a deferred payment plan: *easy credit.* **c.** The time period over which regular payments must be made: *a 30-day credit on all orders.* **3.** *(usually singular).* A cause for pride or recognition: *She's a credit to her team.* **4.** A unit of study: *You need three credits of History to graduate.* **5.** A reputation for being solvent and reliable that indicates that sbdy. is a good risk to buy goods or services on a deferred payment plan or to borrow money: *If your credit is good, you'll have no problem buying a car.* —*tr.v.* **1.a.** To enter (a credit) on the right side of a T account: *credit your last payment.* **b.** To make (a credit entry) in an account: *credit an account.* **2.** To

31

credit column

regard (sbdy.) as having done sthg. or having a particular quality: *Credit her with good intentions.*

credit column (krĕd′ĭt kŏl′əm) *n.* The column in the journal or ledger into which credits are posted.

credit line (krĕd′ĭt līn′) *n.* Another term for **line of credit**.

credit memorandum (krĕd′ĭt mĕm′ə răn′dəm) *n., pl.* **memoranda. 1.** A written statement indicating that a seller is willing to reduce the amount of a buyer's debt. The seller records the amount of the credit memorandum in the Sales Returns and Allowances account. **2.** A business form provided by the seller to a buyer who has either returned a purchase (or part of a purchase) for credit or been granted an allowance for damaged goods.

creditor (krĕd′ĭ tər) *n.* A person to whom money is owed.

creditor's equity (krĕd′ĭ tərz ĕk′wĭ tē) *n.* A claim against the resources of a company; a liability, not an asset. See also **owner's equity**.

credit period (krĕd′ĭt pîr′ē əd) *n.* The length of time the seller allows a buyer before full payment on a charge sale is due.

credit policy (krĕd′ĭt pŏl′ĭ sē) *n., pl.* **policies.** A set of procedures established by a company to ensure that the people and companies it allows to make purchases on credit have the financial resources to pay for what they buy.

crossfooting (krôs′fŏŏt′ĭng) *n.* The addition and subtraction of numbers across a row of columns in a ledger.

cross-reference (krôs′rĕf′ər əns *or* krŏs′rĕf′ər əns) *n.* **1.** The ledger account number in the Posting Reference (Post. Ref.) column of the journal and the journal page number in the Journal Reference (Jrnl.) column of the ledger account. **2.** A note in a book, catalog, index, or file that tells a reader where additional information can be found.

cumulative (kyōōm′yə lā′tĭv *or* kyōōm′yə lə tĭv) *adj.* Increasing or growing by steady addition or in stages: *The cumulative knowledge of our research department is impressive.*

cumulative effect of an accounting change (kyōōm′yə lā′tĭv ĭ fĕkt′ əv ən ə koun′tĭng chānj′) *n.* The effect that a different accounting principle would have had on the net income or prior periods if it had been used instead of the old principle.

cumulative preferred stock (kyōōm′yə lā′tĭv prĭ fûrd′ stŏk′) *n.* Preferred stock on which unpaid dividends accumulate over time and must be paid in any given year before a dividend can be paid to common stockholders.

currency (kûr′ən sē *or* kŭr′ən sē) *n.* Money, either coins or bills, that is used as a medium of exchange. Another term for **cash or change**.

current assets (kûr′ənt ăs′ĕts) *pl.n.* Cash or other assets that are reasonably expected to be converted to cash, sold, or consumed within one year or within the normal operating cycle, whichever is longer.

current liability (kûr′ənt lī′ə bĭl′ĭ tē) *n., pl.* **liabilities.** Debts and obligations expected to be paid in full within one year or within the normal operating cycle, whichever is longer.

current ratio (kûr′ənt rā′shō) *n.* Used as an indicator of a company's liquidity and ability to pay short-term debts. This is found by dividing current assets by current liabilities.

current report (kûr′ənt rĭ pôrt′) *n.* A report (Form 8–K) that publicly held corporations must file with the Securities and Exchange Commission within a few days of a significant event.

cycle

Such events may indicate important changes that affect the future financial performance of the company.

curve (kûrv) *n.* **1.** In mathematics and statistics, a line of a set of points defined by a function drawn on a surface or plane. **2.** A line or surface that bends in a smooth continuous way without sharp angles. **3.** Something that has the shape of a curve: *a curve in the road.*

C-V-P *Abbr.* An abbreviation of cost-volume-profit (analysis).

cycle (sī′kəl) *n.* **1.** A series of events that is repeated on a regular basis: *cycles in our lives; a billing cycle.* **2.** The time during which such a series of events occurs: *a cycle of 30 days.*

Dd

D. *Abbr.* An abbreviation of department.

data processing (dā′tə prŏs′ĕs ĭng) *n.* **1.** The way an accounting system gathers data, organizes the information into useful forms, and issues the resulting information to users. **2.** Sorting, analysis, and other operations performed on data by computers.

date of declaration (dāt′ əv dĕk′lə rā′shən) *n.* The date on which the board of directors of a company formally declares that a dividend is going to be paid. See also **date of payment, date of record.**

date of maturity (dāt′ əv mə tyoor′ĭ tē) *n., pl.* **dates of maturity.** Another term for **maturity date.**

date of payment (dāt′ əv pā′mənt) *n.* The date on which a company pays a dividend to the stockholders of record. See also **date of declaration, date of record.**

date of record (dāt′ əv rĕk′ərd) *n.* The formally declared date on which ownership in the stock of a company is determined. This date determines which owners are entitled to receive a dividend. See also **date of declaration, date of payment.**

debenture bond (dĭ bĕn′chər bŏnd′) *n.* Another term for **unsecured bond.**

debit (dĕb′ĭt) *n.* **1.** A debt charged to and recorded in an account. Debits represent increases in asset, drawing, and expense accounts and decreases in liability, capital, and revenue accounts. **2.** The left side of a **T account.** —*tr.v.* To record an amount on the left side of a T account.

debit card (dĕb′ĭt kärd′) *n.* A card issued by a bank that allows its customers to pay for purchases. The amount of the purchase is deducted directly from the customer's account just as a check would be. The debit card is also called an **ATM card,** but not all ATM cards are debit cards.

debit column (dĕb′ĭt kŏl′əm) *n.* A column in the journal or ledger where debits are posted or entered.

debit memo (dĕb′ĭt mĕm′ō) *n., pl.* **memos.** A memorandum from a bank explaining decreases or debits to a customer's account, such as charges for NSF checks, ATM withdrawals, and service charges. Also called **debit memorandum.**

debit memorandum (dĕb′ĭt mĕm′ə răn′dəm) *n., pl.* **memorandums, memoranda.** Another term for **debit memo.**

debt (dĕt) *n.* Something, especially money, that is owed by one individual or company to another; a liability: *She has so much debt she is unable to secure another loan.*

debt to equity (dĕt′ tōō ĕk′wĭ tē) *n.* A way of measuring the relationship of assets provided by creditors to those provided by owners. It is a long-term or noncurrent ratio found by dividing liabilities by owner's equity.

debt to equity ratio (dĕt′ tōō ĕk′wĭ tē rā′shō) *n.* A way of measuring the relationship of debt financing to equity financing, or the extent to which a company is leveraged. It is found by dividing long-term liabilities by stockholders' equity.

decentralized organization (dē sĕn′trə līzd′ ôr′gə nĭ zā′shən) *n.* An organization that has several operating segments. Operating control of each segment's activities is the responsibility of the segment's manager.

decimal point (dĕs′ə məl point′) *n.* **1.** A period used to separate dollar and cent amounts on unruled paper. On paper with

deferred payment

ruled columns, decimal points are not necessary. **2.** In mathematics, a period placed to the left of a decimal fraction. In .079, for example, 0 is in the first decimal place, 7 is in the second decimal place, and 9 is in the third decimal place.

decision (dĭ sĭzh′ən) *n.* A conclusion or judgment that resolves a conflict: *Has she made a decision about which college she's going to attend?* —**decide** *tr. & intr.v.*

decision analysis (dĭ sĭzh′ən ə năl′ĭ sĭs) *n.* Information on the possible effects of different alternatives that accountants provide to decision makers. Two decision tools that help accountants produce this information are **variable costing** and **incremental analysis**.

decision-making (dĭ sĭzh′ən mā′kĭng) *n.* The act of deciding or the ability to decide sthg.: *Decision-making requires accurate information about the available alternatives.*

decision model (dĭ sĭzh′ən mŏd′l) *n.* A symbolic or numerical representation of the variables and parameters used to evaluate and choose among alternative courses of action.

decision parameter (dĭ sĭzh′ən pə răm′ĭ tər) *n. (usually plural).* An uncontrollable factor and the operating constraints and limitations within a decision model.

decision variable (dĭ sĭzh′ən vâr′ē ə bəl) *n. (usually plural).* A factor that management controls within a **decision model**.

declare (dĭ klâr′) *tr.v.* declared, declaring, declares. **1.** To make (sthg.) known officially; announce: *The company's board of directors will declare its dividends next week.* **2.** To state (sthg.) with great emphasis: *Management declared a company holiday.*

decline (dĭ klīn′) *intr.v.* declined, declining, declines. To decrease gradually in strength, value, or importance: *The cost of a personal computer has been declining.* —*n.* **1.** A gradual decrease in strength or importance; a period of decline: *the decline in productivity.* **2.** A change to a lower value or amount: *a decline in price; a decline in sales.*

declining balance (dĭ klī′nĭng băl′əns) *n.* Another term for **carrying value.**

declining-balance method (dĭ klī′nĭng băl′əns mĕth′əd) *n.* An accelerated method of depreciating a tangible long-lived asset by applying a fixed rate based on some multiple of the straight line rate to its carrying value (the **declining balance**). See also **double-declining-balance method.**

defer (dĭ fûr′) *v.* deferred, deferring, defers. —*tr.* To delay or postpone (sthg.): *We can defer payment until January.* —*intr.* To yield to the wishes, decisions, or opinion of (sbdy.) because of authority or superior knowledge: *She deferred to her parents' wishes and went to a college closer to home.*

deferral (dĭ fûr′əl) *n.* **1.** The postponement of the date (**recognition**) that an expense already paid or incurred, or of a revenue already received, is entered in the ledger. **2.** The delay or postponement of sthg.: *We managed to get a deferral on our loan payment.*

deferred (dĭ fûrd′) *adj.* Delayed; postponed: *We finally got to take our deferred vacation.*

deferred expense (dĭ fûrd′ ĭk spĕns′) *n.* Another term for **prepaid expense.**

deferred income taxes (dĭ fûrd′ ĭn′kəm tăk′sĭz) *pl.n.* The account used to record the difference between the Income Taxes Expense and the Income Taxes Payable accounts.

deferred payment (dĭ fûrd′ pā′mənt) *n.* A payment that has been postponed until a later date.

deficit

deficit (dĕf′ĭ sĭt) *n.* **1.** A debit balance in the Retained Earnings account. **2.** The amount by which an amount of money is less than the required or expected amount: *This business has been running at a deficit for the last two years.*

define (dĭ fīn′) *tr.v.* **defined, defining, defines. 1.** To state the meaning of a word or phrase: *Dictionaries define words.* **2.** To describe or identify (sthg.) clearly: *We'll need to define the responsibilities of the job.*

defined benefit plan (dĭ fīnd′ bĕn′ə fĭt plăn′) *n.* A type of employee pension plan for which the amount of future benefits is fixed, but an employer's contributions vary, depending on assumptions about how much the pension fund will earn. See also **defined contribution plan.**

defined contribution plan (dĭ fīnd′ kŏn′trĭ byōō′shən plăn′) *n.* A type of employee pension plan for which an employer is required to contribute a specific amount every year. That amount is fixed by an agreement between the company and its employees or by a resolution of the board of directors. The amount of future benefits is dependent upon the amount of pension payment the accumulated contributions can support. See also **defined benefit plan.**

definite (dĕf′ə nĭt) *adj.* **1.** Sure to happen: *Is our departure time definite?* **2.** Limited in a clearly defined way: *definite restrictions on using the coupons.* **3.** Precise: *Do you have a definite plan?* —**definitely** *adv.*

definitely determinable liability (dĕf′ə nĭt lē dĭ tûr′mĭn ə bəl lī′ə bĭl′ĭ tē) *n., pl.* **liabilities.** A current liability that can be measured exactly because it is determined by contract or set by law.

deliver (dĭ lĭv′ər) *tr.v.* To take or carry (sthg.) to a specific place or individual: *Has the computer been delivered yet?*

delivered cost of purchases (dĭ lĭv′ərd kôst′ əv pûr′chə sĭz) *pl.n.* An amount entered in the Cost of Goods Sold section of a ledger. It is found by adding the cost of **freight in** to net purchases.

delivery (dĭ lĭv′ə rē *or* dĭ lĭv′rē) *n., pl.* **deliveries. 1.** The act of taking or carrying (sthg.) to a specific place or individual: *How soon can you make the delivery?* **2.** Something taken or carried to a specific place or individual: *I have a delivery for you.*

delivery cycle time (dĭ lĭv′ə rē sī′kəl tīm′) *n.* The time period between acceptance of an order and final delivery of the product.

delivery expense (dĭ lĭv′ə rē ĭk spĕns′) *n.* Another term for **freight out expense.**

delivery time (dĭ lĭv′ə rē tīm′) *n.* The amount of time it takes for a finished product to reach a customer: *We estimate that delivery time of your order will be about three weeks.*

denom. *Abbr.* An abbreviation of denomination.

denomination (dĭ nŏm′ə nā′shən) *n. Abbr.* **denom.** One of a series of coins and currency, such as quarters, dimes, and nickels and $1 and $5 bills, that has a specific cash value: *What are the denominations of the currency you have in your pocket?*

denominator (dĭ nŏm′ə nā′tər) *n.* **1.** In the ABA number, the two numbers below the line or to the right of the slash. In the ABA number 88-2258/1113, 1113 is the denominator. See also **numerator** and **ABA number. 2.** In mathematics, the number written below the line in a common fraction. In the fraction 2/3, 3 is the denominator.

dep. *Abbr.* An abbreviation of department.

detailed income statement

department (dĭ pärt′mənt) *n. Abbr.* **dept., dpt., dep., D.** A part of a larger business that is responsible for carrying out specific tasks or functions: *a human resources department; a shoe department.*

departmental margin (dē′pärt mĕn′tl mär′jĭn) *n.* The contribution of a specific department to a company's income; the gross profit of a department minus its direct expenses.

deplete (dĭ plēt′) *tr.v.* **depleted, depleting, depletes.** To use (sthg.) completely: *Our vacation depleted our savings.*

depletion (dĭ plē′shən) *n.* **1.** The periodic allocation of the cost of a natural resource. **2.** The exhaustion of a natural resource through mining, cutting, pumping, or other extraction, and the way in which the cost is distributed among those who will pay for it, for example, the company responsible for using up the resource.

deposit (dĭ pŏz′ĭt) *tr.v.* To put (money) in a bank or other financial account: *I deposited my paycheck this morning.* —*n. Abbr.* **dep. 1.** Something, such as money, put in a place for safekeeping: *The bank deposit won't be credited until tomorrow.* **2.a.** A partial payment of a cost or debt: *make a deposit on a house.* **b.** An amount of money given to sbdy. as assurance on sthg.: *a security deposit for the apartment.*

deposit in transit (dĭ pŏz′ĭt ĭn trăn′sĭt) *n.* A deposit not recorded on the bank statement because the deposit was made between the time of the bank's closing date for compiling items for its statements and the time the statement is received by the depositor. Another term for **late deposit.**

deposit slip (dĭ pŏz′ĭt slĭp′) *n.* A printed form provided by a bank on which customers can list all items being deposited. Another term for **deposit ticket.**

depreciable asset (dĭ prē′shə bəl ăs′ĕt) *n.* Tangible, long-lived assets, other than land and natural resources, that have a limited useful life.

depreciable cost (dĭ prē′shə bəl kôst′) *n.* The cost of an asset less its residual value.

depreciate (dĭ prē′shē āt′) *tr. & intr.v.* **depreciated, depreciating, depreciates.** To go down in or lessen the value or price of (sthg.): *A new car begins to depreciate as soon as you drive it off the lot. I plan to depreciate my computer over the next five years.*

depreciation (dĭ prē′shē ā′shən) *n.* **1.** An expense based on the expectation that a tangible, long-lived asset (other than land and natural resources) will gradually decline in usefulness due to time, wear and tear, or technological advances that make it obsolete. The cost of the asset is therefore spread out over its estimated useful life. A part of depreciation expense is apportioned to each fiscal period. **2.** The periodic allocation of the cost of a tangible long-lived asset over its estimated useful life. Also called **depreciation expense.**

depreciation base (dĭ prē′shē ā′shən bās′) *n.* The total cost of an asset less its trade-in or salvage value.

dept. *Abbr.* An abbreviation of department.

description column (dĭ skrĭp′shən kŏl′əm) *n.* The column of the general journal where the exact names of the accounts debited and credited are written.

destination (dĕs′tə nā′shən) *n.* The place to which sbdy./sthg. is going or is sent: *Paris is our next destination.*

detailed income statement (dĭ tāld′ ĭn′kəm stāt′mənt) *n.* A complete and explicit statement of an economic entity's

development and exploration costs

financial activities and holdings. See also **condensed financial statement, multistep form, single-step form**.

development and exploration costs (dĭ vĕl′əp mənt ənd ĕk′splə rā′shən kôsts′) *pl.n.* An expense of oil and gas companies for finding and developing resources.

digit (dĭj′ĭt) *n.* **1.a.** One of the ten Arabic number symbols, 0 through 9. **b.** Such a symbol used in a counting system. **2.** A human finger or toe. —**digital** *adj.*

dilute (dī lōōt′ *or* dĭ lōōt′) *tr.v.* **diluted, diluting, dilutes. 1.** To weaken the force, intensity, purity, or condition of (sthg.): *Those bonds may dilute profits.* **2.** To make (a substance) thinner by adding a liquid to it: *We can dilute the paint by adding turpentine.* —**dilution** *n.*

dilutive (dī lōō′tĭv *or* dĭ lōō′tĭv) *adj.* **1.** Tending to weaken the force, intensity, purity, or condition of sthg.: *dilutive stocks.* **2.** Tending to make a substance thinner.

direct (dĭ rĕkt′ *or* dī rĕkt′) *adj.* **1.** Moving in a straight course or line: *a direct route to the office.* **2.** Open and honest: *Be direct in your business dealings.* **3.** Having no people or conditions to interrupt or influence sthg.: *direct shipment.*

direct charge-off method (dĭ rĕkt′ chärj′ôf mĕth′əd) *n.* A way of accounting for uncollectible accounts by directly debiting an expense account when **bad debts** are discovered instead of using the allowance method. This method violates the **matching rule** but is required for federal income tax computations.

direct cost (dĭ rĕkt′ kôst′) *n.* A cost that can be easily and economically traced to a specific product that was completed during an accounting period.

direct costing (dĭ rĕkt′ kôs′tĭng) *n.* Another term for **variable costing**.

direct expense (dĭ rĕkt′ ĭk spĕns′) *n.* An operating (or overhead) expense that can be assigned to a specific department and is under the control of the department head. *The usual way to identify a direct expense is: If the department did not exist, the expense would not exist.* See also **indirect expense**.

direct labor costs (dĭ rĕkt′ lā′bər kôsts′) *pl.n.* The labor cost is for specific work that can be easily and economically traced to an end product.

direct labor efficiency variance (dĭ rĕkt′ lā′bər ĭ fĭsh′ən sē vâr′ē əns) *n.* The difference between actual hours worked and **standard hours** allowed for the good units produced, multiplied by the **standard labor rate**.

direct labor rate standard (dĭ rĕkt′ lā′bər rāt stăn′dərd) *n.* The hourly labor costs expected to be most common during the next accounting period for a specific function or job classification.

direct labor rate variance (dĭ rĕkt′ lā′bər rāt vâr′ē əns) *n.* The difference between the actual labor rate and the standard labor rate, multiplied by the actual labor hours worked.

direct labor time standard (dĭ rĕkt′ lā′bər tīm stăn′dərd) *n.* The expected time required for a department, machine, or process to complete the production of one unit or one batch of output.

direct material (dĭ rĕkt′ mə tîr′ē əl) *n. (usually plural).* A material that will become part of a finished product and can be easily and economically traced to specific product units, for example, sthg. used to manufacture an automobile or a washing machine.

direct materials price standard (dĭ rĕkt′ mə tîr′ē əlz prīs′ stăn′dərd) *n.* A careful estimate of the cost of a specific direct material, such as steel or rivets, in the next accounting period.

direct materials price variance (dĭ rĕkt′ mə tîr′ē əlz prīs′ vâr′ē əns) *n.* The difference between the actual price and the standard price of a specific direct material, multiplied by the actual quantity purchased.

direct materials quantity standard (dĭ rĕkt′ mə tîr′ē əlz kwŏn′tĭ tē stăn′dərd) *n.* An estimate of the expected quantity of direct materials to be used, which is influenced by product engineering specifications, quality of direct materials, age and productivity of machinery, and quality and experience of the work force.

direct materials quantity variance (dĭ rĕkt′ mə tîr′ē əlz kwŏn′tĭ tē vâr′ē əns) *n.* The difference between the actual quantity of direct materials used and the standard quantity, multiplied by the standard price.

direct method (dĭ rĕkt′ mĕth′əd) *n.* The method of converting the income statement from an accrual basis to a cash basis by separately adjusting each item in the income statement. See also **indirect method**.

disclose (dĭ sklōz′) *tr.v.* **disclosed, disclosing, discloses.** To make (sthg.) known: *The company refused to disclose its sales figures.*

disclosure (dĭ sklō′zhər) *n.* **1.** Another term for **full disclosure**. **2.** The act or process of revealing or exposing sthg.: *The company repeated that there will be no disclosure of its profit margin.* **3.** Something revealed, shown, or told for the first time: *Several well-timed disclosures have dramatically increased the value of that firm's stock.*

discontinue (dĭs′kən tĭn′yōō) *tr.v.* **discontinued, discontinuing, discontinues.** To stop doing or producing (sthg.): *We discontinued that model last year.*

discontinued operation (dĭs′kən tĭn′yōōd ŏp′ə rā′shən) *n.* A part of a business that no longer operates.

discount (dĭs′kount *or* dĭs kount′) *n.* **1.** The amount by which the face value of a bond exceeds the **issue price**. This happens when the market interest rate is higher than the face interest rate. **2.** Interest deducted in advance by a bank that makes a loan. **3.** The amount by which the issuing price of a stock falls below the **par value**. —*tr.v.* **1.** To subtract (a percentage) from the cost or price of sthg.: *The dealer discounted 20 percent off the price of the car.* **2.** To sell (sthg.) at a reduced price: *The store is discounting all of its discontinued products.* See also **sales discount, trade discount**.

discounting (dĭs′koun′tĭng *or* dĭs koun′tĭng) *n.* A way of selling notes receivable. The bank that holds the note deducts the interest from the maturity value of the note to determine the proceeds (amount of money) that the seller receives.

discounting notes payable (dĭs′koun′tĭng nōts′ pā′ə bəl) *n.* The way a bank deducts interest in advance when it loans money.

discounting notes receivable (dĭs′koun′tĭng nōts′ rĭ sē′və bəl) *n.* The process by which a company raises cash by selling a note receivable to a bank or **finance company**. The bank deducts the interest from the maturity value of the note to determine the proceeds (amount of money) that the company receives.

discount period (dĭs′kount pîr′ē əd) *n.* The time between the date when a **note receivable** is discounted and the date when it matures.

dishonored check (dĭs ŏn′ərd chĕk′) *n.* Another term for **NSF check**.

dishonored note

dishonored note (dĭs ŏn′ərd nōt′) *n.* A **promissory note** (loan) that the maker cannot or will not pay at the maturity date.

disposal value (dĭ spō′zəl văl′yōō) *n.* Another term for **residual value** or **salvage value**.

dissolution (dĭs′ə lōō′shən) *n.* **1.** The ending of a partnership because of a change in the people who are partners. The remaining partners can form a new partnership that will be a new accounting entity. The transition results primarily in changes in the Capital accounts, while routine business is carried on as usual. **2.** The act or process of breaking sthg. into parts: *A series of bad financial decisions caused the dissolution of the company.* **3.** An ending of a formal contract.

distribution (dĭs′trə byōō′shən) *n.* **1.** The dividing up and giving out of sthg. in regular amounts or shares: *Stock distribution has been put off until next quarter.* **2.** The supplying or sending out of sthg.: *distribution of paychecks.*

distributive share (dĭ strĭb′yə tĭv shâr′) *n.* The share of the net income (or net loss) that is allocated to each partner.

diversified company (dĭ vûr′sə fīd′ kŭm′pə nē) *n., pl.* **companies.** A company that operates in more than one industry. Also called a **conglomerate**.

dividend (dĭv′ĭ dĕnd′) *n.* The distribution of a corporation's earnings, usually cash, to its stockholders. See also **stock dividend.**

dividends in arrears (dĭv′ĭ dĕndz′ ĭn ə rîrz′) *pl.n.* Dividends on cumulative preferred stock that remain **unpaid** in the year they are due.

dividends payable (dĭv′ĭ dĕndz pā′ə bəl) *pl.n.* A liability for payment of a company's earnings to its shareholders. Such a liability does not exist until the board of directors **declares** the dividends.

dividends yield (dĭv′ĭ dĕndz yēld′) *n.* Used to measure the current return to an investor in a stock. This is found by dividing dividends per share by market price per share.

document (dŏk′yə mənt) *n.* **1.** Another term for **source document.** **2.** A written or printed paper that is used to give evidence or information: *The documents related to this issue are on your desk.* —*tr.v.* To prove or support (sthg.) with written or printed evidence: *We haven't been able to document the extent of the fraud.*

double-declining-balance method (dŭb′əl dĭ klī′nĭng băl′əns mĕth′əd) *n.* An accelerated way of depreciating a long-term asset. In this method, a fixed rate that is equal to twice the **straight-line percentage** is applied to the carrying value of the asset.

double-entry accounting (dŭb′əl ĕn′trē ə koun′tĭng) *n.* A system in which each business transaction is recorded in at least two accounts and the accounting equation is kept in balance.

double-entry system (dŭb′əl ĕn′trē sĭs′təm) *n.* An accounting system in which each transaction is recorded with at least one debit and one credit so that the total dollar amount of debits and the total dollar amount of credits equal each other. This is based on the **principle of duality.**

double taxation (dŭb′əl tăk sā′shən) *n.* The act of taxing corporate earnings twice, once as the net income of the corporation and once as the dividends distributed to stockholders.

downsize (doun′sīz′) **downsized, downsizing, downsizes.** *tr.v.* To make (sthg.) smaller: *Manufacturers downsized cars in the 1980s.* —*intr.v.* **1.** To become smaller in terms of workers,

duration of note

managers, or divisions. **2.** To reduce the number of workers in a company significantly: *He's looking for a new job because he was downsized.*

downsizing (doun′sī′zĭng) *n.* The tactic used by corporations to reduce product and other operating expenses by drastically reducing the size of the workforce: *Many companies have resorted to downsizing in order to remain competitive.* Also called **rightsizing, reengineering.**

dpt. *Abbr.* An abbreviation of department.

draw (drô) *tr.v.* **drew** (drōō), **drawn, drawing, draws.** To obtain (sthg.) from a source of supply. *To draw ones wages.* **2.** To write out (a check): *Which bank was the check drawn on?* See also **withdraw** (sense 1).

drawer (drô′ər) *n.* The individual who writes a check: *Who is the drawer on the check?*

drawing (drô′ĭng) *n.* Another term for **withdrawal.**

duality (dōō ăl′ĭ tē) *n.* Another term for **principle of duality.**

due care (dōō kâr′) *n.* The act of carrying out professional responsibilities competently and diligently: *I hope you'll proceed in this matter with due care.*

due date (dōō dāt′) *n.* The date that a note (loan) must be paid in full, usually expressed in days or months.

duration of note (dōō rā′shən əv nōt′) *n.* The number of days between a promissory note's issue date and its maturity date.

Ee

early extinguishment of debt (ûr′lē ĭk stĭng′gwĭsh mənt əv dĕt′) *n.* The retirement of a bond issue before its maturity date.

earned capital (ûrnd′ kăp′ĭ tl) *n.* Another term for **retained earnings**.

earned income credit (ûrnd′ ĭn′kŭm krĕd′ĭt) *n. Abbr.* **EIC** A special income tax credit for certain people who work and have an earned income and modified adjusted gross income below a specified level.

earnings (ûr′nĭngz) *pl.n.* Another term for **primary earnings per share**.

earnings per share (ûr′nĭngz pər shâr′) *pl.n. Abbr.* **EPS** An amount shown on the income statement of a company, used to judge its performance and to compare it with other companies. It is arrived at by dividing net income by the number of shares of common stock outstanding (issued and still in circulation). See also **primary earnings per share**.

economic entity (ĕk′ə nŏm′ĭk ĕn′tĭ tē) *n., pl.* **entities.** A unit, such as a business, a hospital, a nonprofit organization, a club, or a government body, that exists independently and has financial transactions that must be accounted for. Also called **separate entity** or **business entity**.

economics (ĕk′ə nŏm′ĭks *or* ē′kə nŏm′ĭks) *n.* **1.** *(used with a singular verb).* The study of the ways goods and services are produced, transported, sold, and used: *Economics is one of her scholarly interests.* **2.** *(used with a singular or plural verb).* Economic matters, especially those relating to cost and profit: *the economics of running a small business.*

economic unit (ĕk′ə nŏm′ĭk yōō′nĭt) *n.* Another term for **economic entity**.

economist (ĭ kŏn′ə mĭst) *n.* A person whose profession is the study of economics.

effective interest (ĭ fĕk′tĭv ĭn′trĭst) *n.* Another term for **market interest rate**.

effective interest method (ĭ fĕk′tĭv ĭn′trĭst mĕth′əd) *n.* A way of amortizing bond discounts or premiums by applying a constant interest rate—in this case, the market rate at the time the bonds were issued—to the carrying value of the bonds at the beginning of each interest period.

effective interest rate (ĭ fĕk′tĭv ĭn′trĭst rāt′) *n.* The rate of interest actually paid or earned. By law, it must be clearly stated to borrowers and depositors. It reflects the impact of compounding frequency. Also called **true interest rate** or **annual percentage rate (APR)**.

efficiency variance (ĭ fĭsh′ən sē vâr′ē əns) *n.* Another term for **direct labor efficiency variance**.

EFT *Abbr.* An abbreviation of electronic funds transfer.

EIC *Abbr.* An abbreviation of earned income credit.

EIN *Abbr.* An abbreviation of employer identification number.

electronic funds transfer (ĭ lĕk trŏn′ĭk fŭndz′ trăns′fər) *n. Abbr.* **EFT** The transfer of funds from one bank to another through electronic communication.

eliminate (ĭ lĭm′ə nāt′) *tr.v.* **eliminated, eliminating, eliminated.** To get rid of or remove (sbdy./sthg.): *How can we eliminate or reduce the pollution caused by the process of manufacturing paper?*

42

endorsement

eliminating entry (ĭ lĭm′ə nāt′ĭng ĕn′trē) *n.* An entry made on consolidated work sheets to eliminate transactions between parent and subsidiary companies. See also **purchase method.**

elimination entry (ĭ lĭm′ə nā′shən ĕn′trē) *n.* See **eliminating entry.**

embezzle (ĕm bĕz′əl) *tr.v.* **embezzled, embezzling, embezzles.** To steal (money) from an employer: *The cashier embezzled $125,000 from the bank during a ten-year period.* —**embezzlement** *n.*

employee (ĕm ploi′ē *or* ĕm′ploi ē′) *n.* A person who works for wages or salary under the direction and control of an **employer.**

employee earnings record (ĕm ploi′ē ûr′nĭngz rĕk′ərd) *n.* A record of earnings and withholdings for an individual employee.

employee stock ownership plan (ĕm ploi′ē stŏk′ ō′nər shĭp plăn′) *n. Abbr.* **ESOP** A benefit offered by some companies to their employees that allows employees to buy stock in the company at regular intervals.

Employee's Withholding Allowance (Exemption) Certificate (ĕm ploi′ēz wĭth hōl′dĭng ə lou′əns (ĭg zĕmp′shən) sər tĭf′ĭ kĭt) *n.* Another term for **Form W-4.**

employer (ĕm ploi′ər) *n.* A person or an entity that engages the services of another person in exchange for money.

employer identification number (ĕm ploi′ər ī dĕn′tə fĭ kā′shən nŭm′bər) *n. Abbr.* **EIN** The number that is assigned to each employer by the Internal Revenue Service for use in making tax payments.

Employer's Annual Federal Unemployment Tax Return (ĕm ploi′ərz ăn′yōō əl fĕd′ə rəl ŭn′ĕm ploi′mənt tăks′ rĭ tûrn′) *n.* Another term for **Form 940.**

Employer's Quarterly Federal Tax Return (ĕm ploi′ərz kwôr′tər lē fĕd′ə rəl tăks′ rĭ tûrn′) *n.* Another term for **Form 941.**

encumber (ĕn kŭm′bər) *tr.v.* **1.** To burden (sbdy.) with legal or financial obligations: *encumbered by debt.* **2.** To put a heavy load on (sbdy.); burden: *The rider's weight encumbered the horse.* **3.** To hinder or make difficult the action or performance of (sbdy./sthg.): *rules that encumber efficient management.*

encumbrance (ĕn kŭm′brəns) *n.* **1.** In not-for-profit accounting, a way of restricting the amount of money spent so that an organization will not exceed the amounts of money appropriated. **2.** A burden: *Carrying extra weight proved to be an encumbrance for the runner.*

end (ĕnd) *n.* The finish or conclusion of sthg.: *the end of the year.* —*v.* —*tr.* To bring (sthg.) to a conclusion; finish: *She ended the discussion by leaving abruptly.* —*intr.* To come to a finish; conclude: *The meeting ended on a happy note.*

ending (ĕn′dĭng) *n.* The concluding part of sthg., such as a book, movie, or play: *Most people like happy endings.*

ending inventory (ĕn′dĭng ĭn′vən tôr′ē) *n., pl.* **inventories.** Merchandise on hand at the end of an accounting period.

endorse (ĕn dôrs′) *tr.v.* **endorsed, endorsing, endorses. 1.** To write one's name on the back of (a check): *Have you endorsed your paycheck?* **2.** To support or approve of (sbdy./sthg.): *The local newspaper has endorsed a candidate.*

endorsement (ĕn dôrs′mənt) *n.* The process by which the payee transfers ownership of a check to a bank or another party by writing his or her name on the back of it. A check must be endorsed when deposited in a bank because the bank must have

endorsement "without recourse"

legal title to it in order to collect payment from the **drawer** of the check (the person or firm who wrote the check).

endorsement "without recourse" (ĕn dôrs′ mənt wĭth out′ rē′kôrs) *n.* Another term for **qualified endorsement.**

end product (ĕnd′ prŏd′ŭkt) *n.* The result of a completed series of processes or changes: *Increasing tourism will have as its end product increased revenues for the state.*

engineered time (ĕn′jə nîrd′ tīm′) *n.* The standard or predicted machine time needed for making a product.

enter (ĕn′tər) *tr.v.* **1.** To write or record a company's or an organization's financial transaction, such as a debit or a credit, in the ledger. **2.** To come or go into a place: *It was early when the first workers entered the parking lot.* **3.** To pierce; penetrate: *The bullet entered the body at a downward angle.*

enterprise funds (ĕn′tər prīz′ fŭndz′) *pl.n.* In not-for-profit accounting, an account for activities that are available to the public and are financed and operated like a private business. For example, a city might own and operate a water system or recreation center.

entry (ĕn′trē) *n., pl.* **entries. 1.a.** The act of recording a company's or an organization's financial transaction in the ledger: *The clerk hasn't yet finished entry of the day's sales.* **b.** An item when it is entered in a company's or an organization's ledger: *Scroll back; I want to see that last entry again.* **2.** The act or an instance of going into a place: *Entry into the research labs was limited.* **3.** A way or place by which to enter sthg.: *We receive deliveries at our back entry.*

eom *Abbr.* An abbreviation of end-of-month.

EPS *Abbr.* An abbreviation of earnings per share.

equal cash flows (ē′kwəl kăsh′ flōz′) *pl.n.* May refer to projected or actual cash flows. Cash flows that are the same for each year of an asset's life. See also **unequal cash flows.**

equation (ĭ kwā′zhən *or* ĭ kwā′shən) *n.* A mathematical statement that two expressions are equal. It is usually written as a line of symbols on both the right and left sides of an equal sign: $E = mc^2$ *is an equation.*

equip (ĭ kwĭp′) *tr.v.* **equipped, equipping, equips.** To provide (sbdy./sthg.) with what is required to accomplish a specific purpose: *I doubt that he's equipped to handle a crisis. Being properly equipped is essential for starting a business.*

equipment (ĭ kwĭp′mənt) *n.* The things needed or used in a specific activity: *We'll need more equipment to meet our production goal.*

equity (ĕk′wĭ tē) *n.* **1.** Justice; fairness: *Where's the equity in such a plan?* **2.** Another term for **claim** (sense 2). **3.** The value of property after deducting any charges to which it is liable.

equity account (ĕk′wĭ tē ə kount′) *n.* An account that contains the figures showing the value of a business beyond any mortgages or liabilities.

equity method (ĕk′wĭ tē mĕth′əd) *n.* A way of accounting for long-term investments, when the investing company owns 20 percent to 50 percent of another company's voting stock. This method presumes the investing company has significant influence over the other company and should therefore share proportionally in its net income or losses.

equivalent (ĭ kwĭv′ə lənt) *adj.* Equal in value, meaning, or importance: *equivalent salaries.* —*n.* Something that is equal in value, meaning, or importance: *A nickel is the equivalent of five pennies.*

exchange

equivalent production (ĭ kwĭv′ə lənt prə dŭk′shən) *n.* A measure of the number of equivalent **whole units** produced in a period of time. In order to predict the number of completed units, units that are only partially completed are treated as though they were whole units, that is, as the equivalent of whole units. Also called **equivalent units**.

ESOP (ē′sŏp) *Abbr.* An abbreviation of employee stock ownership plan.

estimate (ĕs′tə māt′) *tr.v.* **estimated, estimating, estimates.** To make a judgment about the approximate cost, amount, or size of sthg.: *Can you estimate how much the improvements might cost?* —*n.* (ĕs′tə mĭt) An approximate calculation of the cost, amount, or size of sthg.: *The builder's estimate for the project is too high.*

estimated liabilities (ĕs′tə mā′tĭd lī′ə bĭl′ĭ tēz) *pl.n.* Debts for which the exact dollar amount cannot be known until a later date.

estimated useful life (ĕs′tə mā′tĭd yōōs′fəl līf′) *n.* The total number of **service units** expected from a long-term asset. Service units may be measured in terms of the number of years a given tangible asset can be expected to be useful, the number of units expected to be produced, the number of miles expected to be driven, or similar measures.

estimation (ĕs′tə mā′shən) *n.* **1.** A judgment about the approximate cost, quantity, or size of (sthg.): *What is the current estimation of profits for the next quarter?* Another term for **forecasting**. **2.** An opinion or judgment: *In your estimation, what is the best way to handle the situation?*

ethics (ĕth′ĭks) *n.* (*used with a singular or plural verb.*) A code of conduct used to judge whether everyday actions are right or wrong.

ex. *Abbr.* An abbreviation of exchange.

exceed (ĭk sēd′) *tr.v.* To be greater than (sthg.): *Our expenses exceeded our estimate.*

excess (ĭk sĕs′ *or* ĕk′sĕs′) *n.* **1.** The amount or quantity that is more than what is actually needed; a surplus: *We bought too many boxes this year, and we don't know what to do with the excess.* **2.** The amount or degree that one quantity is greater than another: *The package weighed in excess of four pounds.* —*adj.* Being more than what is usual or needed: *excess baggage; excess cost.*

excess capacity (ĕk′sĕs kə păs′ĭ tē) *n., pl.* **capacities.** Machinery and equipment not being used but kept on standby.

exch. *Abbr.* An abbreviation of exchange.

exchange (ĭks chānj′) *v.* **exchanged, exchanging, exchanged.** *Abbr.* **exch.** —*tr.* **1.** To give (sthg.), such as money, for sthg. received; trade: *I exchanged my gold coins for her painting.* **2.** To turn in (sthg.) for another, similar item: *She exchanged the TV that didn't work for one that did.* —*intr.* To be received as currency: *Last week the British pound exchanged for $2.00.* —*n. Abbr.* **exch., ex. 1.** The act or an instance of making an exchange: *We made a profitable exchange.* **2.** A place where things are exchanged, especially a financial center where securities or products are bought and sold: *the stock exchange.* **3.a.** A system of payments in which **instruments**, such as **negotiable drafts**, are used instead of money. **b.** The fee charged for using such a system of payments. **4.** Another term for **bill of exchange**. **5.** Another term for **exchange rate**. **6.** The amount of difference in the actual value of two or more currencies or between the values of the same currency at two or more places.

exchange gain

exchange gain or **loss** (ĭks chānj′ gān′ or lôs′) *n.* A gain or loss arising from exchange rate fluctuations; the net gain or loss reported on the income statement.

exchange of value (ĭks chānj′ əv văl′yōō) *n.* A business transaction between two or more parties that involves the giving or receiving of one thing of value in return for something else of value, such as a purchase, sale, payment, collection, or loan. Another term for **exchange transaction**. See also **nonexchange transaction**.

exchange rate (ĭks chānj′ rāt′) *n.* The ratio at which a unit of currency from one nation can be exchanged for the unit of currency of another nation; the value of one currency in terms of another. Also called **rate of exchange**.

exchange transaction (ĭks chānj′ trăn săk′shən) *n.* A business transaction that involves an exchange of value. Another term for **exchange of value**. See also **nonexchange transaction**.

excise (tax) (ĕk′sīz (tăks′)) *n.* A government tax on production, sale, or use of certain items or services: *an excise on liquor and tobacco.*

excise taxes payable (ĕk′sīz tăk′sīz pā′ə bəl) *pl.n.* The amount of money a retail business must collect and send periodically to the appropriate government agency. The amount of tax collected is a liability until it is sent to the government.

ex-dividend (ĕks′dĭv′ĭ dĕnd) *n.* The period beginning four days prior to the date of record and the date of payment, when the right to a dividend already declared on the stock remains with the person who sells the stock and does not transfer to the person who buys it.

exempt (ĭg zĕmpt′) *tr.v.* [*from*] To free (sbdy.) from a debt or an obligation; excuse: *We can exempt you from this exercise, if you wish.* —*adj.* Freed from a duty or an obligation that is required of others: *She is exempt from paying taxes on the first $2,000 in income.*

exemption (ĭg zĕmp′shən) *n.* An amount of an employee's annual earnings not subject to income tax: *The federal government allows every taxpayer an exemption.* Also called **withholding allowance**.

expend (ĭk spĕnd′) *tr.v.* **1.** To spend (money): *How much did we expend for entertainment?* **2.** To use (sthg.): *You've already expended a lot of energy on this problem.*

expenditure (ĭk spĕn′də chər) *n.* **1.** The act or process of spending or using sthg.: *the expenditure of tax dollars.* **2.** An amount spent: *account for all expenditures.* **3.** A payment or an obligation to make future payment for an asset or a service: *business expenditures for travel.*

expense (ĭk spĕns′) *n.* **1.** Something spent on a specific item or for a particular purpose: *an enormous expense of valuable time.* **2.** A loss for the sake of sthg. gained; a sacrifice: *at the expense of one's health.* **3.** A spending of money: *Food is our largest expense.* **4. expenses.** The amount of money spent by an employee in performing a job, especially while away from the office: *Travel expenses usually include food and lodging.* **5.** Something requiring one to spend money: *Owning a car is a big expense.* **6.** A decrease in owner's equity that results from the costs of goods and services used up in the course of earning revenues. **7.** A cost related to the earning of revenue, including wages, rent, interest, and advertising, that can be paid in cash or at a later time. Also called **cost of doing business, expired costs**. See also **accounts payable**.

extraordinary repair

expense center (ĭk spĕns' sĕn'tər) *n.* Another term for **cost center.**

expire (ĭk spīr') *intr.v.* **expired, expiring, expires. 1.** To come to an end: *Our lease expired yesterday.* **2.** To no longer be valid: *Your driver's license has expired.* **3.** To die: *When the ambulance arrived, he'd already expired.* —**expiration** *n.*

expired (ĭk spīrd') *adj.* **1.** No longer valid: *an expired rental contract.* **2.** Dead: *an expired friend.*

expired cost (ĭk spīrd' kôst') *n.* Another term for **expense** (sense 7).

explain (ĭk splān') *v.* —*tr.* **1.** To make (sthg.) easier to understand or to provide more details: *explain the rules of a game.* **2.** To give (reasons) for (sthg.); justify: *explain one's behavior.* —*intr.* To make sthg. more specific or easier to understand: *Must I explain?* —**explanation** *n.* —**explanatory** *adj.*

explanatory note (ĭk splăn'ə tôr'ē nōt') *n.* One of the notes included in a company's financial statement to meet the requirements of **full disclosure.** An explanatory note explains items such as seasonal financing, the details of specific accounts or entries, taxes on income, and stockholders' equity.

external (ĭk stûr'nəl) *adj.* **1.** Being outside or on the outside: *external repairs to a factory roof.* **2.** Relating to an outer surface: *This medicine is for external use only.* **3.** Acting or coming from outside: *external forces.*

external failure costs (ĭk stûr'nəl fāl'yər kôsts') *pl.n.* The costs incurred when defects are discovered after a product or service has been delivered to a customer; a cost of nonconformance.

extinguish (ĭk stĭng'gwĭsh) *tr.v.* **1.** To settle or pay off (a debt): *Can we extinguish outstanding debts by the end of the year?* **2.** To put out (a fire): *We managed to extinguish the fire on the second floor.* **3.** To put an end to (sthg.); destroy: *Months of low sales extinguished the company's hopes to recover financially.* —**extinguishment** *n.*

extraordinary (ĭk strôr'dn ĕr'ē or ĕk'strə ôr'dn ĕr'ē) *adj.* Very unusual: *an extraordinary expense.*

extraordinary item (ĭk strôr'dn ĕr'ē ī'təm) *n.* An event or a transaction that is both unusual in nature and infrequent in occurrence.

extraordinary repair (ĭk strôr'dn ĕr'ē rĭ pâr') *n.* A major repair that increases the estimated residual value of a long-term asset or extends the estimated useful life of an asset. See also **ordinary repair.**

Ff

face (fās) *adj.* Showing or visible on an outer surface of sthg., such as a note or bill: *face value.* —*n.* **1.** The front of the head: *He had a surprised look on his face.* **2.** An outer surface: *the face of a building.*

face interest rate (fās' ĭn'trĭst rāt') *n.* The rate of interest paid to bondholders based on the face value of the bonds.

face value (fās' văl'yōō) *n.* **1.** The face amount of a note or bond on which interest is charged or paid. Another term for **principal. 2.** The arbitrary amount imprinted on each bond or share of stock, used to determine the legal capital of a corporation. Another term for **par value. 3.** The apparent value or meaning of sthg.: *You'll have to take my comments at face value.*

factor (făk'tər) *n.* **1.** An entity that buys accounts receivable: *We need to find a factor to raise funds.* **2.** Something that helps cause a certain result; an element: *His contacts were certainly a factor in his success.* **3.** In mathematics, one of two or more numbers or expressions that are multiplied to obtain a given product. —*tr.v.* [*in*] To consider (sthg.) as relevant to a decision: *Have you factored in overtime as part of the labor cost?*

factoring (făk'tə rĭng) *n.* The selling or transferring of accounts receivable to another business entity: *A company's acceptance of credit cards is an example of factoring.*

factory (făk'tə rē) *n., pl.* **factories.** A building or group of buildings in which goods are manufactured; a plant: *They're going to build a new factory on that land.*

factory burden (făk'tə rē bûr'dn) *n.* See **factory overhead budget, Factory Overhead Control account, factory overhead costs,** and **predetermined overhead rate.**

factory overhead budget (făk'tə rē ō'vər hĕd bŭj'ĭt) *n.* A detailed schedule of anticipated manufacturing costs, other than direct materials and direct labor costs, that must be incurred to meet the production expectations of a future period.

Factory Overhead Control account (făk'tə rē ō'vər hĕd kən trōl' ə kount') *n.* A general ledger account that contains the cumulative total of all types of factory overhead costs incurred as well as factory overhead costs applied to the products produced.

factory overhead costs (făk'tə rē ō'vər hĕd kôsts') *pl.n.* Various production-related costs that cannot be practically or conveniently traced to an end product. Also called **manufacturing overhead, factory burden,** and **indirect manufacturing costs.**

Factory Payroll account (făk'tə rē pā'rōl ə kount') *n.* An account in which wages and salaries are entered.

fair (fâr) *adj.* **1.** Without prejudice; just: *a fair appraisal of the property.* **2.** Not very good; mediocre: *a fair job review.*

Fair Labor Standards Act (fâr' lā'bər stăn'dərdz ăkt') *n.* A federal law that sets minimum wage levels and regulates overtime pay. Also called **Wages and Hours Law.**

fair market value (fâr' mär'kĭt văl'yōō) *n.* The present worth of an asset, or the amount that would be received if the asset were sold to an outsider on the open market.

FASB *Abbr.* An abbreviation of Financial Accounting Standards Board.

federal income taxes (fĕd'ər əl ĭn'kŭm tăk'sĭz) *pl.n.* Taxes on net income that must be paid to the federal government by individuals and businesses.

financial leverage

Federal Insurance Contributions Act (fĕd′ər əl ĭn shoor′əns kŏn′trə byoo′shəns ăkt′) *n. Abbr.* **FICA** The federal act that requires workers to contribute a percentage of their income to Social Security and Medicare.

Federal Reserve Board (fĕd′ər əl rĭ zûrv′ bôrd′) *n.* The group of directors that supervises the Federal Reserve System.

Federal Reserve System (fĕd′ər əl rĭ zûrv′ sĭs′təm) *n.* The U.S. banking system that consists of 12 federal reserve banks located in different geographical regions. It has broad powers over the money supply and the credit structure in the United States.

Federal Unemployment Tax (fĕd′ər əl ŭn′ĕm ploi′mənt tăks′) *n. Abbr.* **FUTA** A payroll tax levied on employers, by the federal government to pay for programs to help unemployed workers.

fee (fē) *n.* A charge or payment for a service or privilege.

FICA (fī′kə *or* fē′kə) *Abbr.* An abbreviation of Federal Insurance Contribution Act.

FICA taxes (fī′kə tăk′sĭz) *pl.n.* Social Security taxes plus Medicare taxes paid by both employee and employer under the provisions of the Federal Insurance Contributions Act. The proceeds are used to pay old-age and disability pensions and fund the Medicare program.

FIFO (fī′fō) *Abbr.* An abbreviation of first-in, first-out.

FIFO costing approach (fī′fō kôs′tĭng ə prōch′) *n.* A process costing method in which cost flow follows product flow. The first products to be introduced into the production process are the first products to be completed. Costs assigned to those first products are the first costs to be transferred out of the production center or department.

finance (fə năns′ *or* fī′năns′) *n.* **1.** The science of the management of money and other financial assets: *the world of finance.* **2. finances.** Money resources; funds: *The company's finances are in bad shape.* —*tr.v.* **financed, financing, finances.** To provide or obtain funds or capital for (sthg.): *How can we finance the needed improvements?*

finance company (fə năns′ kŭm′pə nē) *n., pl.* **companies.** A company that makes loans to people and businesses.

financial (fə năn′shəl *or* fī năn′shəl) *adj.* Relating to finance: *the financial pages; financial difficulties.*

financial accounting (fə năn′shəl ə koun′tĭng) *n.* The process of generating and communicating accounting information in the form of financial statements to those outside an organization.

Financial Accounting Standards Board (fə năn′shəl ə koun′tĭng stăn′dərdz bôrd′) *n. Abbr.* **FASB** The most important body responsible for developing and issuing rules on accounting practices, called Statements of Financial Accounting Standards.

financial activity (fə năn′shəl ăk tĭv′ĭ tē) *n.* An activity undertaken by management to obtain adequate funds to begin and to continue operating a business.

financial highlights (fə năn′shəl hī′līts) *pl.n.* A section of a firm's annual report that presents important financial statistics for a 10-year period, usually accompanied by illustrative graphs.

financial information (fə năn′shəl ĭn′fər mā′shən) *n.* Another term for **accounting information**.

financial leverage (fə năn′shəl lĕv′ər ĭj) *n.* The ability to increase earnings for stockholders by earning more on assets

financial position

than is paid in interest on debt incurred to finance the assets. Also called **trading on the equity**.

financial position (fə năn′shəl pə zĭsh′ən) *n.* The resources or assets (equities) owned by an economic unit at a point in time. These are offset by the claims against those resources and owner's equity, as shown by a balance sheet.

financial statement (fə năn′shəl stāt′mənt) *n.* A report prepared by accountants, the primary means of communicating important accounting information to external decision makers. This report summarizes the financial affairs of a business and includes an income statement, statement of owner's equity, balance sheet, and statement of cash flows.

financial statement analysis (fə năn′shəl stāt′mənt ə năl′ĭ sĭs) *n., pl.* **analyses**. All the techniques used to show important relationships among figures in a financial statement.

financing (fə năn′sĭng *or* fī′năn sĭng) *n.* Money provided by an individual, a bank, or a group to support a purchase: *bank financing.*

financing activity (fə năn′sĭng ăk tĭv′ĭ tē) *n., pl.* **activities**. A business activity that involves obtaining resources from or returning resources to owners and providing them with a return on their investment, and obtaining resources from creditors and repaying the amount borrowed or settling the obligation in some other way.

finish (fĭn′ĭsh) *v.* — *tr.* **1.** To reach or come to the end of (sthg.): *finish a race.* **2.** To bring (sthg.) to an end; complete: *finish balancing the budget.* **3.** To consume all of (sthg.); use up: *finish the available lumber.* — *intr.* **1.** To come to an end: *Has the production cycle finished?* **2.** To reach the end of sthg., such as a task or relationship: *We worked on the account all night, but we didn't finish.* — *n. (usually singular).* The end of sthg.: *the finish of the third quarter tax estimates.*

finished (fĭn′ĭsht) *adj.* Completed: *a finished project.*

finished goods (fĭn′ĭsht gŏŏdz′) *pl.n.* The products that have been made and are ready for sale.

finished goods inventory (fĭn′ĭsht gŏŏdz′ ĭn′vən tôr′ē) *n.* The quantity of finished goods on hand and available for sale at the end of an accounting period.

finished goods inventory account (fĭn′ĭsht gŏŏdz′ ĭn′vən tôr′ē ə kount′) *n.* An inventory account unique to manufacturing operations. This account holds the costs of all completed products that have not been sold.

firm (fûrm) *n.* A business partnership, especially when it is unincorporated. Another term for **business** (sense 3), **business entity, company, economic entity**. See also **corporation**.

first-in, first-out method (fûrst′ĭn′ fûrst′out′ mĕth′əd) *n. Abbr.* **FIFO** A way of figuring inventory cost based on the assumption that the costs of the first items acquired should be assigned to the first items sold. See also **last-in, first-out method**.

fiscal (fĭs′kəl) *adj.* Relating to finance or finances: *fiscal responsibility.*

fiscal period (fĭs′kəl pĭr′ē əd) *n.* Another term for **fiscal year**.

fiscal year (fĭs′kəl yĭr′) *n.* Any 12-month accounting period used by an economic entity, for example, a fiscal year can begin on January 1 and end on December 31.

$500 rule (fīv′ hŭn′drĭd dŏl′ər rōōl′) *n.* A rule pertaining to small employers who accumulate less than a $500 tax liability during a quarter. No deposits are required. This liability may be paid with the tax return for the period.

follow-up principles of budgeting

fixed (fĭkst) *adj.* **1.** Not changing; constant: *fixed assets.* **2.** Firmly in position; stationary: *a roomful of fixed cubicles.* **3.** Having a result that has been illegally controlled: *a fixed election.*

fixed assets (fĭkst' ăs'ĕts) *n.* Tangible long-term assets used in the continuing operation of a business that are unlikely to change for a long time. Another term for **property, plant, and equipment.**

fixed budget (fĭkst' bŭj'ĭt) *n.* A budget that shows the desired operating results and provides a goal for use in determining monthly and weekly operating plans. Also called **static budget.** See also **flexible budget.**

fixed costs (fĭkst' kôsts') *pl.n.* Costs that remain constant within a defined range of activity, volume, or time period.

fixed manufacturing costs (fĭkst' măn'yə făk'chər ĭng kôsts') *pl.n.* Production costs that stay fairly constant during the accounting period.

flexibility (flĕk'sə bĭl'ĭ tē) *n.* **1.** The ability to take care of the kinds of transactions a company commonly encounters. **2.** The ability to change easily: *the flexibility of rubber.* **3.** Of the human body, the ability to bend and twist easily: *a gymnast's flexibility.*

flexibility principle (flĕk'sə bĭl'ĭ tē prĭn'sə pəl) *n.* The principle that holds that the design of an accounting system must be flexible enough to allow the volume of transactions to grow and organizational changes to be made.

flexible (flĕk'sə bəl) *adj.* **1.** Able to be bent or twisted; pliable: *a flexible hose.* **2.** Able to change or be changed: *a flexible plan. My time is flexible.* —**flexibly** *adv.* —**flexibility** *n.*

flexible budget (flĕk'sə bəl bŭj'ĭt) *n.* A budget that provides predicted information that can be adjusted automatically when changes in the level of output occur; a summary of expected costs for a range of activity levels. Also called **variable budget.** See also **fixed budget.**

flexible budget formula (flĕk'sə bəl bŭj'ĭt fôr'myə lə) *n.* An equation for figuring the correct budgeted or standard cost for any level of productive activity. It is the variable costs per unit of measure multiplied by the number of units, plus the total budgeted fixed costs.

flexible manufacturing system (flĕk'sə bəl măn'yə făk'chər ĭng sĭs'təm) *n. Abbr.* **FMS** A single, multifunctional machine or an integrated set of computerized machines or systems designed to complete a series of operations automatically.

FMS *Abbr.* An abbreviation of flexible manufacturing system.

FOB, F.O.B., f.o.b. *Abbr.* An abbreviation of free on board.

FOB destination (ĕf'ō bē' dĕs'tə nā'shən) *n.* A shipping term that means that the seller bears transportation costs to the place of delivery.

FOB shipping point (ĕf'ō bē' shĭp'ĭng point') *n.* A shipping term that means that the buyer bears transportation costs from the point of origin.

folio column (fō'lē ō kŏl'əm) *n.* The column used to note the journal page where an original entry can be found. Another term for **posting reference column.**

follow-up principles of budgeting (fŏl'ō ŭp prĭn'sə pəlz əv bŭj'ĭ tĭng) *pl.n.* The accounting principles that are part of the control aspect of budgeting, including the importance of continuously checking the accuracy of a budget and correcting it when necessary.

foot

foot (fŏŏt) *n.* The bottom or lowest part of sthg.: *the foot of the column.* —*tr.v.* To total a column of numbers: *Have you footed those columns yet?*

footing (fŏŏt'ĭng) *n.* The working totals of columns of numbers.

forecast (fôr'kăst') *tr.v.* To tell in advance (sthg. that might or will happen): *forecast the weather; forecast the economy.* —*n.* A prediction about future events or conditions: *a weather forecast; an economic forecast.*

forecasted balance sheet (fôr'kăs'tĭd băl'əns shēt') *n.* A balance sheet that projects the financial position of a business for a future period.

forecasted income statement (fôr'kăs'tĭd ĭn'kŭm stāt'mənt) *n.* An income statement that projects the net income of a business for a future period.

forecasting of cash flow (fôr'kăs'tĭng əv kăsh' flō') *n.* Projecting the cash receipts and the cash payments for a future period.

foreign (fôr'ĭn *or* fŏr'ĭn) *adj.* **1.** Relating to or from another country: *foreign companies.* **2.** Conducted or involved with other countries: *foreign investments.*

foreign currency (fôr'ĭn kûr'ən sē) *n.* Cash or cash equivalents that belong to a foreign country.

foreign subsidiary (fôr'ĭn səb sĭd'ē ĕr'ē) *n., pl.* **subsidiaries.** A foreign company in which another company owns a controlling interest.

Form 8-K (fôrm' āt kā') *n.* A report that publicly held corporations must file with the Securities and Exchange Commission within a few days of a significant event. Such events may indicate important changes that affect the future financial performance of the company. Another term for **current report.**

Form 10-K (fôrm' těn kā') *n.* A standard annual report form that publicly held corporations must file with the Securities and Exchange Commission. The report contains more information than the published annual report.

Form 10-Q (fôrm' těn kyōō') *n.* A quarterly report that publicly held corporations must file with the Securities and Exchange Commission. The report presents important facts about interim financial performance.

Form 940 (fôrm' nīn fôr'tē) *n.* An annual report filed by employers showing total wages paid to employees, total wages subject to federal income tax, total federal unemployment tax, and other information. Also called **Employer's Annual Federal Unemployment Tax Return.**

Form 941 (fôrm nīn'fôr'tē wŭn') *n.* A report showing the tax liability for withholdings of employees' federal income tax and FICA tax and the employer's share of FICA tax. Total tax deposits made in the quarter are also listed on the **Employer's Quarterly Federal Income Tax Return.**

Form W-2 (fôrm dŭb'əl yōō tōō') *n.* A form containing information about employee earnings and tax deductions for the year. Also called **Wage and Tax Statement.**

Form W-3 (fôrm dŭb'əl yōō thrē') *n.* An annual report sent to the Social Security Administration listing the total wages and tips, total federal income tax withheld, total Social Security and Medicare taxable wages, total Social Security and Medicare tax withheld, and other information for all employees of a firm. Also called the **Transmittal of Wage and Tax Statements.**

Form W-4 (fôrm dŭb'əl yōō fôr') *n.* A form that specifies the number of exemptions claimed by each employee and that

52

fund

gives the employer the authority to withhold money for an employee's federal income taxes and FICA taxes. Also called **Employee's Withholding Allowance (Exemption) Certificate.**

franchise (frăn′chīz′) *n.* The right granted to someone, usually for a fee, to sell or distribute a company's goods or services in a certain area: *a restaurant franchise.*

fraud (frôd) *n.* **1.** Dishonesty practiced in order to make unfair or unlawful profit: *He was convicted of mail fraud.* **2.** A person who is deceitful or tries to trick others: *The doctor was found to be a fraud.*

fraudulent (frô′jə lənt) *adj.* Gained by or engaging in fraud; dishonest: *a fraudulent insurance claim.*

fraudulent financial reporting (frô′jə lənt fə năn′shəl rĭ-pôr′tĭng) *n.* The intentional preparation of misleading financial statements.

free cash flow (frē′ kăsh′ flō′) *n.* The amount of cash that remains after deducting the funds a company must commit to continue operating at its planned level. This is found by deducting dividends and net capital expenditures from net cash flows from operating activities. It is used to measure the amount of cash generated by an economic entity after allowing for its commitments.

free on board (frē′ ŏn bôrd′) *adj. & adv. Abbr.* **FOB, F.O.B., f.o.b.** Without charge to the buyer for delivery on board or into a carrier at a specified location.

freight charges (frāt′ chär′jĭz) *pl.n.* Another term for **freight in.**

freight in (frāt′ ĭn′) *n.* Transportation charges on merchandise purchased for resale. Also called **freight in expense, transportation expense,** or **transportation in.**

freight out (frāt′ out′) *n.* Transportation charges on merchandise sold; an operating expense. Also called **delivery expense** or **freight out expense.**

full-costing (fool′kôs′tĭng) *n.* A method of accounting for the costs of exploration and development of oil and gas resources. In this method all costs, those associated with both successful and unsuccessful exploration, are recorded as assets and depleted over the estimated life of the producing resources. Another term for **absorption costing.** See also **successful efforts.**

full cost profit margin (fool′ kôst′ prŏf′ĭt mär′jĭn) *n.* The difference between total revenue and total costs traceable to the work cell or product.

full disclosure (fool′ dĭ sklō′zhər) *n.* The accounting convention that requires that financial statements and their notes present all information relevant to the users' understanding of the company's financial condition.

function (fŭngk′shən) *n.* A group of activities that have a common purpose or objective.

functional (fŭngk′shə nəl) *adj.* **1.** Relating to a specific activity: *the functional responsibilities of a manager.* **2.** In working order: *a functional time clock.* **3.** Intended to be used in a particular way or a specific location.

functional currency (fŭngk′shə nəl kûr′ən sē) *n., pl.* **currencies.** The currency of the country where a subsidiary conducts most of its business.

functional depreciation (fŭngk′shə nəl dĭ prē′shē ā′shən) *n.* A way that tangible assets lose their usefulness to companies by becoming obsolete or inadequate. See also **physical depreciation.**

fund (fŭnd) *n.* **1.** A sum of money set aside for a specific purpose: *a retirement fund; a scholarship fund.* **2. funds.** Avail-

fundamental accounting equation

able money; ready cash: *Will our funds last until the end of the month?* —*tr.v.* To provide money for (sthg.): *fund new construction.*

fundamental accounting equation (fŭn′də mĕn′tl ə koun′-tĭng ĭ kwā′zhən) *n.* Another term for **accounting equation.**

fund balance account (fŭnd′ băl′əns ə kount′) *n.* A capital or equity account.

FUTA (fyōō′tə) *Abbr.* An abbreviation of Federal Unemployment Tax Act.

future value (fyōō′chər văl′yōō) *n.* *(usually singular).* The amount that an investment will be worth at a future date if it is invested at compound interest.

Gg

G&A *Abbr.* An abbreviation of general and administrative (expense budget).

GAAP *Abbr.* An abbreviation of generally accepted accounting principles.

gain (gān) *v.* —*tr.* To obtain (sbdy./sthg.): *gain work experience.* **2.** To get an increase of (sthg.): *Sales gained momentum.* —*intr.* To increase; grow: *Land often gains in value.* —*n.* **1.** An increase in wealth or money: *He made a nice gain on his investment.* **2.** Progress; advancement: *Social gains require public support.*

Gain on Disposal of Plant and Equipment (gān′ ŏn dĭ spō′zəl əv plănt′ ănd ĭ kwĭp′mənt) *n.* The income account in which a gain is recorded when a firm sells or trades in an asset and receives an amount in excess of the book value for that asset. It appears under Other Income in the income statement.

GASB *Abbr.* An abbreviation of Governmental Accounting Standards Board.

general and administrative expense budget (jĕn′ər əl ənd ăd mĭn′ĭ strā′tĭv ĭk spĕns′ bŭj′ĭt) *n. Abbr.* **G&A** A detailed plan of operating expenses, other than those of manufacturing and selling, needed to support overall business operations for a future period.

general expenses (jĕn′ər əl ĭk spĕn′sĭz) *pl.n.* Expenses incurred in the administration of a business, including office expenses and any expenses that are not wholly classified as Selling Expenses or Other Expenses.

general fund (jĕn′ər əl fŭnd′) *n.* A kind of account used by state and local governments that contains information on the revenues and operating activities. For example, a city's general fund covers administration, fire, police, sanitation, and other services.

general journal (jĕn′ər əl jûr′nəl) *n.* The simplest and most flexible type of journal. It is used to record all transactions chronologically so that individual transactions and errors can be more easily identified. Also called **book of original entry, journal.**

general ledger (jĕn′ər əl lĕj′ər) *n.* The book or computer file that contains all of a company's accounts arranged in the order of the chart of accounts. Also called **ledger.**

general ledger software (jĕn′ər əl lĕj′ər sôft′wâr′) *n.* Computer programs that direct the computer to carry out the major accounting functions.

generally accepted accounting principles (jĕn′ər ə lē ăk sĕp′tĭd ə koun′tĭng prĭn′sə pəlz) *pl.n. Abbr.* **GAAP** The conventions, rules, and procedures that define accepted accounting practice at a particular time.

general partners (jĕn′ər əl pärt′nərz) *pl.n.* Partners who actively and publicly participate in the transactions of a firm and have unlimited liability.

going concern (gō′ĭng kən sûrn′) *n.* The assumption, unless there is evidence to the contrary, that a business entity will continue to operate indefinitely.

goods available for sale (gŏŏdz′ ə vā′lə bəl fôr sāl′) *pl.n.* **1.** The sum of beginning inventory and the net cost of purchases during a period. **2.** The total goods available for sale to customers during an accounting period.

goods flow

goods flow (go͝odz′ flō′) *n.* The actual physical movement of goods in the operations of a company. See also **cost flow**.

goodwill (go͝od′wĭl′) *n.* **1.** The excess of the cost of a group of assets, usually a business, over the fair market value of the net assets if they were purchased individually. Also called **goodwill from consolidation**. **2.** An attitude of kindness or friendliness. **3.** A good relationship of a business with its customers.

goodwill from consolidation (go͝od′wĭl′ frŭm kən sŏl′ĭ dā′shən) *n.* Another term for **goodwill**.

Governmental Accounting Standards Board (gŭv′ərn-měn′tl ə koun′tĭng stăn′dərdz bôrd′) *n. Abbr.* **GASB** The board responsible for issuing accounting standards for state and local governments.

gross (grōs) *adj.* Having nothing subtracted; total: *gross profit.* —*n., pl.* **gross. 1.** The entire amount of income before any deductions have been made: *The company's gross is impressive.* **2.** A group of 144 items; 12 dozen: *a gross of hammers.* —*tr.v.* To earn (money) as total profit or income before deductions: *The company grossed over $4 billion this year.*

gross margin (grōs′ mär′jĭn) *n.* The difference between net sales and cost of goods sold. Also called **gross profit**.

gross margin pricing (grōs′ mär′jĭn prī′sĭng) *n.* An approach to cost-based pricing in which the price is computed using the percentage of a product's total production costs.

gross pay (grōs′ pā′) *n.* The total amount of an employee's pay before deductions.

gross payroll (grōs′ pā′rōl) *n.* The total wages and salaries earned by employees, including payroll deductions.

gross proceeds (grōs′ prō′sēdz) *pl.n.* The total amount of income before any deductions have been made.

gross profit (grōs′ prŏf′ĭt) *n.* Another term for **gross margin**.

gross profit method (grōs′ prŏf′ĭt měth′əd) *n.* A way of estimating the cost of inventory based on the assumption that the ratio of gross margin for a business remains relatively stable from year to year.

gross sales (grōs′ sālz′) *pl.n.* The total amount of sales for cash and on credit accumulated during a specific accounting period.

group depreciation (gro͞op′ dĭ prē′shē ā′shən) *n.* The grouping of similar items to calculate depreciation.

Hh

half-year convention (hăf′ yîr′ kən vĕn′shən) *n.* Taking only one-half of a year's depreciation on a long-lived asset, regardless of when it was purchased during the year.

hardware (härd′wâr′) *n.* The mechanical equipment and related components needed to operate a computerized data processing system.

held-to-maturity security (hĕld′tōō mə tyōōr′ĭ tē sĭ kyōōr′ĭ tē) *n.* A debt security that management intends to hold to its maturity or payment date and whose cash value is not needed until that date.

hierarchy (hī′ə rär′kē *or* hī′rär′kē) *n., pl.* **hierarchies.** A group of people or things organized according to rank or grade: *the hierarchy of positions in a corporation.*

high-low method (hī′lō′ mĕth′əd) *n.* A common, simple way of separating variable from fixed costs. It identifies a linear relationship between activity level and cost by analyzing the highest and lowest volumes in an accounting period and their related costs. The change in cost between the two sets of data is divided by the change in volume to find the variable cost component of the semivariable or mixed cost. This amount, in turn, is used to compute the fixed costs at each level of activity.

historical (hĭ stôr′ĭ kəl *or* hĭ stŏr′ĭ kəl) *adj.* Relating to or having happened in the past: *historical records; historical research.*

historical cost (hĭ stôr′ĭ kəl kôst′) *n.* The cost of a business transaction at the **point of recognition,** used to assign value to business transactions. Another term for **original cost.**

home base (hōm′ bās′) *n.* **1.** A base of operations; headquarters: *It's time to report to home base.* **2.** *Baseball.* Home plate.

home base network (hōm′ bās′ nĕt′wûrk) *n.* A computer network in which many microcomputers are linked to a central switching point, or home base. Also called **star network.**

horizontal (hôr′ĭ zŏn′tl *or* hŏr′ĭ zŏn′tl) *adj.* **1.** Parallel to the plane of the horizon; level: *a horizontal line.* **2.** In the same level in a hierarchy: *a horizontal transfer for an employee.*

horizontal analysis (hôr′ĭ zŏn′tl ə năl′ĭ sĭs) *n., pl.* **analyses.** A technique for analyzing financial statements that involves the computation of changes in both dollar amounts and percentages from the previous year to the current year.

Ii

IASC *Abbr.* An abbreviation of International Accounting Standards Committee.

ideal (ī dē′əl *or* ī dēl′) *adj.* **1.** Perfect; the best possible: *an ideal day for seeing customers.* **2.** Existing only in the mind; imaginary: *ideal work situation.* —*n.* **1.** A standard of perfection: *Justice is a social ideal.* **2.** A person or thing regarded as an example of excellence or perfection: *He's my ideal of what a manager should be.*

ideal capacity (ī dē′əl kə păs′ĭ tē) *n.* The maximum productive output for a given period, assuming all machinery and equipment are operating at optimum speed, without interruption. Another term for **theoretical capacity**.

ideal measure (ī dē′əl mĕzh′ər) *n.* Another term for **rule-of-thumb measure**.

idle (īd′l) *adj.* Not working or being used: *an idle factory.*

idle cash (īd′l kăsh′) *n.* Cash that is not being used at a specific time: *Idle cash should be invested.*

IMA *Abbr.* An abbreviation of Institute of Management Accountants.

imprest (ĭm′prĕst) *n.* An advance or a loan of money, especially for performing services for a government: *A petty cash fund is one type of imprest.*

imprest system (ĭm′prĕst sĭs′təm) *n.* A way of controlling small cash disbursements by establishing a fund at a fixed amount and periodically reimbursing the fund by the amount necessary to restore the original cash balance.

impute (ĭm pyōōt′) *tr.v.* **imputed, imputing, imputes.** **1.** To charge (sbdy./sthg.) with responsibility or blame for sthg.: *The worker imputed the ruined products to a faulty machine.* **2.** To attribute to or credit (sbdy./sthg.): *the intelligence imputed to management.*

imputed interest (ĭm pyōō′tĭd ĭn′trĭst) *n.* A rate of interest assigned to a long-term note when it does not have an explicit rate of interest stated. It is based on the normal interest cost of a company.

in arrears (ĭn ə rîrz′) *adv.* Not paid at the time originally agreed to and overdue: *Your loan is in arrears.*

in balance (ĭn băl′əns) *adj.* Of ledgers, journals, or accounts, having the total of all debits recorded equal to the total of all credits recorded.

in circulation (ĭn sûr′kyə lā′shən) *adv.* Still being passed from one individual to another: *Some silver coins remain in circulation.*

income (ĭn′kŭm) *n.* The amount of money received for work, for the sale of products or goods, or from financial investments: *My income from investments raised my taxes this year.* See also **receipts** (sense 2).

income from operations (ĭn′kŭm frŭm ŏp′ə rā′shənz) *n.* Gross margin with operating expenses subtracted. Also called **operations income**.

income statement (ĭn′kŭm stāt′mənt) *n.* The financial statement that summarizes the revenues earned and the expenses incurred by a business over a period of time as a net income or loss, which is found by subtracting total expenses from total revenue.

indirect manufacturing costs

income summary (ĭn'kŭm sŭm'ə rē) *n.* A temporary account used during the **closing** process that holds a summary of all revenues and expenses before the net income or loss is transferred to the Capital account. Also called **clearing account** or **revenue and expense summary**.

income tax (ĭn'kŭm tăks') *n., pl.* **taxes.** A tax on the income of an individual or a business entity that is paid to a government.

income tax allocation (ĭn'kŭm tăks ăl'ə kā'shən) *n.* A method to account for the difference between income tax expense (based on accounting income) and the actual income taxes payable (based on taxable income).

increment (ĭn'krə mənt *or* ĭng'krə mənt) *n.* **1.** An increase in number, size, amount, or extent: *an increment in sales.* **2.** One of a series of regular increases: *raise wages by increments.*

incremental (ĭn'krə měn'tl *or* ĭng'krə měn'tl) *adj.* Gradually increasing: *incremental income.*

incremental analysis (ĭn'krə měn'tl ə năl'ĭ sĭs) *n., pl.* **analyses.** *(usually singular).* A technique used in decision analysis that compares alternatives by focusing on the differences in their projected revenues and costs.

incur (ĭn kûr') *tr.v.* **incurred, incurring, incurs.** To acquire or become responsible for (sthg.): *The company incurred new debts when they bought that old factory.*

independence (ĭn'dĭ pěn'dəns) *n.* **1.** An ethical principle that an accountant must avoid all relationships that impair or appear to impair his or her objectivity. **2.** The quality or condition of being able to act on one's own without external control or support: *financial independence.*

independent (ĭn'dĭ pěn'dənt) *adj.* Not controlled, supported, or guided by others: *an independent evaluation of the situation.*

independent auditors' report (ĭn'dĭ pěn'dənt ô'dĭ tərz rĭ-pôrt') *n.* The section of an annual report in which the independent certified public accountants describe the nature of the audit (**scope section**) and state an opinion about how fairly the financial statements have been presented (**opinion section**).

independent contractor (ĭn'dĭ pěn'dənt kŏn'trăk'tər) *n.* A person who is engaged only for a definite job or service and who is not an employee of the firm for which the service is provided, for example, an appliance repairperson, a plumber, a freelance artist, or a CPA.

index number (ĭn'děks nŭm'bər) *n.* In trend analysis, a number against which changes in related items over a period of time are measured. It is calculated by setting the base year equal to 100 percent.

indirect cost (ĭn'dĭ rěkt' kôst') *n.* Any cost that cannot be conveniently and economically traced to a specific department; a manufacturing cost that is not easily traced to a specific product and must be assigned using an allocation method. For example, a property tax is an indirect expense because it is incurred by the entire company, not a single department. Another term for **indirect expense**.

indirect expense (ĭn'dĭ rěkt' ĭk spěns') *n.* Another term for **indirect cost**. See also **direct expense**.

indirect labor costs (ĭn'dĭ rěkt' lā'bər kôsts') *pl.n.* Labor costs for production-related activities that cannot be connected with or conveniently and economically traced to a specific end product.

indirect manufacturing costs (ĭn'dĭ rěkt' măn'yə făk'chər-ĭng kôsts') *pl.n.* Various production-related costs that cannot

indirect materials

be practically or conveniently traced to an end product. Another term for **factory overhead costs**.

indirect materials (ĭn′dĭ rĕkt′ mə tĭr′ē əlz) *pl.n.* Minor materials and other production supplies that cannot be conveniently and economically traced to specific products.

indirect method (ĭn′dĭ rĕkt′ mĕth′əd) *n.* The procedure for converting the income statement from an accrual basis to a cash basis. This is done by adjusting net income for items that do not affect cash flows, including depreciation, amortization, depletion, gains, losses, and changes in current assets and current liabilities. See also **direct method**.

industry norm (ĭn′də strē nôrm′) *n.* A way of adjusting for the limitations of using past performance as a measure of a company's performance. This is done by comparing the company to other companies in the same industry.

initial public offering (ĭ nĭsh′əl pŭb′lĭk ô′fər ĭng) *n. Abbr.* **IPO** A common stock issue of a company that is selling its stock to the public for the first time.

input (ĭn′pŏŏt′) *n.* **1.** The ideas, money, or effort put into a process or project: *We want to get input from as many people as possible.* **2.** The data or programs put into a computer for processing: *Our results will only be as accurate as our input.* —*tr.v.* **inputted** or **input, inputting, inputs.** To enter (data or a program) into a computer: *It'll take hours to input all those figures.*

input device (ĭn′pŏŏt′ dĭ vīs′) *n.* An original document that contains all the information for each business transaction.

insider (ĭn sī′dər) *n.* A person who has information or special knowledge or access to private information because he or she is in a position to acquire it: *Insiders know that labor problems have increased during the year.*

insider trading (ĭn sī′dər trā′dĭng) *n.* Making use of inside information about a company or an industry in order to make money buying or selling its stock. It is unethical and usually illegal.

inspect (ĭn spĕkt′) *tr.v.* **1.** To look at (sthg.) carefully: *Please inspect the document for errors.* **2.** To look at or review (sbdy./sthg.) formally or officially: *inspect a factory for safety violations.* —**inspection** *n.* —**inspector** *n.*

inspection time (ĭn spĕk′shən tīm′) *n.* The time spent looking for product flaws or reworking defective units.

installment (ĭn stôl′mənt) *n.* **1.** One of a series of regular payments on a loan or purchase: *He paid for the car in monthly installments.* **2.** The practice of paying for sthg. in a series of regular payments: *He bought the car on installment.*

installment accounts receivable (ĭn stôl′mənt ə kounts′ rĭ sē′və bəl) *pl.n.* Accounts receivable that are payable in a series of scheduled time payments.

installment note payable (ĭn stôl′mənt nōt pā′ə bəl) *n.* A long-term note paid off in a series of scheduled payments, of which part is interest and part is repayment of principle.

Institute of Management Accounts (ĭn′stĭ tōōt əv măn′ĭj mənt ə kounts′) *n. Abbr.* **IMA** A professional organization made up primarily of management accountants.

instrument (ĭn′strə mənt) *n.* A legal document used for a specific purpose, such as paying for goods received. A check is an example of an instrument.

int. *Abbr.* An abbreviation of: **1.** Interest. **2.** Interim.

intangible asset (ĭn tăn′jə bəl ăs′ĕt) *n.* A long-term asset that has no physical substance but that has a value based on

internal control structure

rights, privileges, or advantages coming to or belonging to the owner. **Goodwill** is an intangible asset. See also **tangible asset**.

integrity (ĭn tĕg′rĭ tē) *n.* An ethical principle that requires honesty, frankness, and placing service and the public trust before personal gain.

intercompany payables (ĭn′tər kŭm′pə nē pā′ə bəlz) *pl.n.* When either a parent company or a subsidiary company owes money to the other, the payables entries on the debtor's balance sheet that have to be eliminated, because it does not make sense for a company to owe money to itself.

intercompany receivables (ĭn′tər kŭm′pə nē rĭ sē′və bəlz) *pl.n.* When either a parent company or a subsidiary company owes money to the other, the receivables entries on the creditor's balance sheet that have to be eliminated, because it does not make sense for a company to owe money to itself.

interest (ĭn′trĭst *or* ĭn′tər ĭst) *n. Abbr.* **int. 1.** A cost for borrowing money or the return (amount earned) for lending money, depending on whether one is the borrower or the lender, usually a percentage of the amount borrowed (principal). **2.** The cost associated with the use of money for a specific period of time: *The cost of accumulated interest could drive the company into bankruptcy.* **3.** Ownership in sthg.: *We have a 25 percent interest in the company.*

interest allowances (ĭn′trĭst ə lou′ən sĭz) *pl.n.* Ways of distributing net income, like **salary allowances**, that encourage partners to leave their money in a company rather than withdrawing it. This is done by paying partners interest on their capital investments.

interest coverage ratio (ĭn′trĭst kŭv′ər ĭj rā′shō) *n.* A way of measuring the degree of protection that a creditor has from a debtor's default on interest payments. It is found by dividing the sum of the net income of a business before taxes plus interest expense by the total interest expense.

interest income (ĭn′trĭst ĭn′kŭm) *n.* Income from savings accounts, investments, or stock dividends.

interest on partners' capital (ĭn′trĭst ŏn pärt′nərz kăp′ĭ tl) *n.* Financial return to a business's partners for the use of their capital. See also **interest allowances**.

interest rate (ĭn′trĭst rāt′) *n.* An amount of money charged for borrowing money or paid for the use of sbdy. else's money.

interim (ĭn′tər ĭm) *n. Abbr.* **int.** An interval of time between one process, event, or period and another: *In the interim, the company appointed an acting president.*

interim financial statement (ĭn′tər ĭm fə năn′shəl stāt′mənt) *n.* A financial statement prepared for an accounting period of less than one year, usually quarterly or monthly. Also called **quarterly report** or **interim statement**.

interim period (ĭn′tər ĭm pîr′ē əd) *n.* An **accounting period** that is less than a year, for example, a month or a quarter.

interim statement (ĭn′tər ĭm stāt′mənt) *n. (usually singular).* Another term for **interim financial statement**.

internal (ĭn tûr′nəl) *adj.* Located inside sthg.; inner; interior: *the internal workings of a clock; the internal operations of a company.*

internal control (ĭn tûr′nəl kən trōl′) *n.* All the policies and procedures a company uses to protect its assets, check the accuracy and reliability of its accounting data, promote operational efficiency, and encourage adherence to its policies.

internal control structure (ĭn tûr′nəl kən trōl′ strŭk′chər) *n.* A structure established to protect the assets of a business

internal failure costs

and to provide reliable accounting records. This consists of an established environment, controlled by management, the accounting system, and control procedures.

internal failure costs (ĭn tûr′nəl fāl′yər kôsts′) *pl.n.* The costs that are incurred by a company when defects are discovered before a product or service is delivered to a customer; a **cost of nonconformance.**

Internal Revenue Code (ĭn tûr′nəl rĕv′ə no͞o kōd′) *n.* A U.S. government document that contains the thousands of rules governing the preparation of federal income taxes. This document is frequently revised.

Internal Revenue Service (ĭn tûr′nəl rĕv′ə no͞o sûr′vĭs) *n. Abbr.* **IRS** A U.S. government agency that interprets and enforces the tax laws that govern the assessment and collection of revenue for the running the federal government.

International Accounting Standards Committee (ĭn′tər-năsh′ə nəl ə koun′tĭng stăn′dərdz kə mĭt′ē) *n. Abbr.* **IASC** The organization that encourages worldwide cooperation in the development of uniform accounting principles. It approves international standards of accounting.

Internet (ĭn′tər nĕt′) *n.* A worldwide network of computers: *The Internet is very profitable for many companies.*

inventoriable (ĭn′vən tôr′ē ə bəl) *adj.* Available in inventory to be produced or sold: *inventoriable products.*

inventoriable costs (ĭn′vən tôr′ē ə bəl kôsts′) *pl.n.* Another term for **product costs.**

inventory (ĭn′vən tôr′ē) *n., pl.* **inventories. 1.** A complete list of goods or possessions, especially of goods and materials available for sale: *Have you finished all the inventories?* **2.** All of the products of a business available (in stock) for sale to customers: *We can't allow our inventory to drop below a certain level.* **3.** The process of making a list of goods or products for sale, or the period of time when such a list is made: *Inventory may take several weeks.* —*tr.v.* **inventoried, inventorying, inventories.** To make (an itemized report or record of all the products available for sale): *We can inventory these toys this afternoon.* See also **physical inventory, periodic inventory system, perpetual inventory system.**

inventory cost (ĭn′vən tôr′ē kôst′) *n.* The total price paid to acquire an asset. This includes the invoice price less purchase discounts, plus freight in or transportation and applicable taxes or tariffs.

inventory turnover (ĭn′vən tôr′ē tûrn′ō′vər) *n.* A ratio used to indicate the number of times a company's average inventory is sold during an accounting period. It is found by dividing the cost of goods sold by average inventory.

inventory valuation (ĭn′vən tôr′ē văl′yo͞o ā′shən) *n.* Determining the cost of goods or products available for sale to customers. See also **average-cost method, first-in, first-out method,** and **last-in, first-out method.**

invest (ĭn vĕst′) *tr. & intr.v.* To put money into sthg., such as property, stocks, or a business, in order to earn interest or make a profit: *Where should I invest my money? Many people have invested in mutual funds.*

investee (ĭn vĕs′tē *or* ĭn′vĕs tē′) *n.* A company in which another company invests money.

investing (ĭn vĕs′tĭng) *n.* **1.** The practice of putting money into sthg., such as property, in order to earn interest or make a profit: *Her investing has really paid off for her.* **2.** The job of putting

item-by-item method

other people's money into sthg. that will earn them interest or make a profit: *He's in investing now.*

investing activity (ĭn vĕs′tĭng ăk tĭv′ĭ tē) *n.* **1.** An activity undertaken by management to spend capital in ways that are productive and will help to achieve a business's objectives. This includes the acquisition and sale of long-term assets and marketable securities other than cash equivalents, and the making and collecting of loans.

investment (ĭn vĕst′mənt) *n.* **1.** The act of investing money to earn interest or to make a profit: *Investment in small-cap stocks has paid off this year.* **2.** An amount of money invested: *My investment in junk bonds bankrupted me.* **3.** Something in which money is invested: *Replacing worn-out equipment is a good business investment.* **4. investments.** Assets, usually long-term, that are not used in the normal operation of a business and that management does not intend to convert to cash within the next year.

investment center (ĭn vĕst′mənt sĕn′tər) *n.* A center whose manager is responsible for profit generation and, in addition, can make significant decisions about the assets the center uses.

investor (ĭn vĕs′tər) *n.* A company or a person who puts money or capital into a business in order to make money.

invoice (ĭn′vois′) *n.* A form sent to the purchaser by the **vendor** (seller) that describes the quantity and price of the goods or services delivered and the terms of payment. —*tr. & intr.v.* **invoiced, invoicing, invoices.** To send a form to a purchaser or client that describes both the quantity and price of the products or services delivered and specifies the payment terms: *Have you invoiced the factory for our latest delivery?*

IPO *Abbr.* An abbreviation of initial public offering.

IRS *Abbr.* An abbreviation of Internal Revenue Service.

issue (ĭsh′ōō) *n.* **1.** The act of circulating, distributing, or publishing sthg.: *an issue of municipal bonds.* **2.** Something produced, offered, or published, such as a single copy of a magazine: *Do you have the first issue of that magazine?* **3.a.** Something being talked about, debated, or argued: *political issues.* **b.** The most important or essential point: *a human rights issue.* —*v.* **issued, issuing, issues.** —*intr.* To accumulate over a period of time (said of, for example, profits or proceeds from doing business): *Not enough profit issued from the sale of stock.* —*tr.* To publish or distribute (sthg.) as an official act or declaration: *The company will have to issue more stock to raise money.*

issued stock (ĭsh′ōōd stŏk′) *n.* The number of shares of stock that have been put into circulation. This amount is equal to outstanding shares plus treasury stock. Also called **issued shares.**

issue price (ĭsh′ōō prīs′) *n.* The price of a share of stock when it is initially offered.

item-by-item method (ī′təm bī ī′təm mĕth′əd) *n.* A way of valuing inventory. In this method cost and market price are compared for each item in inventory, with each item then valued at its lower price.

Jj

JIT *Abbr.* An abbreviation of just-in-time (operating philosophy).

JIT/FMS environment (jā′ī tē′ĕf′ĕm ĕs′ ĕn vī′rən mənt) *n.* An operating environment created by a flexible manufacturing system functioning within the just-in-time operating philosophy.

job (jŏb) *n.* **1.** A task that must be done: *I have a job for you if you're bored.* **2.** A position at which sbdy. works to earn a living: *Do you enjoy your job?* **3.** Something that has been produced by work: *I think she'll do a fine job.*

job card (jŏb′ kärd′) *n.* A record of the time spent by each employee on a particular job.

job order (jŏb′ ôr′dər) *n.* A customer order for a specific number of specially designed, made-to-order products.

job order cost card (jŏb′ ôr′dər kôst′ kärd′) *n.* A document on which all costs incurred in the production of a particular job order are recorded. It is part of the subsidiary ledger for the Work in Process Inventory Control account.

job order cost system (jŏb′ ôr′dər kôst′ sĭs′təm) *n.* A product costing system used by companies that make large, unique, or special-order products. The costs of materials, labor, and factory overhead are traced to and assigned to specific job orders or batches.

joint (joint) *adj.* Shared or carried by two or more people or groups: *Finishing the project has been a joint effort.*

joint cost (joint′ kôst′) *n.* A cost that relates to two or more products or services produced from a common input or raw material and that can be assigned only by means of arbitrary cost allocation after the products or services become identifiable. Also called **common cost.**

journal (jûr′nəl) *n. Abbr.* Jrnl. **1.** A daily record of events; a diary or log: *He's kept a journal since he was nine years old.* **2.** A periodical, such as a newspaper or magazine. **3.** The simplest and most flexible type of record of transactions. It is used to record all transactions chronologically so that individual transactions and errors can be more easily identified. Also called **general journal** or **book of original entry.**

journal entry (jûr′nəl ĕn′trē) *n.* A notation in the general journal. It records a single transaction.

journalize (jûr′nə līz′) *tr.v.* **journalized, journalizing, journalizes.** To record (financial transactions) in a journal: *Have the current costs been journalized yet?*

journalizing (jûr′nə lī′zĭng) *n.* The process of recording transactions in a journal.

just-in-time (jŭst′ĭn tīm′) *n. Abbr.* JIT An overall operating philosophy of inventory management in which all resources, including materials, personnel, and facilities, are used only as needed.

just-in-time operating environment (jŭst′ĭn tīm′ ŏp′ə-rā′tĭng ĕn vī′rən mənt) *n.* An inventory management system in which companies try to reduce their levels of inventory by working with suppliers to coordinate and schedule deliveries so that goods arrive just at the time they are needed.

just-in-time operating philosophy (jŭst′ĭn tīm′ ŏp′ə rā′tĭng fĭ lŏs′ə fē) *n.* An overall operating philosophy that requires that all resources, including materials, personnel, and facilities, be used only as needed. The objectives are to improve productivity and eliminate waste.

Ll

labor (lā′bər) *n.* **1.** Physical or mental effort; work: *the labor of running a marathon.* **2.** A specific task or piece of work: *Baking that cake was a labor of love.* **3.** People who work for wages, spoken of as a group: *Labor won't like the new contract.* —*intr.v.* To work: *labor in the fields.* —**laborer** *n.*

labor budget (lā′bər bŭj′ĭt) *n.* A schedule that identifies the labor needs for a future period and the labor costs of meeting those needs.

labor cost (lā′bər kôst′) *n.* The expenses incurred as a result of paying wages and salaries, providing benefits, and other direct and indirect costs.

labor rate (lā′bər rāt′) *n.* The amount of money per hour paid to people who perform the same job.

land (lănd) *n.* **1.** Property; real estate: *Land is a good investment.* **2.** The part of the earth's surface that is not covered by water: *Only one-third of the earth's surface is land.* —*tr.v.* To secure sthg. that is very desirable: *We landed the big account!*

Land Improvements account (lănd′ ĭm prōōv′mənts ə kount′) *pl.n.* An asset account covering expenditures for improvements to real estate that are not as permanent as the land or are not directly associated with a building. These include driveways, parking lots, trees and shrubs, fences, and outdoor lighting systems.

last-in, first-out method (lăst′ĭn′ fûrst′out′ mĕth′əd) *n. Abbr.* **LIFO** An inventory cost method based on the assumption that the costs of the last items purchased should be assigned to the first items sold. See also **first-in, first-out method.**

late deposit (lāt′ dĭ pŏz′ĭt) *n.* A deposit not recorded on the bank statement because the deposit was made between the time of the bank's closing date for compiling items for its statements and the time the statement is received by the depositor. Another term for **deposit in transit.**

launder (lŏn′dər) *tr.v.* **1.** To hide the source or nature of (illegal funds) by using an intermediate agent to disguise them: *launder money.* **2.** To wash (clothes).

LCM rule (ĕl′sē ĕm′ rōōl′) *n.* Another term for **lower-of-cost-or-market rule.**

Ld. *Abbr.* An abbreviation of: **1.** Limited (sense 1). **2.** A limited company.

lead-time (lēd′tīm′) *n.* The interval of time between the beginning of a project or policy and the appearance of results: *We'll need more lead-time to allow for delays.*

lease (lēs) *n.* A written agreement allowing a person, group, or business to use a specific property for a specified period of time in exchange for rent or some other consideration: *We signed the lease on our new apartment yesterday.* —*tr.v.* **leased, leasing, leases. 1.** To grant the use of (property) in exchange for money or some other consideration: *She's leased her summer home.* **2.** To hold or use (property) by renting it: *We leased computer equipment.*

leasehold (lēs′hōld′) *n.* A right to occupy land or buildings under a long-term rental contract. —**leaseholder** *n.*

leasehold improvement (lēs′hōld′ ĭm prōōv′mənt) *n.* An improvement to leased property that becomes the property of the lessor at the end of the lease.

ledger

ledger (lĕj′ər) *n.* The book or computer file that contains all of a company's accounts arranged in the order of the chart of accounts. Another term for **general ledger.**

ledger account (lĕj′ər ə kount′) *n.* A complete record of the transactions recorded in each individual account.

ledger account form (lĕj′ər ə kount′ fôrm′) *n.* A form of account that has four columns: one column for debit entries, one column for credit entries, and two columns (debit and credit) for showing the balance of the account.

ledger balance of cash (lĕj′ər băl′əns ŭv kăsh′) *n.* The balance of the Cash account in the general ledger before it is reconciled with the bank statement.

legal (lē′gəl) *adj.* **1.** Relating to the law: *legal issues.* **2.** Allowed by law; legitimate: *legal drugs.* **3.** According to certain rules: *Is that a legal play in soccer?*

legal capital (lē′gəl kăp′ĭ tl) *n.* The number of shares of stock issued by an economic entity times the par value; the minimum amount that can be reported as contributed capital. See also **par value.**

lessee (lĕ sē′) *n.* A person who rents property from sbdy. under a lease for a specified amount of money for a specific length of time. See also **lessor.**

lessor (lĕs′ər) *n.* A person who rents property to sbdy. under a lease for a specified amount of money for a specific length of time. See also **lessee.**

letter to stockholders (lĕt′ər tōō stŏk′hōl′dərz) *n.* A letter that begins a company's annual report. In this letter the company's top officers describe the company's performance and future prospects for its stockholders.

leverage (lĕv′ər ĭj *or* lē′vər ĭj) *n.* **1.** The use of borrowed funds (credit) to increase the profit from an investment: *The company gained leverage by taking on new debt.* **2.** An advantage in position or in power: *An advanced degree will give you greater leverage on the job market.* —*tr.v.* To provide (a company with money for some activity) by going into debt: *leverage a buyout.*

levy (lĕv′ē) *tr.v.* **levied, levying, levies.** To impose or collect (a tax): *levy a tax on imports.* —*n., pl.* **levies. 1.** The act of levying a tax: *a new levy on foreign products.* **2.** The money collected as a tax, tariff, or other kind of fee: *How much is the new levy on gasoline?*

liability (lī′ə bĭl′ĭ tē) *n., pl.* **liabilities.** A legal obligation of a business, the result of past transactions, to pay cash, transfer assets, or provide services to other entities in the future; debts, or the amounts owed to creditors.

liable (lī′ə bəl) *adj.* **1.** Legally obligated or responsible for sthg.: *You'll be liable for court costs.* **2.** Likely: *You're liable to need more equipment soon.*

license (lī′səns) *n.* **1.** An exclusive right to a formula, technique, process, or design: *The company holds the license for all products sold at the event.* **2.** Legal evidence that sbdy. is qualified to do sthg.: *a driver's license.* —*tr.v.* **licensed, licensing, licenses.** To give (sbdy.) permission for (sthg.) or to do sthg.: *The state licenses drivers.*

life (līf) *n.* The length of time sthg., such as a corporation, continues to exist. The life of a corporation is set by its **charter** and is regulated by state laws.

LIFO (lī′fō) *Abbr.* An abbreviation of last-in, first-out.

LIFO liquidation (lī′fō lĭk′wĭ dā′shən) *n.* The reduction of inventory levels at year's end below beginning-of-the-year lev-

liquidate

els for businesses using the LIFO inventory method. Income is increased by the amount current prices exceed the historical cost of the inventory. See also **last-in, first-out method**.

limit (lĭm′ĭt) *n*. A point or line beyond which sthg. ends: *place a limit on overtime.* —*tr.v.* To place a limit on (sbdy./sthg.): *Limit your speech to five minutes.*

limited (lĭm′ĭ tĭd) *adj.* **1.** *Abbr.* **ltd., Ltd., Ld.** Relating to or being a limited company. **2.** Small in area; not big: *limited space for growth.* **3.** Not able to perform at the highest level; not having the best talent for sthg.: *a limited ability to forecast sales.*

limited access (lĭm′ĭ tĭd ăk′sĕs) *n.* Access to sthg., such as assets, accounting records, or a warehouse, granted only to certain people judged to be trustworthy by management.

limited company (lĭm′ĭ tĭd kŭm′pə nē) *n., pl.* **companies.** *Abbr.* **ltd., Ltd., Ld.** *British.* A company, usually registered in the United Kingdom, that is organized to protect its owners from financial responsibility.

limited liability (lĭm′ĭ tĭd lī′ə bĭl′ĭ tē) *n.* The obligation of owners of a corporation, who are liable only for the amount of their investment and are not liable for the corporation's debts. Limited liability restricts the ability of a small corporation to borrow money. This is because lenders cannot lay claim to the assets of the individual owners and so limit their loans to the level of assets owned by the company.

limited life (lĭm′ĭ tĭd līf′) *n.* The characteristic of a partnership that any event that changes the partnership agreement—including the admission, withdrawal, or death of a partner—terminates the partnership.

limited partnership (lĭm′ĭ tĭd pärt′nər shĭp′) *n.* A form of participation in which limited partners' liabilities are limited to their investment and general partners with unlimited liability operate the business.

linear (lĭn′ē ər) *adj.* **1.** Relating to or resembling a straight line: *linear thought.* **2.** Consisting of or using lines: *a linear design.* **3.** Relating to the length of sthg.: *a unit of linear measurement.*

linear approximation (lĭn′ē ər ə prŏk′sə mā′shən) *n.* An accounting method used to convert **nonlinear variable costs** into **linear variable costs**. It relies on the concept of **relevant range**.

linear variable costs (lĭn′ē ər vâr′ē ə bəl kôsts′) *pl.n.* Expenses for which there is an assumed linear relationship between cost and volume, and for which it is assumed that costs increase or decrease as volume goes up or down.

line of credit (līn′ əv krĕd′ĭt) *n., pl.* **lines of credit.** An arrangement with a commercial bank that allows a company to borrow funds as needed. Also called **credit line**.

liquid (lĭk′wĭd) *n.* A substance that is not a solid or a gas and that has molecules that move freely in the space it occupies: *Milk is a liquid.* —*adj.* **1.** Easily changed into cash: *liquid assets.* **2.** In a liquid state: *liquid rocket fuel.*

liquid asset (lĭk′wĭd ăs′ĕt) *n.* A cash asset or an asset that can be easily converted into cash.

liquidate (lĭk′wĭ dāt′) *v.* **liquidated, liquidating, liquidates.** —*tr.* **1.** To pay for (sthg.) in full: *liquidate one's debts.* **2.** To convert into cash: *We're liquidating some of our stock holdings.* —*intr.* To close (a business) by settling its accounts and dividing up its remaining assets among owners: *The furniture store is liquidating.*

liquidating dividend

liquidating dividend (lĭk′wĭ dā′tĭng dĭv′ĭ děnd′) *n.* A dividend that exceeds retained earnings, usually paid when a corporation goes out of business or reduces its operations.

liquidation (lĭk′wĭ dā′shən) *n.* The process of going out of business. This involves the sale of the assets, payment of the liabilities, and distribution of the remaining cash to the owners: *Sometimes, liquidation is the only choice a company has.*

liquidity (lĭ kwĭd′ĭ tē) *n.* **1.** Available money on hand to pay bills when they are due and to take care of unexpected needs for cash. **2.** The quality of being easily changed into cash: *an investment with high liquidity.*

list (lĭst) *n.* **1.** A series of names, words, or other items that occur one right after the other: *a list of employee identification numbers.* **2.** A large number: *a list of memorized dates.* —*v.* —*tr.* **1.** To make a list of (sthg.): *list your job requirements.* **2.** To put on a list; register: *list each item received.* —*intr.* To have a stated price that usually appears in a catalog or price list: *That radio lists for $12.*

list price (lĭst′ prĭs′) *n.* The basic or standard price of a product, usually provided in a written document, such as a catalog. List price is often subject to a discount.

loan (lōn) *n.* **1.** An amount of money supplied to sbdy. in exchange for payment of interest and repayment of principal: *a bank loan.* **2.** Something given to sbdy. else on a temporary basis: *the loan of my car.* —*tr.v.* To give (sbdy.) sthg. on a temporary basis, with the understanding that it will be returned or repaid: *She loaned me money for lunch.*

local income tax (lō′kəl ĭn′kŭm tăks′) *n.* A tax on income, usually a percentage of amount or value, levied by a city or county government.

long-lived asset (lông′lĭvd′ ăs′ĕt) *n.* Another term for **long-term asset**.

long-term asset (lông′tûrm′ ăs′ĕt) *n.* An asset that has the following characteristics: (1) it has a useful life of more than one year; (2) it is acquired for use in the operation of a business; and (3) it is not intended for resale to customers. Includes tangible assets, such as property, plant, and equipment, and intangible assets, such as goodwill. This is a category of long-term assets. Also called **noncurrent asset**.

long-term debt (lông′tûrm′ dĕt′) *n.* Another term for **long-term liability**.

long-term investment (lông′tûrm′ ĭn věst′mənt) *n.* An investment that management plans to hold for more than one year.

long-term liability (lông′tûrm′ lī′ə bĭl′ĭ tē) *n., pl.* **liabilities.** A debt that falls due more than one year in the future or beyond the normal operating cycle, or that is to be paid out of noncurrent assets.

lookback period (lŏŏk′băk′ pĭr′ē əd) *n.* A measure of past tax liabilities used to determine the frequency of payment of present tax liabilities. See also **monthly deposit schedule rule.**

loss (lôs *or* lŏs) *n.* **1.** A person or thing that has been lost: *sustain huge financial losses.* **2.** The act or an instance of losing sthg.: *loss of a job.* **3.** The pain or damage caused by losing sbdy./sthg.: *The manager's death was a loss to all of us.*

Loss on Disposal of Plant and Equipment (lôs′ ŏn dĭ spō′zəl ŭv plănt′ ənd ĭ kwĭp′mənt) *n.* The account in which a loss is recorded when a firm sells or trades in an asset and receives an amount less than the book value for that asset. It

ltd.

appears under Other Revenues and Expenses in the income statement.

lower-of-cost-or-market (LCM) rule (lō′ər əv kôst′ôr mär′-kĭt (ĕl′sē ĕm′) rōōl′) *n.* A method of valuing inventory at an amount below cost if the replacement (market) value is less than cost.

LP column (ĕl′ pē′ kŏl′əm) *n.* Another term for **posting reference column.** Also called **folio column.**

ltd. or **Ltd.** *Abbr.* An abbreviation of: **1.** Limited (sense 1). **2.** A limited company.

Mm

MACRS (mā'kərz) *Abbr.* An abbreviation of Modified Accelerated Cost Recovery System.

made-to-order (mād'tōō ôr'dər) *adj.* **1.** Made according to the specific instructions of a customer; custom-made: *a made-to-order furniture business.* **2.** Perfect: *a made-to-order job situation.*

magnetic ink character recognition (măg nĕt'ĭk ĭngk kăr'ək tər rĕk'əg nĭsh'ən) *n. Abbr.* **MICR** The characters the bank uses to print the number of the depositor's account and the bank's number at the bottom of checks and deposit slips. The bank also prints the amount of the check in MICR when the check is deposited. A number written in these characters can be read by electronic equipment used by banks to clear checks.

major category method (mā'jər kăt'ĭ gôr'ē mĕth'əd) *n.* A lower-of-cost-or-market method of valuing inventory in which the total cost and total market value for each category of items are compared. Each category is then valued at its lower amount.

make-or-buy decision analysis (māk'ôr bī' dĭ sĭzh'ən ə năl'ĭ sĭs) *n.* In management, a way of deciding whether to make or buy some or all of the parts used in product assembly operations by identifying how much each option would cost and which option would be the most profitable.

maker (mā'kər) *n.* An individual or a firm that signs a promissory note.

manage (măn'ĭj) *v.* **managed, managing, manages.** —*tr.* To have control over (sbdy./sthg.): *He manages a bookstore.* —*intr.* **1.** To run a business: *The goal of the course is to learn to manage effectively.* **2.** To get along, often with some difficulty: *I don't know how we managed to finish on time.*

management (măn'ĭj mənt) *n.* **1.** The act of controlling sbdy./sthg.: *His management of that department has been less than efficient.* **2.** Collectively, the people who have overall responsibility for operating a business and meeting its profitability and liquidity goals: *Management uses the information prepared by accountants to make decisions.*

management accounting (măn'ĭj mənt ə koun'tĭng) *n.* The process of producing accounting information for the internal use of a company's management.

management by exception (măn'ĭj mənt bī ĭk sĕp'shən) *n.* The practice of locating and analyzing only the areas of unusually good or unusually bad performance.

management information system (măn'ĭj mənt ĭn fər mā'shən sĭs'təm) *n. Abbr.* **MIS** The interconnected subsystems that provide the information needed to run a business.

manual (măn'yōō əl) *adj.* Operated or performed using the hands: *manual controls.* —*n.* A small book of instructions for doing or operating sthg.: *a computer manual.* —**manually** *adv.*

manual data processing (măn'yōō əl dā'tə prŏs'ĕs ĭng) *n.* A system of accounting in which data for each transaction are entered by hand from a **source document** into the general journal (input device) and each debit and credit is posted by hand to the correct ledger account (processor and memory device) for the eventual preparation of financial statements (output devices).

manufacture (măn'yə făk'chər) *tr.v.* **manufactured, manufacturing, manufactures.** To make or process (a product),

marketable security

especially by using machines: *This company manufactures metal containers.* —*n.* The act of making sth.: *the manufacture of metal containers.* —**manufacturer** *n.*

manufacturing or **manufacturing business** (măn'yə făk'chər ĭng *or* măn'yə făk'chər ĭng bĭz'nĭs) *n.* 1. A business engaged in the making or processing of sth.: *I'm in manufacturing.* 2. Collectively, all of the businesses that make products: *The manufacturing business requires reliable sources for raw materials.*

manufacturing cost flow (măn'yə făk'chər ĭng kôst' flō') *n.* The flow of manufacturing costs (direct materials, direct labor, and factory overhead) as they appear repeatedly in the Materials, Work in Process, and Finished Goods inventory accounts to the Cost of Goods Sold account.

manufacturing costs (măn'yə făk'chər ĭng kôsts') *pl.n.* All of the expenses related to the production process, including direct materials costs, direct labor costs, and factory overhead.

manufacturing overhead (măn'yə făk'chər ĭng ō'vər hĕd') *n.* Another term for **factory overhead costs.**

Manufacturing Summary (măn'yə făk'chər ĭng sŭm'ə rē) *n.* The account used to make adjustments to Raw Materials Inventory and Work in Progress Inventory accounts. It is similar to the **Income Summary account.**

marginal (mär'jə nəl) *adj.* 1. Not making enough money: *a marginal business.* 2. Written or printed in the margin: *marginal notes.* 3. Barely acceptable; not good enough to meet some standard of excellence: *marginal quality.* —**marginally** *adv.*

marginal cost (mär'jə nəl kôst') *n.* The change in total cost caused by a one-unit change in output.

marginal cost curve (mär'jə nəl kôst' kûrv') *n.* A graphic curve that represents marginal costs. It is produced by measuring and plotting the rate of change in total cost at different levels of activity.

marginal revenue (mär'jə nəl rĕv'ə nōō) *n.* The change in total revenue caused by a one-unit change in output.

marginal revenue curve (mär'jə nəl rĕv'ə nōō kûrv') *n.* A graphic curve that represents marginal revenues by measuring and plotting the rate of change in total revenues at different levels of activity.

markdown (märk'doun') *n.* A reduction in price; an amount deducted from the original retail price: *We can get better markdowns if we shop more.*

mark down (märk' doun') *tr.v.* To lower the price of (sth.): *In the spring, stores usually mark winter coats down for quicker sale.*

market (mär'kĭt) *n.* 1. A public place where goods are regularly bought and sold: *a farmers' market.* 2. A stock market: *The market was up today.* 3. The business of buying and selling a product: *the real estate markets in urban areas.* 4.a. A region or country where goods are sold: *automobiles for foreign markets.* b. A particular group of buyers: *the college market for computers.* 5. A desire to buy; demand for sth.: *a weak market for bicycles.* 6. Current replacement cost of inventory: *sell coffee at market.* Also called **market value** or **replacement value.** —*tr.v.* To sell or offer (sth.) for sale: *market a product.*

marketable (mär'kĭ tə bəl) *adj.* Ready for sale or of interest to buyers or employers: *She has many marketable skills.* —**marketability** *n.*

marketable security (mär'kĭ tə bəl sĭ kyŏŏr'ĭ tē) *n.* A short-term investment intended to be held until needed to pay current obligations. Also called **short-term investment.**

market interest rate

market interest rate (mär′kĭt ĭn′trĭst rāt′) *n.* The rate of interest paid in the market on bonds of similar risk. Also called **effective interest rate**.

market transfer price (mär′kĭt trăns′fər prīs′) *n.* A transfer price based on the price that could be charged if a segment of a company could buy from or sell to an external party.

market value (mär′kĭt văl′yōō) *n.* **1.** The price investors are willing to pay for a share of stock on the open market. Also called **market**. **2.** The current replacement cost. Another term for **replacement value**.

markup (märk′ŭp′) *n.* The amount added to the price of a product by a retailer to arrive at a selling price: *a huge markup on clothing.*

mark up (märk′ ŭp′) *tr.v.* To mark (sthg.) for sale at a higher price: *That store usually marks everything up.*

master (măs′tər) *n.* A person who consistently performs an activity in a skilled way: *a master at adding columns.* —*adj.* Most important; primary: *the master control.* —*tr.v.* **1.** To bring (sthg.) under control: *master one's emotions.* **2.** To become skilled at or in the use of (sthg.): *master a language.*

master budget (măs′tər bŭj′ĭt) *n.* A set of period budgets that have been consolidated into forecasted financial statements for an entire company.

match (măch) *n.* A person or thing that is exactly the same as or equal to another: *That company is no match for the competition.* —*v.* —*tr.* **1.** To be like or go well with (sthg.): *The wallpaper matches the rug in her office.* —*intr.* To be alike or equal: *These figures don't match.*

matching issue (măch′ĭng ĭsh′ōō) *n.* The problem of assigning revenues and expenses to the appropriate accounting period in order to measure net income accurately.

matching principle or **rule** (măch′ĭng prĭn′sə pəl *or* rōol′) *n.* The accounting principle that the revenue for one time period must be matched or compared with the expenses for the same time period.

material (mə tîr′ē əl) *n.* **1.** The substance or substances from which sthg. is made: *made of inferior material.* **2. materials.** The tools and supplies needed to perform a task: *educational materials.* —*adj.* Having a clear connection with sthg. else; important: *Do you think this fact is material to our earlier discussion?*

materiality (mə tîr′ē ăl′ĭ tē) *n.* The accounting convention that requires that an item or event in a **financial statement** be important to the users of financial statements. An item is material if there is a reasonable expectation that knowing about it would influence the decisions of users of the financial statements.

materials cost (mə tîr′ē əlz kôst′) *n.* The direct and indirect expenses incurred in ordering, receiving, storing, and using materials to produce a product.

Materials Inventory account (mə tîr′ē əlz ĭn′vən tôr′ē ə kount′) *n.* An inventory account made up of the balances of materials, parts, and supplies on hand at a given time. Also called **Stores account, Raw Materials Inventory account,** or **Materials Inventory Control account.**

materials purchase/usage budget (mə tîr′ē əlz pûr′chĭs yōō′sĭj bŭj′ĭt) *n.* A detailed plan that is developed from information in the production budget and from anticipated changes in the levels of materials inventory. This budget identifies the

merchandise

amount and timing of raw materials and parts to be purchased and used to meet production needs. (A merchandise purchasing budget is used by retail businesses.) See also **merchandise purchasing budget.**

materials requisition (mə tîr′ē əlz rĕk′wĭ zĭsh′ən) *n.* A form used within a company to authorize the use of stored materials and parts in the production operation. It describes the types and quantities of goods needed and received, and it requires an authorized signature.

mature (mə tyŏŏr′ *or* mə tŏŏr′ *or* mə chŏŏr′) *adj.* **1.** Having reached its due date: *a mature savings bond.* **2.** Completely grown or ripe: *mature fruit.* **3.** Having the mental and emotional qualities thought to be appropriate in an adult: *a mature approach to life.* **4.** Completely planned: *a mature scientific proposal.* —*intr.v.* matured, maturing, matures. **1.** To become due for payment: *This bond matures next year.* **2.** To reach full growth or development: *Do you think he'll ever mature?*

maturity (mə tyŏŏr′ĭ tē *or* mə tŏŏr′ĭ tē *or* mə chŏŏr′ĭ tē) *n.* **1.** The time at which payment of a loan or bond becomes due: *The loan reaches maturity in two years.* **2.** Full growth: *Some trees reach maturity faster than others.*

maturity date (mə tyŏŏr′ĭ tē dāt′) *n.* The date on which a promissory note is due. Also called **date of maturity.**

maturity value (mə tyŏŏr′ĭ tē văl′yōō) *n.* The total proceeds of a promissory note, including principle and interest, at the maturity date.

measure (mĕzh′ər) *n.* **1.** The size or amount of sthg. in relation to a standard: *a measure of liquid.* **2.** A unit of measurement specified by a standard scale, such as an inch or a liter: *A mile is a measure of distance.* **3.** A standard for evaluating sthg. or a basis for comparison: *Money is the most popular measure of success.* —*v.* measured, measuring, measures. —*tr.* **1.** To find the size, amount, volume, or degree of (sthg.): *measure a room.* **2.** To serve as a measure of (sthg.): *Yards and miles measure distance.* **3.** [*off; out*] To mark off or distribute (sthg.) by using a standard measure: *measure off two feet.* —*intr.* **1.** To have a specific amount, size, volume, or degree: *The room measures 144 square feet.* **2.** To find out the amount, size, volume, or degree: *You should measure twice before cutting a board.*

measurement (mĕzh′ər mənt) *n.* **1.** The act of measuring: *careful measurement of a space.* **2.** Numbers that represent the size, amount, speed, or volume of sthg. as a result of measuring: *compare the measurements of two rooms.*

medical (mĕd′ĭ kəl) *adj.* Relating to the study or practice of medicine: *medical school; a medical problem.*

medical insurance (mĕd′ĭ kəl ĭn shŏŏr′əns) *n.* A kind of insurance bought to cover all or some portion of a person's medical expenses for an illness, injury, or disease.

medical insurance withholding (mĕd′ĭ kəl ĭn shŏŏr′əns wĭth hōl′dĭng) *n.* An amount of money that an employee contributes at specific times from wages or salary to pay for all or part of the cost of medical insurance coverage.

Medicare taxes (mĕd′ĭ kâr′ tăk′sĭz) *pl.n.* Federal government taxes levied on employees and employers. The proceeds are used for medical insurance for eligible people age 65 or over.

merchandise (mûr′chən dīz′ *or* mûr′chən dīs′) *n.* Items that can be bought or sold; commercial goods: *display merchandise attractively.* —*tr.v.* (mûr′chən dīz′) merchandised,

73

merchandise inventory

merchandising, merchandises. 1. To buy and sell (goods). **2.** To promote the sale of (goods), for example, by advertising: *merchandise a new computer.*

merchandise inventory (mûr′chən dīz′ ĭn′vən tôr′ē) *n.* The goods on hand at any one time that are available for sale to customers in the regular course of business.

merchandise purchasing budget (mûr′chən dīz′ pûr′chə-sĭng bŭj′ĭt) *n.* Similar to a materials purchase/usage budget but used by retail businesses. See also **materials purchase/usage budget.**

merchandising business (mûr′chən dī′zĭng bĭz′nĭs) *n.* A business that earns income by buying products or merchandise at wholesale prices and selling them at retail prices. Also called **retail business.**

MICR *Abbr.* An abbreviation of magnetic ink character recognition.

microeconomic pricing model (mī′krō ĕk′ə nŏm′ĭk prī′sĭng mŏd′l) *n.* An accounting model that is based on the economic theory that profit will be greater when the difference between total revenue and total cost is the greatest.

midmonth convention (mĭd′mŭnth′ kən vĕn′shən) *n.* The accounting practice of taking half a month of an asset's depreciation during the first month of the first year that the asset was put in operation.

midquarter convention (mĭd′kwôr′tər kən vĕn′shən) *n.* The accounting practice of taking half a quarter of an asset's depreciation when the total property placed in service during the last three months (last quarter) of the year is more than 40 percent of all the property placed in service that year. All property placed in service during any quarter (three-month period) of a given tax year is treated as though it had been placed in service at the midpoint of the quarter.

minority (mə nôr′ĭ tē *or* mə nŏr′ĭ tē *or* mī nôr′ĭ tē *or* mī nŏr′-ĭ tē) *n., pl.* **minorities. 1.** The smaller of two groups that form a whole: *a minority of stockholders.* **2.** A racial, religious, political, or other group that differs from the majority of people in a country: *the rights of minorities.*

minority interest (mə nôr′ĭ tē ĭn′trĭst) *n.* The amount recorded on a consolidated balance sheet that represents the holdings of stockholders who own less than 50 percent of the voting stock of a subsidiary.

minute book (mĭn′ĭt bo͝ok′) *n.* A written narrative of all actions taken at official meetings of the board of directors. It is a source document for dividend accounting entries.

minutes (mĭn′ĭts) *pl.n.* An official record of what was discussed and what was decided during a meeting.

MIS *Abbr.* An abbreviation of management information system.

mix (mĭks) *v.* —*tr.* To combine (things) into a single mass by pouring, stirring, or shaking: *mix the ingredients for paint.* —*intr.* To become combined: *Oil and water don't mix.* —*n.* A combination of different things: *The company style is a mix of old and new.*

mixed (mĭkst) *adj.* **1.** Combined into a single mass or whole: *a drink of mixed juices.* **2.** Made up of various elements: *The plan got mixed reviews.*

mixed costs (mĭkst′ kôsts′) *pl.n.* Costs that result when both variable and fixed costs are charged to the same general ledger account, such as the Repair and Maintenance account. Repair and maintenance workers may be employed full-time (fixed

multinational

cost) and extra help hired when needed (variable cost). See also **semivariable costs**.

Modified Accelerated Cost Recovery System (mŏd′ə fīd′ ăk sĕl′ə rā′tĭd kôst′ rĭ kŭv′ə rē sĭs′təm) *n. Abbr.* **MACRS** A mandatory system of depreciation for income tax purposes, enacted by Congress in 1986. This system requires a cost recovery allowance to be computed (1) on the unadjusted cost of property being recovered and (2) over a period of years set by law for all property of similar types.

modified cash basis (mŏd′ə fīd′ kăsh′ bā′sĭs) *n.* An accounting method that is used to record income only when it is received in cash. Most expenses are recorded only when they are paid in cash. Exceptions are made for expenditures on items having a useful life of more than one year and for certain prepaid items, such as expenditures for supplies and insurance premiums, which can be prorated, or spread out over the fiscal periods covered. Expenditures for long-lived items are recorded as assets and later depreciated as an expense over their useful lives.

modify (mŏd′ə fī′) *tr. & intr.v.* **modified, modifying, modifies.** To be changed or to change (sthg.); alter: *The company modified its plans for expansion.*

money laundering (mŭn′ē lôn′dər ĭng) *n.* The use of an intermediate agent, such as a bank, to disguise the source of money received from illegal activities: *Offshore banks are often used for money laundering.*

money measure (mŭn′ē mĕzh′ər) *n.* The recording of all business transactions in terms of money.

monthly deposit schedule rule (mŭnth′lē dĭ pŏz′ĭt skĕj′ool rool′) *n.* An accounting rule pertaining to an employer whose total amount of reported taxes for the four quarters in the **lookback period** is not more than $50,000. Taxes must be paid by the fifteenth day of the following month.

mortgage (môr′gĭj) *n.* A long-term debt that is secured by real property. It is usually paid in equal monthly installments, of which part is interest and part is repayment of principal: *a $200,000 mortgage.* —*tr.v.* **mortgaged, mortgaging, mortgages.** To promise (property) as security for the repayment of a loan: *He mortgaged his house to start a new business.*

move (moov) *tr. & intr.v.* **moved, moving, moves. 1.** To change place or position: *I'll move the meeting to a later time.* **2.** To make progress: *The construction is moving smoothly now.* **3.** To make a formal request or proposal in a meeting: *I move we table the issue until next week.* **4.** To do sthg.; take action: *We have to move quickly if we want to buy the property.* —*n.* **1.** Act of moving: *The move will cost us in terms of productivity. He made a move as though to leave.* **2.** An action intended to achieve a goal: *Any move now has inherent problems.*

moving average method (moo′vĭng ăv′ər ĭj mĕth′əd) *n.* A modified version of the **weighted-average-cost method**. It is used to compute the average cost of a **perpetual inventory**. The firm determines the moving-average unit price each time the firm buys more units. See also **average-cost method**.

moving time (moo′vĭng tīm′) *n.* The time spent moving a product from one operation or department to another.

multinational (mŭl′tē năsh′ə nəl) *adj.* **1.** Having the central offices or smaller divisions of a business in more than two countries: *a multinational corporation.* **2.** Involving more than two countries: *a multinational treaty.* —*n.* A company that operates in more than two countries.

multinational corporation

multinational corporation (mŭl′tē nāsh′ə nəl kôr′pə rā′shən) *n.* A company that operates in more than one country. Also called **transnational corporation.**

multistep form (mŭl′tē stĕp′ fôrm′) *n.* A form of condensed income statement that arrives at net income in the same steps as a detailed income statement. Also called **condensed financial statement, detailed income statement, multistep statement, multistep income statement.** See also **single-step form.**

mutual (myōō′chōō əl) *adj.* **1.** Having the same relationship to each other: *Their dislike is mutual.* **2.** Shared in common: *They have many mutual friends.*

mutual agency (myōō′chōō əl ā′jən sē) *n.* The ability of each partner in a company to act as an agent of the company. Each partner has the power to commit the entire firm to a binding contract.

Nn

n/10 (nĕt′tĕn′) *adj.* Notation used to indicate that payment of an invoice is due 10 days after the date on the invoice. (Read as *net ten*.)

n/10 eom (nĕt′tĕn′ ĕnd′ ŭv mŭnth′) *adj.* Notation used to indicate that payment of an invoice is due 10 days after the end of the month in which the invoice is dated. (Read as *net ten end-of-month*.)

n/30 (nĕt′thûr′tē) *adj.* Notation used to indicate that payment of an invoice is due 30 days from the date on the invoice. (Read as *net thirty*.)

natural resource (năch′ər əl rē′sôrs) *n.* A long-term asset, such as timber, oil, or gas, that is different from land because the asset is purchased for the economic value that can be taken from the land and used up rather than for the value associated with the land's location. A natural resource is subject to depletion rather than depreciation. Also called **wasting asset**.

negotiable (nĭ gō′shə bəl) *adj.* **1.** Able to be transferred from one person to another by delivery or by delivery and endorsement: *negotiable securities.* **2.** Easy or possible to negotiate or be negotiated: *negotiable salary.*

negotiable draft (nĭ gō′shə bəl drăft′) *n.* A type of legal document used instead of money to pay for sthg. A check is an example of a negotiable draft.

negotiate (nĭ gō′shē āt′) *v.* **negotiated, negotiating, negotiates.** —*tr.* To talk about (sthg.) with the hope of reaching an agreement on it: *negotiate a contract.* —*intr.* To talk with others in order to reach an agreement: *Compromise is essential when people negotiate.* —**negotiation** *n.* —**negotiator** *n.*

negotiated transfer price (nĭ gō′shē ā′tĭd trăns′fər prīs′) *n.* A transfer price that is arrived at through bargaining between the managers of the buying and selling divisions or segments.

net[1] (nĕt) *adj.* Remaining after all subtractions have been made: *net income after expenses.* —*n.* The net amount of sthg., especially money or income, after liabilities have been deducted: *The company's net has increased this year.* —*tr.v.* **netted, netting, nets.** To bring (sthg.) in as profit after all liabilities have been deducted: *She netted a huge profit on the sale.*

net[2] (nĕt) *n.* **1.** The linking of two or more computers by telephone lines or other connection so that the computers can share information. Another term for **network** (sense 1). **2.** A loose, openwork fabric made of threads or ropes woven or knotted together at regular points. —*tr.v.* **netted, netting, nets.** To catch or get (sthg.) in a net or as if in a net: *net a great job.*

Net (nĕt) *n.* The Internet: *surf the Net.*

net assets (nĕt′ ăs′ĕts) *pl.n.* A claim by the owner of a business to its assets (owner's equity); what would be left after all liabilities had been paid (assets minus liabilities). See also **net worth** and **residual equity**.

net cash inflow (nĕt′ kăsh′ ĭn′flō′) *n.* The amount of expected increases in cash receipts (inflows) over increases in cash payments (outflows) resulting from a proposed capital expenditure. Used in evaluating capital expenditure proposals by projecting future cash flows.

net cost of purchases (nĕt′ kôst′ əv pûr′chə sĭz) *n.* The net expense of all purchases, less returns, allowances, and dis-

77

net income

counts for early payment (if allowed by suppliers) plus any freight-in charges on the purchases.

net income (nĕt' ĭn'kŭm) *n.* **1.** The amount of an individual's earnings after all deductions, such as taxes, medical costs, or business expenses, have been subtracted from the gross income. **2.** The net increase in owner's equity that results from business operations and accumulates in the Capital account; revenues less expenses when revenues exceed expenses over a period of time. **3.** For merchandising companies, what is left after deducting operating expenses from gross margin.

net loss (nĕt' lôs') *n.* **1.** The difference between expenses and revenues when expenses exceed revenues over a period of time. **2.** The net decrease in owner's equity that results from business operations when expenses exceed revenues, accumulated in the Capital account.

net of taxes (nĕt' ŭv tăk'sĭz) *n.* Taking into account the expense of applicable taxes, usually income taxes, on an item to determine how it will affect the financial statements.

net pay (nĕt' pā') *n.* Gross pay minus deductions. Also called **take-home pay.**

net payroll (nĕt' pā'rōl') *n.* The amount paid to employees after all payroll deductions have been subtracted from gross wages.

net present value method (nĕt' prĕz'ənt văl'yōō mĕth'əd) *n.* A capital investment evaluation method that discounts future cash flows to their present value. The present value of all the future cash flows is compared with the amount of the proposed expenditure to determine if the investment should be made.

net proceeds (nĕt' prō'sēdz) *pl.n.* The amount of money received after all expenses have been paid: *the net proceeds from the sale of the property.*

net purchases (nĕt' pûr'chĭ sĭz) *pl.n.* Total purchases less any deductions, such as purchases returns and allowances and purchases discounts.

net realizable value of accounts receivable (nĕt' rē'ə lī'zə bəl văl'yōō əv ə kounts' rĭ sē'və bəl) *n.* The balance of Accounts Receivable after deducting the balance of Allowance for Doubtful Accounts. Also called **book value of accounts receivable.**

net sales (nĕt' sālz') *pl.n.* The **gross proceeds** from sales of merchandise less sales returns and allowances and any discounts. Also called **sales** on income statements.

network (nĕt'wûrk') *n.* **1.** The linking of two or more computers by telephone lines or other connection so that the computers can share information. Also called **net²** (sense 1). **2.** A system made up of parts, lines, or routes that cross or intersect each other: *a transportation network.* **3.** A group of people who are in regular contact with each other: *a large network of friends.* —*v.* —*intr.* To meet regularly with people in order to advance one's career: *He networks constantly to stay up-to-date.* —*tr.* To link (computers) together so that they can communicate and share information.

net worth (nĕt' wûrth') *n.* **1.** The residual interest in the assets of a business entity that remains after deducting the entity's liabilities; an owner's right to or investment in a business. Also called **residual equity, owner's equity,** or **residual interest. 2.** Assets minus liabilities: *As part of the town's approval process, we had to determine our net worth.*

nominal (nŏm'ə nəl) *adj.* So small that it is meaningless or not worth serious consideration: *charge a nominal price for a service.*

nonparticipating preferred stock

nominal accounts (nŏm′ə nəl ə kounts′) *pl.n.* Accounts that show the accumulation of revenues and expenses over one accounting period. At the end of the accounting period, these account balances are transferred to owner's equity. Also called **nominal-equity accounts** or **temporary accounts**.

nominal-equity accounts (nŏm′ə nəl ĕk′wĭ tē ə kounts′) *pl.n.* Another term for **temporary accounts**.

nominal value (nŏm′ə nəl văl′yōō) *n.* Another term for **par value**.

noncash expense (nŏn′kăsh′ ĭk spĕns′) *n.* An expense that did not require a cash outlay during the period under review such as depreciation expense.

noncash investing and financing transactions (nŏn′kăsh′ ĭn vĕs′tĭng ənd fə năn′sĭng trăn săk′shənz) *pl.n.* Significant investing and financing transactions that do not involve an actual cash inflow or outflow but involve only long-term assets, long-term liabilities, or stockholders' equity, such as the exchange of a long-term asset for a long-term liability or the settlement of a debt by the issue of capital stock.

nonconformance (nŏn′kən fôr′məns) *n.* A cost of quality, caused when it is necessary to correct the flaws or other problems in a product or service.

noncumulative preferred stock (nŏn′ kyōōm′yə lā′tĭv prĭ-fûrd′ stŏk′) *n.* A preferred stock that does not oblige the issuer to pay a dividend to preferred stockholders unless it is declared. See also **cumulative preferred stock**.

noncurrent asset (nŏn′kûr′ənt ăs′ĕt) *n.* All assets other than current assets. Also called **long-term asset**.

nonexchange transaction (nŏn′ĭks chānj′ trăn săk′shən) *n.* An economic event that can affect the business entity the same way an **exchange transaction** does, but it does not involve an exchange of value, such as a loss from fire or flood, physical wear and tear on machinery and equipment, or the daily accumulation of interest.

nonfinancial data (nŏn′fə năn′shəl dā′tə) *pl.n.* Information that is important to management but that concerns aspects of business that are not the result of financial transactions. Such information includes: (1) increasing the quality of the firm's products or services; (2) increasing efficiency by reducing the time (and, thereby, the cost) of creating and delivering products or services; (3) satisfying customers; (4) reducing costs.

noninventoriable cost (nŏn′ĭn vən tôr′ē ə bəl kŏst′) *n.* The cost of resources consumed during an accounting period. These cannot be inventoried. Also called **period cost**.

nonlinear (nŏn lĭn′ē ər) *adj.* Not in a straight line: *nonlinear thought.*

nonlinear variable costs (nŏn lĭn′ē ər vâr′ē ə bəl kôsts′) *pl.n.* Expenses that do not have a linear relationship in proportion to sthg. else. For example, labor costs can vary depending on the number of hours used to produce a product, the number of employees working on sthg., and the efficiency of the employees and machines in use.

nonoperating items (nŏn ŏp′ə rā′tĭng ī′təmz) *pl.n.* Items that appear on the bottom half of a company's income statement, such as discontinued operations, extraordinary gains or losses, or effects of accounting changes, that are not directly related to operating items but can affect a company's net income.

nonparticipating preferred stock (nŏn′pär tĭs′ə pā′tĭng prĭ-fûrd′ stŏk′) *n.* Stock for which the dividends are limited to the regular or stated rate.

nonprofit organization

nonprofit organization (nŏn prŏf′ĭt ôr′gə nĭ zā′shən) *n.* A financial entity that does not seek or produce a profit. See also **not-for-profit**.

nontraffic-sensitive costs (nŏn′trăf′ĭk sĕn′sĭ tĭv kôsts′) *pl.n. Abbr.* **NTS** Relating to telecommunications costs that are not connected with the amount of traffic, such as the costs associated with the subscriber lines running between the telephone user and the exchange company's switching equipment, executive salaries, office expenses, and accounting charges. Such costs are treated as **fixed costs**. See also **traffic-sensitive costs**.

nonvalue-adding activity (nŏn′văl′yōō ăd′ĭng ăk tĭv′ĭ tē) *n., pl.* **activities**. An activity that is related to production or service and adds cost to a product but, from a customer's perspective, does not increase its value.

nonvalue-adding cost (nŏn′văl′yōō ăd′ĭng kôst′) *n.* The cost of an operating or a support activity that adds cost to a product but does not increase its market value.

no-par stock (nō′pär′ stŏk′) *n.* Capital stock that does not have a par value. See also **par value** and **stated value**.

normal (nôr′məl) *adj.* Standard, typical, or usual: *a normal cost of doing business.*

normal balance (nôr′məl băl′əns) *n.* The usual balance of an account; also the side (**debit** or **credit**) that increases the account; the plus side of a **T account**.

normal capacity (nôr′məl kə păs′ĭ tē) *n.* The average annual level of operating capacity needed to meet expected sales demand.

normal markup (nôr′məl märk′ŭp′) *n.* The usual amount, or percentage, that a business adds to the cost of an item to determine its selling price.

note (nōt) *n.* **1.** A detailed explanation added to a company's financial statement in order to meet the requirements of full disclosure and to help readers interpret some of the more complex items. There are three kinds of notes: (1) summary of significant accounting policies; (2) explanatory notes; (3) supplementary information. **2.a.** A piece of paper money; a bill. **b.** A certificate representing an amount of money, issued by a government or bank. **3.** *(usually plural).* A short written record of sthg. heard, seen, or read in order to help the memory: *Do you have the notes from today's meeting?* **4.** A short informal message: *I left a note on your desk.* **5.** An explanation or a comment at the bottom of a page or at the end of a chapter in a book that provides information to the reader.

notes payable (nōts′ pā′ə bəl) *pl.n.* Collective term for written promissory notes that are due in less than one year. These are owed by the entity who promises payment (maker) to other entities **(payees)**.

notes receivable (nōts′ rĭ sē′və bəl) *pl.n.* Collective term for written promissory notes that are due in less than one year and are held by the entity to whom payment is promised **(payee)**.

notes receivable register (nōts′ rĭ sē′və bəl rĕj′ĭ stər) *n.* A supplementary record in which a firm lists details of promissory notes that are receivable.

notes to the financial statements (nōts′ tōō thə fə năn′shəl stāt′mənts) *pl.n.* The section of a corporate annual report containing information that aids users in interpreting the financial statements. Another term for **note** (sense 1).

not-for-profit (nŏt′fər prŏf′ĭt) *adj.* About or relating to an organization that is established to accomplish a specific purpose,

numerator

such as a foundation, charity, or private group, in which no profit is sought. —*n.* Such an organization. See also **nonprofit organization.**

notice (nō'tĭs) *n.* An announcement about sthg., usually written down: *Did you get the notice about the change of the meeting time? Try to give me a week's notice if you plan to visit.* —*tr.v.* **noticed, noticing, notices.** To perceive or become aware of (sthg.): *Have you noticed the new furniture in my office?*

notice of maturity (nō'tĭs əv mə tyŏŏr'ĭ tē) *n., pl.* **notices of maturity.** A notice specifying the terms and due date of a promissory note that has been left with a bank for collection. Such a notice is mailed by the bank to the maker.

not sufficient funds (nŏt' sə fĭsh'ənt fŭndz) *pl.n. Abbr.* **n.s.f., N.S.F., NSF** Lacking enough money to cover sthg., such as a check.

NSF *Abbr.* An abbreviation of not sufficient funds.

n.s.f. or **N.S.F.** *Abbr.* An abbreviation of not sufficient funds.

NSF check (ĕn'ĕs ĕf' chĕk') *n.* A check drawn against an account in which there is not enough money to honor it. Such a check is returned by the payee's bank to the drawer's bank because of nonpayment. Also called **dishonored check.**

NTS *Abbr.* An abbreviation of nontraffic-sensitive (costs).

numerator (nōō'mə rā'tər) *n.* **1.** In an ABA number, the number above or to the left of the line. In the ABA number 88-2258/1113, 88-2258 is the numerator. See also **denominator** and **ABA number. 2.** In mathematics, the number above the line in a common fraction. In the fraction 2/3, 2 is the numerator.

Oo

objective (əb jĕk′tĭv) *adj.* **1.** Existing in a physical form: *objective facts.* **2.** Not influenced by emotion or personal feelings: *Give me an objective opinion of the situation.* —*n.* A specific goal or purpose: *What is your objective in calling him?* —**objectively** *adj.* —**objectiveness** *n.*

objectivity (ŏb′jĕk tĭv′ĭ tē) *n.* In accounting, the principle of impartiality and intellectual honesty.

obligation (ŏb′lĭ gā′shən) *n.* **1.** A debt owed as payment for a special service: *The company already has too many obligations.* **2.** A legal, moral, or social duty: *the obligation to vote.*

obsolescence (ŏb′sə lĕs′əns) *n.* The process of becoming out-of-date. This is a contributor, along with physical deterioration, to the limited useful life of tangible assets, such as machinery.

obsolete (ŏb′sə lēt′) *adj.* No longer in use or in fashion; out-of-date: *obsolete technology.*

$100,000 one day rule (wŭn hŭn′drĭd thou′zənd dŏl′ər wŭn′ dā′ rool) *n.* A rule pertaining to employers whose accumulated tax is $100,000 or more on any day during a deposit period, either monthly or semiweekly. The taxes must be deposited the next day, and the employer then becomes a semiweekly depositor and remains so for at least the remainder of the calendar year and for the following calendar year.

on hand (ŏn′ hănd′) *adj.* Present or available: *How many trucks do we have on hand?*

on-line (ŏn′līn′) *adj. & adv.* **1.** Under the control of a central computer, as in a manufacturing process: *Most aspects of packaging are done on-line.* **2.** Connected to a computer network: *My job requires me to be on-line a great deal.* **3.** Accessible using a computer or a computer network: *on-line databases.*

on-line processing (ŏn′līn′ prŏs′ĕs ĭng) *n.* The form of data processing in which remote terminals are linked to a central processor and files are updated virtually as transactions occur. See also **network** (sense 1).

open (ō′pən) *adj.* **1.** Not shut or closed: *an open door.* **2.** Not restricted or limited: *an open tournament.* **3.** Available: *The position is still open.* **4.** Ready for business: *Are you open on Saturdays?* —*tr. & intr.v.* **1.** To make (sthg.) or become no longer shut: *open a window. The door is opening.* **2.** To begin the operation of (sthg.), such as a business, or start to operate: *open a restaurant. The restaurant is opening later this week.*

open corporation (ō′pən kôr′pə rā′shən) *n.* A corporation in which ownership is widely distributed through a stock exchange or **over-the-counter** markets to a large number of stockholders. Also called **public corporation** or **publicly held corporation**.

operate (ŏp′ə rāt′) *v.* **operated, operating, operates.** —*intr.* **1.** To perform a function; work: *How does this machine operate?* **2.** To perform surgery: *Many doctors prefer to operate early in the morning.* —*tr.* **1.** To control the functioning of (sthg.): *operate a bulldozer.* **2.** To direct the affairs of (sthg.): *operate a business.*

operating activity (ŏp′ə rā′tĭng ăk tĭv′ĭ tē) *n.* A business activity undertaken by management in the course of running a business. Such an activity affects net income. Examples

organization costs

include employing managers and workers, buying and producing goods or services, and paying taxes to one or more levels of government.

operating assets (ŏp′ə rā′tĭng ăs′ĕts) *pl.n.* Another term for **property, plant, and equipment**; also **long-term** or **long-lived assets.**

operating capacity (ŏp′ə rā′tĭng kə păs′ĭ tē) *n.* The highest limit of a company's ability to produce goods or services, given its existing resources.

operating costs (ŏp′ə rā′tĭng kôsts′) *pl.n.* The costs that arise in the course of operating a business.

operating cycle (ŏp′ə rā′tĭng sī′kəl) *n.* A series of transactions that include purchases of merchandise inventory, sales of merchandise inventory for cash or on credit, and collection of the cash from the sales. The operating cycle also includes the time it takes to sell and collect for products sold. This is found by adding average days' inventory on hand to the average days' sales uncollected.

operating effectiveness reporting (ŏp′ə rā′tĭng ĭ fĕk′tĭv nĭs rĭ pôr′tĭng) *n.* A report that focuses on the nonvalue-adding activities of a business in order to increase its effectiveness. Such reports typically include the **processing time, lead-time,** and **waste time** involved in delivering a product or service.

operating expense (ŏp′ə rā′tĭng ĭk spĕns′) *n.* An expense other than cost of goods sold that is incurred in running a business.

operating lease (ŏp′ə rā′tĭng lēs′) *n.* A short-term or cancelable lease in which the risk of ownership lies with the **lessor,** and for which payments are recorded as a rent expense.

operations (ŏp′ə rā′shənz) *pl.n.* Normal business activities.

operations income (ŏp′ə rā′shənz ĭn′kŭm) *n.* Another term for **income from operations.**

opinion section (ə pĭn′yən sĕk′shən) *n.* The part of the auditors' report that presents the audit's conclusions regarding the presentation of a company's financial statements.

opportunity (ŏp′ər tōō′nĭ tē) *n., pl.* **opportunities. 1.** A good time or occasion for a specific purpose: *This is your opportunity to ask for a raise.* **2.** A chance for progress or improvement: *the opportunity to go to college.*

opportunity cost (ŏp′ər tōō′nĭ tē kôst′) *n.* A potential benefit that is given up because one course of action is taken instead of another.

ordinary (ôr′dn ĕr′ē) *adj.* Not remarkable; usual: *an ordinary day at work; ordinary expenses.*

ordinary annuity (ôr′dn ĕr′ē ə nōō′ĭ tē) *n.* A series of equal payments made at the end of equal intervals of time, with compound interest on these payments.

ordinary repair (ôr′dn ĕr′ē rĭ pâr′) *n.* An expense, usually of a recurring nature, that is necessary to maintain an asset in good operating condition. See also **extraordinary repair.**

organization (ôr′gə nĭ zā′shən) *n.* **1.** The act of arranging sthg. in an orderly way: *the organization of a company picnic.* **2.** The condition of being systematically arranged: *a high level of organization.* **3.** The way in which sthg. is systematically arranged: *the organization of successful corporations.* **4.** A group of people joined together for work or for a common purpose: *a political organization.*

organization costs (ôr′gə nĭ zā′shən kôsts′) *pl.n.* The costs of forming a corporation. These include, for example, incorporation

organize

fees, attorneys' fees, the printing of stock certificates, and accountants' fees.

organize (ôr′gə nīz′) *v.* **organized, organizing, organizes.** —*tr.* **1.** To arrange (sthg.) in an orderly way: *organize financial records.* **2.** To form or set up (a group) that has a common purpose: *organize a club.* —*intr.* **1.** To engage in the process of forming or joining a group: *The administrative assistants are organizing the company picnic.* **2.** To bring workers in a company or an industry into a union: *The workers have been organizing for months.*

original (ə rĭj′ə nəl) *adj.* **1.** Existing before all others; first: *The original plan has been changed.* **2.** New; not copied: *an original idea.*

original cost (ə rĭj′ə nəl kôst′) *n.* Another term for **historical cost.**

other assets (ŭth′ər ăs′ĕts) *pl.n.* The balance sheet category that includes various types of assets (investments, for example) other than current assets and property, plant, and equipment.

other postretirement benefits (ŭth′ər pōst rĭ tīr′mənt bĕn′ə fĭts) *pl.n.* Health care and other nonpension benefits paid to a worker after retirement but earned while the employee is still working.

other revenues and expenses (ŭth′ər rĕv′ə nōoz ənd ĭk spĕn′sĭz) *pl.n.* The section of a **multistep income statement** that includes nonoperating revenues and expenses.

output (out′pŏot′) *n.* **1.** An amount of sthg. produced, especially during a given period of time: *Factory output increased last quarter.* **2.a.** The energy, power, or work produced by a system or machine: *the output of an engine.* **b.** The information that a computer produces: *Check the computer output carefully.*

output device (out′pŏot′ dĭ vīs′) *n.* Another term for **financial statement.**

outsource (out′sôrs′) *tr.v.* **outsourced, outsourcing, outsources.** To purchase (essential services or products) from another company: *They're outsourcing management of their inventory.*

outsourcing (out′sôr′sĭng) *n.* The act or an instance of purchasing essential products or services from another company: *Outsourcing can be more cost-effective.*

outstanding (out stăn′dĭng *or* out′stăn′dĭng) *adj.* **1.** Unusually good; excellent: *The speaker gave an outstanding presentation.* **2.** Not settled or paid: *an outstanding debt.*

outstanding check (out stăn′dĭng chĕk′) *n.* A check that has been written by the **drawer** and deducted on his or her records but has not reached the bank for payment and is not deducted from the bank balance by the time the bank issues its statement.

outstanding stock (out stăn′dĭng stŏk′) *n.* Another term for **shares outstanding.**

overdraft (ō′vər drăft′) *n.* **1.** The act of trying to withdraw more money from an account than is in it: *an overdraft on a checking account.* **2.** The amount overdrawn: *a $100 overdraft.*

overhead (ō′vər hĕd′) *n.* The operating expenses of a business, such as rent, insurance premiums, taxes, and electricity: *Overhead could drive us into bankruptcy.* Also called **overhead expense.** —*adj.* Located above the level of the head: *an overhead light.* —*adv.* Above a person's head: *You'll find the files stored overhead.*

overhead efficiency variance (ō′vər hĕd′ ĭ fĭsh′ən sē vâr′ē əns) *n.* The difference between the actual direct labor hours

owner's withdrawals

worked and the standard labor hours allowed, multiplied by the standard variable overhead rate.

overhead expense (ō′vər hĕd′ ĭk spĕns′) *n.* Another term for **overhead**.

overhead spending variance (ō′vər hĕd′ spĕn′dĭng vâr′ē-əns) *n.* The difference between the actual overhead costs incurred and the amount that should have been spent, based on actual hours worked or other productive input measures.

overhead volume variance (ō′vər hĕd vŏl′yo͞om vâr′ē əns) *n.* The difference between the factory overhead budgeted for the level of production achieved and the overhead applied to production using the standard variable and fixed overhead rates.

over-the-counter (ō′vər thə koun′tər) *adj.* **1.** Sold to customers at retail and without any special restrictions: *an over-the-counter medicine.* **2.** Not listed or available for sale on an officially recognized stock exchange, but traded in direct negotiations between buyers and sellers: *over-the-counter stocks.* —**over the counter** *adv.: Aspirin is sold over the counter.*

own (ōn) *adj.* Belonging to oneself: *my own room.* —*n.* Something that belongs to sbdy.: *He built the machine, but the idea was her own.* —*tr.v.* To have or possess (sthg.): *own a car.* —**owner** *n.*

owner's equity (ō′nərz ĕk′wĭ tē) *n.* The residual interest in the assets of a business entity that remains after deducting the entity's liabilities; an owner's right to or investment in a business. See also **residual equity**.

owner's equity account (ō′nərz ĕk′wĭ tē ə kount′) *n.* An account, such as Capital or Withdrawals, that is used to record how much interest in the assets of a company an owner has or how much money has been withdrawn from the business for personal use.

owner's investments (ō′nərz ĭn vĕst′mənts) *pl.n.* The assets that an owner puts into a business.

owner's withdrawals (ō′nərz wĭth drô′əlz) *pl.n.* The assets that an owner takes out of a business.

Pp

paid-in capital (pād'ĭn' kăp'ĭ tl) *n.* Any amount paid for stock in excess of the stated, or par, value per share. See also **contributed capital**.

Paid-in Capital in Excess of Par Value (pād'ĭn kăp'ĭ tl ĭn ĭk sĕs' əv pär' văl'yōō) *n.* An account in which any amount in excess of **par value** received from the issuing of stock is recorded.

parameter (pə răm'ĭ tər) *n. (usually plural).* A fixed limit or boundary: *What are the parameters of the problem?*

parent company (pâr'ənt kŭm'pə nē) *n.* An investing company that owns a controlling interest in another company.

participate (pär tĭs'ə pāt') *intr.v.* **participated, participating, participates.** To join with or be involved in an activity with other people: *She participated in the company's pension plan.* —**participation** *n.*

participating preferred stock (pär tĭs'ə pā'tĭng prĭ fûrd' stŏk') *n.* Preferred stock whose holders share in any extra dividends distributed by the corporation after the regular dividend has been paid to holders of preferred stock and a specified dividend has been paid to holders of common stock.

participative budgeting (pär tĭs'ə pā'tĭv bŭj'ĭt ĭng) *n.* The process of preparing a budget in which all levels of personnel participate in a meaningful, active way.

partner's equity (pärt'nərz ĕk'wĭ tē) *n.* An owner's equity in a partnership.

partnership (pärt'nər shĭp') *n.* A business owned by two or more people.

partnership agreement (pärt'nər shĭp' ə grē'mənt) *n.* The contractual relationship between partners that lists and defines the details of the partnership.

partner's salary (pärt'nərz săl'ə rē) *n.* Payment to a partner for direct services the partner has rendered to a company.

party (pär'tē) *n., pl.* **parties.** A person or group involved in the same activity or legal proceeding: *a party to the agreement.*

par value (pär' văl'yōō) *n.* The arbitrary amount printed on each bond or share of stock, used to determine the legal capital of a corporation. Also called **face value** or **nominal value**.

par-value stock (pär'văl'yōō stŏk') *n.* Stock in which a uniform face value, indicating the amount per share to be entered in the Capital Stock account, is printed on the stock certificates.

past performance (păst' pər fôr'məns) *n.* A way of forecasting a company's future performance, using the trend of past sales, expenses, net income, cash flow, and return on investment: *Based on past performance, it looks as if this company is in trouble.*

patent (păt'nt) *n.* An exclusive right granted by the federal government to make a particular product or use a specific process for a period of 17 years.

pay (pā) *tr. & intr.v.* **paid, paying, pays.** To give money to sbdy. in exchange for goods or services: *Have you paid the light bill? I'm paying for lunch.* —*n.* Money given in exchange for work done; wages; salary: *He makes good pay at that company.*

payable (pā'ə bəl) *adj.* **1.** Requiring payment on a specific date; due: *bills payable on the first of the month.* **2.** Spec-

86

period cost

ifying payment to a particular person: *Make the check payable to her.*

payables (pā′ə bəlz) *pl.n.* Liabilities; debts.

payback (pā′băk′) *n.* The money or other return gained from an activity: *He'll expect payback for his help.*

payback period method (pā′băk pĭr′ē əd mĕth′əd) *n.* A way of judging capital investments that bases the decision to invest in capital equipment on the minimum length of time it will take to earn back in cash the amount of the initial investment.

payee (pā ē′) *n.* **1.** The person to whom a check is payable. **2.** The party receiving payment, such as a note receivable or an account receivable.

payment (pā′mənt) *n.* **1.** The act of paying for sthg.: *Payment in full is required in advance.* **2.** An amount of money paid: *monthly payments.*

payroll (pā′rōl′) *n.* **1.** A list that contains all the employees working for a company and the amounts they should be paid: *How many employees are there on the payroll?* **2.** The total amount of money paid to employees at a given time: *That company is having trouble meeting its payroll.* **3.** The department of a company that handles concerns related to a payroll: *See payroll to change your W-4.*

payroll accounting (pā′rōl′ ə koun′tĭng) *n.* The calculations, records, and control requirements for payroll accounts.

payroll bank account (pā′rōl băngk′ ə kount′) *n.* A special checking account used to pay a company's employees.

payroll liabilities (pā′rōl lī′ə bĭl′ĭ tēz) *pl.n.* The costs of labor and related taxes for a company.

payroll register (pā′rōl rĕj′ĭ stər) *n.* A detailed listing of a firm's total payroll that is prepared each pay period.

payroll tax expense (pā′rōl tăks′ ĭk spĕns′) *n.* A general expense account used for recording the employer's matching portion of the FICA tax, the federal unemployment tax, and the state unemployment tax.

P/E *Abbr.* An abbreviation of price/earnings ratio.

pension (pĕn′shən) *n.* An amount of money paid regularly to workers who are retired: *He lives on his monthly pension.*

pension fund (pĕn′shən fŭnd′) *n.* A fund established through contributions from an employer, and sometimes employees, from which payments are made to employees after retirement, while they are on disability, or to their survivors after they die.

pension plan (pĕn′shən plăn′) *n.* A contract between a company and its employees under which the company agrees to pay benefits to the employees after they retire.

PERC (pûrk) *Abbr.* An abbreviation of preferred equity redemption convertible (stock).

percentage of net sales method (pər sĕn′tĭj əv nĕt′ sālz′ mĕth′əd) *n.* A way of estimating uncollectible accounts, based on the assumption that a predictable proportion of each dollar of sales will not be collected.

period (pĭr′ē əd) *n.* An interval of time with a specified length or characterized by certain conditions: *accounting period.* —**periodic** *adj.*

period budget (pĭr′ē əd bŭj′ĭt) *n.* A forecast of the operating results for a segment or function of a company for a specific period.

period cost (pĭr′ē əd kôst′) *n.* **1.** A cost that is incurred during an accounting period to support the activities of the company, is not connected with the production process, and results from the

periodic inventory system

purchase of sthg. that was consumed during the period. **2.** The cost of resources that are consumed during an accounting period and that cannot be inventoried. Also called **noninventoriable cost.**

periodic inventory system (pîr′ē ŏd′ĭk ĭn′vən tôr′ē sĭs′təm) *n.* A system for determining inventory on hand by a physical count that is taken at the end of an accounting period. See also **perpetual inventory system.** Also called **periodic inventory method.**

periodicity (pîr′ē ə dĭs′ĭ tē) *n.* The recognition that net income for any period less than the life of the business, although tentative, is still a useful estimate of net income for that period.

permanent (pûr′mə nənt) *adj.* Lasting or intended to last for an indefinite period of time; enduring: *a permanent job.*

permanent accounts (pûr′mə nənt ə kounts′) *pl.n.* Balance sheet accounts, for example, assets, liabilities, and the owner's **capital account,** that have balances extending beyond the end of an accounting period. Also called **real accounts.**

perpetual inventory system (pər pĕch′ŏō əl ĭn′vən tôr′ē sĭs′təm) *n.* A system for determining inventory by keeping continuous records of the quantity and, usually, the cost of individual items as they are bought and sold. Also called **perpetual inventory method.**

personal identification number (pûr′sə nəl ī dĕn′tə fĭ kā′shən nŭm′bər) *n.* *Abbr.* **PIN** A number containing at least four digits that is assigned to various kinds of financial accounts, for example, for use with ATM cards. The number is required to access the funds in such accounts.

personnel (pûr′sə nĕl′) *n.* **1.** *(used with a plural verb).* All the people who are employed by an organization, a business, or a service: *Personnel have to notify management about changes of address.* **2.** *(used with a singular verb).* The part of an organization responsible for hiring, training, and other matters connected with employees: *Personnel has a new manager.*

petty cash (pĕt′ē kăsh′) *n.* A small amount of cash that a company keeps on hand to pay for minor expenses in an office: *Pay for the stamps out of petty cash.*

petty cash fund (pĕt′ē kăsh′ fŭnd′) *n.* Another term for **petty cash.**

petty cash payments record (pĕt′ē kăsh′ pā′mənts rĕk′ərd) *n.* A written record that lists the amount of each petty cash voucher and the accounts to which it should be charged.

petty cash voucher (pĕt′ē kăsh′ vou′chər) *n.* A form that lists the date, amount, and purpose of a withdrawal. The form is signed by the person who withdrew the money and by the person in charge of the fund.

physical depreciation (fĭz′ĭ kəl dĭ prē′shē ā′shən) *n.* A way that tangible assets lose their usefulness to a company by wearing out. An example of such an asset is a truck that can no longer be repaired. Also called **functional depreciation.**

physical deterioration (fĭz′ĭ kəl dĭ tîr′ē ə rā′shən) *n.* Limitations on the useful life of a depreciable tangible asset, such as a machine or building. This results from use and from exposure to the elements.

physical inventory (fĭz′ĭ kəl ĭn′vən tôr′ē) *n.* An actual count of all merchandise on hand at the end of an accounting period. Also called **inventory.** See also **periodic inventory system, perpetual inventory system.**

physical volume method (fĭz′ĭ kəl vŏl′yōōm mĕth′əd) *n.* A way of distributing joint costs to specific products or services.

pre-

This method uses a measure of physical volume (for example, units, pounds, liters, grams) as the basis for allocation.

PIN (pĭn) *Abbr.* An abbreviation of personal identification number.

plant (plănt) *n.* **1.** A building or group of buildings where sthg. is made or processed; factory: *a plastics plant.* **2.** The equipment, including machinery, tools, instruments, fixtures, and the buildings containing them, necessary for a manufacturing or an industrial process: *the physical plant of a soup company.*

plant asset (plănt′ ăs′ĕt) *n.* Another term for **property, plant, and equipment.** Also called **long-term** or **long-lived asset.**

point of recognition (point′ əv rĕk′əg nĭsh′ən) *n.* The time when a business transaction is actually entered in the ledger.

portfolio (pôrt fō′lē ō′) *n.* A group of loans or investments designed to average the returns and risks of a creditor or an investor: *a balanced stock portfolio.*

post (pōst) *tr.* To make the necessary entries in a ledger or to transfer (an item) to a ledger: *Has the payment been posted to the account?*

post- *prefix.* A prefix that means after in time: *a post-holiday meeting.*

post-closing trial balance (pōst′klō′zĭng trī′əl băl′əns) *n.* A trial balance prepared at the end of an accounting period after all adjusting and closing entries have been posted; a final check on the balance of the ledger.

posting (pō′stĭng) *n.* The process of transferring journal entry information from the journal to the ledger.

posting reference column (pō′stĭng rĕf′ər əns kŏl′əm) *n. Abbr.* **Post. Ref.** The column used to note the journal page where an original entry can be found.

Post. Ref. *Abbr.* An abbreviation of posting reference column.

postretirement (pōst′rĭ tīr′mənt) *n.* The period after a person has retired from his or her job or profession, usually at a specified age.

postretirement benefits (pōst′rĭ tīr′mənt bĕn′ə fĭts) *pl.n.* The benefits provided to a retired person. These include health care and regular financial support.

potential (pə tĕn′shəl) *adj.* Able to happen; possible: *a potential delay in delivery.* —*n.* An ability to grow, develop, or come into existence: *the potential for expanding a business.*

potential dilution (pə tĕn′shəl dī lōō′shən) *n.* The possibility of reducing a stockholder's share in a company by converting stocks or bonds or exercising stock options and thereby increasing the total shares outstanding.

potentially dilutive securities (pə tĕn′shə lē dī lōō′tĭv sĭ kyōōr′ĭ tēz) *pl.n.* Stock options, warrants and rights, and convertible preferred stocks or bonds that have the potential to dilute earnings per share.

practical (prăk′tĭ kəl) *adj.* **1.** Relating to experience, practice, or use rather than theory, studies, or ideas: *a practical knowledge of geometry.* **2.** Having or showing good judgment; sensible: *a practical budget that allows for emergencies.*

practical capacity (prăk′tĭ kəl kə păs′ĭ tē) *n.* The theoretical production capacity of a facility that is reduced by normal and expected work stoppages, such as machine breakdowns and down time.

pre- *prefix.* A prefix that means: **1.** Earlier; before: *pretax income.* **2.** In advance: *prepaid invoices.*

predetermine

predetermine (prē'dĭ tûr'mĭn) *tr.v.* **predetermined, predetermining, predetermines.** To decide or establish (sthg.) in advance: *Can you predetermine the costs at this stage?*

predetermined (prē'dĭ tûr'mĭnd) *adj.* Decided or established in advance: *a predetermined production rate.*

predetermined overhead rate (prē'dĭ tûr'mĭnd ō'vər hĕd rāt') *n.* A rate that is used as a way of estimating and assigning overhead costs to products or jobs for each department or operating unit before the end of an accounting period.

preempt (prē ĕmpt') *tr.v.* **1.** To seize or take (sthg.) for oneself before others do: *preempt other bidders on the project.* **2.** To take the place of (sbdy./sthg.); displace: *The President's speech will preempt our regular programming.*

preemption (prē ĕmp'shən) *n.* **1.** The right to purchase sthg. before others: *Your preemption of the land will lower its value.* **2.** The seizure or appropriation of sthg., such as property: *the government's preemption of residents' homes to build the highway.*

preemptive (prē ĕmp'tĭv) *adj.* **1.** Relating to or characteristic of preemption: *a preemptive bid.* **2.** Having or granted by the right of preemption: *preemptive authority.* **3.** Having or characterized by the power to seize or take precedence: *a preemptive business offer.*

preemptive right (prē ĕmp'tĭv rīt') *n.* A stockholder's right to maintain the same proportionate ownership in a corporation in the future as she or he has originally. The stockholder has the right to subscribe to a new issue of stock in the same proportion as her or his present ownership.

prefer (prĭ fûr') *tr.v.* **preferred, preferring, prefers.** To like (sbdy./sthg.) better than sbdy./sthg. else: *I prefer to write early in the morning.*

preferred equity redemption convertible stock (prĭ fûrd' ĕk'wĭ tē rĭ dĕmp'shən kən vûr'tə bəl stŏk') *n. Abbr.* **PERC** A preferred stock that (1) pays higher dividends, (2) must be retired at the end of three years, and (3) provides flexibility through a call feature. It is issued in order to improve a company's equity capital ratio.

preferred stock (prĭ fûrd' stŏk') *n.* Stock that has preference over common stock in terms of dividends and the distribution of assets.

premium (prē'mē əm) *n.* **1.** The amount paid or payable for an insurance policy: *The premiums for the insurance policy are only $10 a month.* **2.** An unusual or high value: *Many people place a premium on punctuality.* **3.** The amount by which the issue price of a bond exceeds its face value. This happens when the market interest rate is lower than the face interest rate.

prepaid expense (prē'pād' ĭk spĕns') *n.* An expense paid in advance that has not yet expired; an **asset account.**

prepay (prē pā') *tr.v.* **prepaid, prepaying, prepays.** To pay for (sthg.) in advance: *She prepaid her mortgage in five years.*

present value (prĕz'ənt văl'yōō) *n.* The amount that must be invested now at a given rate of interest to produce a given future value.

prevention costs (prĭ vĕn'shən kôsts') *pl.n.* The expenses connected with the prevention of defects and failures in products and services; a cost of conformance.

price (prīs) *n.* The amount of money asked or given to buy sthg.: *Prices on new cars continue to rise.* —*tr.v.* **priced, pric-**

process

ing, prices. **1.** To decide how much to charge for (sthg.): *price new merchandise.* **2.** To find out how much (sthg.) costs: *price pickup trucks.*

price/earnings ratio (prīs' ûr'nĭngz rā'shō) *n. Abbr.* **P/E** A ratio that is used as a way of measuring investor confidence in a company and comparing stocks for profitability. It is found by dividing market price per share by earnings per share.

price standard (prīs' stăn'dərd) *n.* An estimate of how much certain direct materials will cost in the next accounting period. This estimate is made by the purchasing agent. It takes into account possible price increases, changes in available quantities, and new sources of supply.

price variance (prīs' vâr'ē əns) *n.* The difference between the actual price and the standard price of direct materials, multiplied by the amount purchased.

pricing (prī'sĭng) *n.* The act of assigning a cost to sthg.: *Pricing must take many factors into account.*

primary (prī'mĕr'ē *or* prī'mə rē) *adj.* **1.** First in importance, rank, or quality: *the primary function of a door.* **2.** First in time; original: *the primary stages of a project.* **3.** Basic; essential: *primary needs.*

primary earnings per share (prī'mĕr'ē ûr'nĭngz pər shâr') *pl.n.* Earnings per share computed for companies with a complex capital structure. It is arrived at by dividing net income by the number of shares of common stock outstanding plus any potentially dilutive shares considered to be common stock equivalents. See also **earnings per share.**

prin. *Abbr.* An abbreviation of: **1.** Principal. **2.** Principle.

principal (prĭn'sə pəl) *adj. Abbr.* **prin. 1.** First or highest in importance, rank, worth, or degree: *of principal concern.* **2.** Relating to a financial principal: *a principal payment.* — *n.* **1.** A person who heads a school. **2.** A sum of money owed on a note, on which interest is charged: *the principal of a mortgage.* **3.** A main participant in a situation or business: *She is a principal in the architectural firm.*

principle (prĭn'sə pəl) *n. Abbr.* **prin. 1.** A rule or standard for judging sthg.: *accounting principles.* **2.** A rule or law concerning a natural or mechanical process: *the principles of physics.*

principle of duality (prĭn'sə pəl əv dōō ăl'ĭ tē) *n.* The assumption that every financial event has two aspects, such as effort and reward or source and use, that balance each other. See also **double-entry system.**

prior (prī'ər) *adj.* Coming before in time, order, or importance: *prior commitments.*

prior period adjustments (prī'ər pîr'ē əd ə jŭst'mənts) *pl.n.* Events or transactions that relate to earlier accounting periods but that could not be determined in the earlier periods.

privatize (prī'və tīz') *tr.v.* **privatized, privatizing, privatizes.** To change (an industry or a business) from public or governmental control to private ownership: *privatize gas companies.* —**privatization** *n.*

proceeds (prō'sēdz) *pl.n.* **1.** The amount of money earned by a business or fundraising activity; the yield: *Proceeds will go to charity.* **2.** The principle of a loan less the discount.

process (prŏs'ĕs) *n., pl.* **processes.** A series of actions, changes, or functions that lead to a desired result: *a manufacturing process.* —*tr.v.* **1.** To put (sthg.) through an established series of steps: *process a job application.* **2.** To prepare, treat,

process cost system

or change (sthg.) by means of a special series of steps: *process copper ore.*

process cost system (prŏs′ĕs kôst′ sĭs′təm) *n.* A product costing system used by companies that produce large amounts of similar products or that have a continuous production flow. The costs of direct materials, direct labor, and factory overhead are first traced to a process or work cell and then assigned to the products produced by that process or work cell.

processing (prŏs′ĕs ĭng) *n.* **1.** The preparation, treatment, or altering of sthg. in order to make it available for sale: *the processing of chicken.* **2.** The arithmetic and nonarithmetic functions of a computer: *data processing.*

processing time (prŏs′ĕs ĭng tīm′) *n.* The actual amount of time a product is being worked on.

processor and memory device (prŏs′ĕs ər ən mĕm′ə rē dĭ vīs′) *n.* The book or computer file that contains all of a company's accounts arranged in the order of the chart of accounts. An **account** (sense 1) and a **general ledger** are examples of processor and memory devices.

process value analysis (prŏs′ĕs văl′yōō ə năl′ĭ sĭs) *n. Abbr.* **PVA** The process of identifying all operating activities and relating them to events that cause the need for the activities and the resources that are consumed. This enables management to identify those activities that add value (**value-adding activities**) and those that simply add cost (**nonvalue-adding activities**).

produce (prə dōōs′) *tr.v.* **produced, producing, produces. 1.** To bring forth (sthg.): *Oak trees produce acorns.* **2.** To create (sthg.) by mental or physical effort: *produce a winning team.* **3.** To manufacture (sthg.): *produce metal doors.* (prŏd′ōōs) —*n.* Farm products, especially fruit and vegetables: *This store has the freshest produce.*

product (prŏd′əkt) *n.* Something brought forth or created by nature or human effort: *farm products; soap products.*

product contribution (prŏd′əkt kŏn′trĭ byōō′shən) *n.* The amount that a specific product has contributed to paying for the fixed costs of producing it but that cannot be directly traced to it.

product contribution reporting (prŏd′əkt kŏn′trĭ byōō′shən rĭ pôr′tĭng) *n.* An accounting report that tells management how much a specific product has contributed to paying for the untraceable fixed costs involved in producing it. Sometimes product contribution can also include traceable fixed costs.

product costs (prŏd′əkt kôsts′) *pl.n.* Inventoriable production costs consisting of the three elements of manufacturing cost: direct materials, direct labor, and factory overhead.

production (prə dŭk′shən) *n.* **1.** The act or process of creating sthg.: *automobile production; the production of capital.* **2.** An item that has been created or manufactured: *a literary production.* **3.** (*usually singular*). An exaggerated display: *Don't make a production out of this.*

production budget (prə dŭk′shən bŭj′ĭt) *n.* A detailed schedule that identifies the products or services that must be produced or provided to meet budgeted sales and inventory needs.

production cycle (prə dŭk′shən sī′kəl) *n.* The process involved in making a product available for shipment.

production cycle time (prə dŭk′shən sī′kəl tīm′) *n.* The time it takes for production personnel to make the product available for shipment to the customer.

profit margin

production flow (prə dŭk′shən flō′) *n.* An established series of stages in the creation or manufacture of a product as it moves from one cost unit of a company to the next.

production method (prə dŭk′shən mĕth′əd) *n.* A method of depreciation that assumes that depreciation is solely the result of use. This method allocates depreciation based on the units of output or use during each period of an asset's useful life.

product line (prŏd′əkt līn′) *n.* **1.** The place in a factory where products are made. **2.** The products themselves, spoken of as a group: *several new product lines.*

product line profitability reporting (prŏd′əkt līn′ prŏf′ĭ tə-bĭl′ĭ tē rĭ pôr′tĭng) *n.* Accounting for all the costs involved in producing an item, including manufacturing and delivery costs.

product unit cost (prŏd′əkt yōō′nĭt kôst′) *n.* The manufacturing cost of a single unit of product. This is the total cost of direct materials, direct labor, and factory overhead for a job divided by the total units produced.

profession (prə fĕsh′ən) *n.* **1.** An occupation that requires a lot of training and specialized study: *the profession of law.* **2.** The act of declaring: *professions of loyalty.*

professional (prə fĕsh′ə nəl) *adj.* **1.** Relating to a specialized occupation: *professional groups.* **2.** Showing specialized skill: *a professional repair job.* **3.** Receiving money for doing sthg.: *professional consultant.* **4.** Behaving according to the standards of a profession: *That wasn't very professional.* —*n.* **1.** A person who earns a living in a profession: *an accounting professional.* **2.** A person who has a lot of skill or experience in a specific activity: *Let's hire a professional to do the analysis.*

professional enterprise (prə fĕsh′ə nəl ĕn′tər prīz′) *n.* A business that offers a specialized service for a fee, such as a medical, legal, or architectural firm.

professional ethics (prə fĕsh′ə nəl ĕth′ĭks) *n.* (*used with a singular or plural verb*). A code of conduct that applies to the practice of a profession.

profit (prŏf′ĭt) *n.* **1.** The money made in a business venture: *A healthy business should show a profit.* **2.** The increase in owner's equity that results from business operations. —*intr.v.* **1.** To gain an advantage: *profit from stock investments.* **2.** To increase owner's equity by engaging in business activities, such as manufacturing a product or providing a service.

profitable (prŏf′ĭ tə bəl) *adj.* Able to produce a profit; money-making: *a profitable business.*

profitability (prŏf′ĭ tə bĭl′ĭ tē) *n.* The ability to earn enough income to attract and hold investment capital.

profitability accounting (prŏf′ĭ tə bĭl′ĭ tē ə koun′tĭng) *n.* Another term for **responsibility accounting**.

profitability management (prŏf′ĭ tə bĭl′ĭ tē măn′ĭj mənt) *n.* The process of setting appropriate prices on merchandise, purchasing merchandise at favorable prices and terms, and maintaining acceptable levels of expenses.

profit center (prŏf′ĭt sĕn′tər) *n.* A responsibility center whose manager is responsible for revenues, costs, and resulting profits.

profit geometry (prŏf′ĭt jē ŏm′ĭ trē) *n.* A single graph that portrays an entire company's break-even history. The information in the graph is based on a companywide analysis.

profit margin (prŏf′ĭt mär′jĭn) *n.* Used to measure the percentage of each sales dollar that results in net income. This is found by dividing net income by net sales.

profit margin pricing (prŏf′ĭt mär′jĭn prī′sĭng) *n.* An approach to cost-based pricing in which price is computed using a percentage of a product's total costs and expenses.

program (prō′grăm′) *tr. & intr.v.* **programmed, programming, programs.** To write the instructions for specific computer software in a computer. —*n.* The set of instructions and steps that brings about the desired results in a computerized data processing system.

promise (prŏm′ĭs) *n.* **1.** A declaration that one will or will not do a specific thing; a vow: *It's foolish to make a promise you can't keep.* **2.** Indication of sthg. good to come or of future success: *a young company that shows promise.* —*v.* **promised, promising, promises.** —*tr.* To declare (sthg.) with a pledge; vow: *She promised to be here on time.* —*intr.* To make or give sbdy. a promise: *Do you promise?*

promissory note (prŏm′ĭ sôr′ē nōt′) *n.* A written promise to pay a definite sum at a definite future time: *She signed the promissory note on the loan.*

property, plant, and equipment (prŏp′ər tē plănt′ ənd ĭ kwĭp′mənt) *n.* Long-term tangible assets used in the continuing operation of a business for a long time. Also called **fixed, long-term** or **long-lived, operating, plant,** or **tangible assets.**

proprietor (prə prī′ĭ tər) *n.* An owner and often manager of a business: *a restaurant proprietor.*

proprietorship (prə prī′ĭ tər shĭp′) *n.* The state of being the owner of a business: *a sole proprietorship.*

proxy (prŏk′sē) *n., pl.* **proxies.** A legal document, signed by a stockholder, giving another party the right to vote his or her shares.

public (pŭb′lĭk) *adj.* **1.** Relating to people in general or a community: *public safety.* **2.** Kept for or used by the people or community: *a public swimming pool.* **3.** Open or available to everyone: *a public speech.* —*n.* The community or people as a whole: *open to the public.*

public corporation (pŭb′lĭk kôr′pə rā′shən) *n.* A corporation in which ownership is widely distributed through a stock exchange or **over-the-counter** markets to a large number of stockholders. Also called **open corporation.**

publicly held corporation (pŭb′lĭk lē hĕld′ kôr′pə rā′shən) *n.* Another term for **public corporation.**

pull-through production (pool′throo′ prə dŭk′shən) *n.* A production system in which a customer's order causes the purchase of materials and the scheduling of production for the required products. See also **push-through method.**

purchase (pûr′chĭs) *tr.v.* **purchased, purchasing, purchases.** To get (sthg.) in exchange for money; buy: *purchase a new microwave oven.* —*n.* **1.** Something that is bought: *The car was an expensive purchase.* **2.** The act of buying: *a land purchase.*

purchase method (pûr′chĭs mĕth′əd) *n.* A way of consolidating financial statements so that intercompany accounts are eliminated. Examples include the investment the parent company has in the subsidiary, and accounts receivable or payable the parent company has from or to the subsidiary. This method is used when the investing company owns more than 50 percent of a subsidiary.

purchase order (pûr′chĭs ôr′dər) *n.* A form prepared by a company's purchasing department and sent to a vendor. The form contains descriptions of the items ordered, their expected price, terms, and shipping date, and other shipping instructions.

94

purchase order lead-time (pûr′chĭs ôr′dər lēd′tīm′) *n.* The time it takes for raw materials and parts to be ordered and received so that production can begin.

purchase request (pûr′chĭs rĭ kwĕst′) *n.* Another term for **purchase requisition.**

purchase requisition (pûr′chĭs rĕk′wĭ zĭsh′ən) *n.* A form that begins the purchasing process by identifying a need for raw materials or parts. It describes the items and quantities needed, and it must be approved by a qualified manager or supervisor. Also called **purchase request.**

Purchases (pûr′chĭ sĭz) *pl.n. (used with a singular verb).* A temporary account used under the periodic inventory system to record the total cost of all merchandise purchased for resale during an accounting period.

purchases discounts (pûr′chĭ sĭz dĭs′kounts′) *pl.n.* Discounts taken by merchants in return for prompt payment for merchandise purchased for resale. The Purchases Discounts account is a contra account.

purchases journal (pûr′chĭ sĭz jûr′nəl) *n.* A single-column or multicolumn special-purpose journal that is used to record all purchases on credit.

Purchases Returns and Allowances (pûr′chĭ sĭz rĭ tûrns′ ənd ə lou′ən sĭz) *n.* A contra account used under the periodic inventory system to accumulate cash refunds, credits on account, and other allowances made by suppliers for unsatisfactory or incorrect merchandise that was originally purchased for resale.

purchasing agent (pûr′chĭ sĭng ā′jənt) *n.* The person in a business who is responsible for buying supplies and materials that are needed to operate the business.

push-through method (pŏŏsh′thrŏŏ′ mĕth′əd) *n.* A production system in which products are manufactured in long production runs and stored in anticipation of customers' orders. See also **pull-through method.**

PVA *Abbr.* An abbreviation of process value analysis.

Qq

qualified (kwŏl′ə fīd′) *adj.* **1.** Having the proper or necessary training for sthg., such as a job: *a qualified applicant.* **2.** Having restrictions; limited: *a qualified success.*

qualified endorsement (kwŏl′ə fīd′ ĕn dôrs′mənt) *n.* An endorsement in which the holder (**payee**) of a check avoids future liability in case the drawer of the check does not have sufficient funds to cover the check. This is done by adding the words "pay to the order of" and "**without recourse**" to the endorsement on the back of the check.

qualify (kwŏl′ə fī′) *v.* **qualified, qualifying, qualifies.** —*tr.* To be evidence that (sbdy.) is eligible for sthg., such as a position or task: *Your degree qualifies you for a more challenging position in the company.* —*intr.* To be or become eligible for sthg.: *Have you qualified for the retirement benefits?*

qualitative (kwŏl′ĭ tā′tĭv) *adj.* Relating to quality, especially as distinguished from quantity or amount: *Because both products cost the same, the difference may be qualitative.*

qualitative characteristics (kwŏl′ĭ tā′tĭv kăr′ək tə rĭs′tĭks) *pl.n.* Standards for judging the quality of information that accountants give to decision makers. The most important qualitative characteristics are **understandability** and **usefulness**. To be useful, information must be relevant and reliable.

quality (kwŏl′ĭ tē) *n., pl.* **qualities. 1.** An operating environment in which a company's product or service meets a customer's specifications the first time it is produced or delivered. **2.** A characteristic or feature that distinguishes one thing from another: *There's a special quality to his writing.* **3.** Excellence; superiority: *a store that sells only quality clothing.* **4.** The degree or grade of excellence: *meat of poor quality.*

quality of earnings (kwŏl′ĭ tē əv ûr′nĭngz) *n.* The amount of an individual's earnings after all deductions, such as taxes, medical costs, or business expenses, have been subtracted from the gross income. Another term for **net income** (sense 1).

quantity (kwŏn′tĭ tē) *n., pl.* **quantities. 1.** An amount or number: *large quantities of goods available.* **2.** A large amount or number: *produce oil in quantity.*

quarter (kwôr′tər) *n.* Three-month intervals of the year, as follows: first quarter: January, February, and March; second quarter: April, May, and June; third quarter: July, August, and September; fourth quarter: October, November, December. Also called **calendar quarter**.

quarterly report (kwôr′tər lē rĭ pôrt′) *n.* Another term for **interim financial statement**.

queue (kyōō) *n.* A line of people or things: *parts in a queue on the production line.*

queue time (kyōō′ tīm′) *n.* The time a product spends waiting to be worked on once it arrives at the next operation or department.

quick asset (kwĭk′ ăs′ĕt) *n.* Something that is cash or can easily be converted into cash, for example, current Notes Receivable or Marketable Securities. Inventory is considered a quick asset.

quick ratio (kwĭk′ rā′shō) *n.* The relationship of a company's current assets that can be converted into cash to its current liabilities. Also **acid-test ratio**.

Rr

R&D *Abbr.* An abbreviation of research and development.

rate of exchange (rāt′ əv ĭks chānj′) *n., pl.* **rates of exchange.** The ratio at which a unit of currency from one nation can be exchanged for the unit of currency of another nation; the value of one currency in terms of another. Also called **exchange rate.**

rate of return (rāt′ əv rĭ tûrn′) *n.* The amount of profit or interest earned on an investment, usually expressed as a percentage, such as an interest rate; the cost of capital; the cost of money.

rate standard (rāt′ stăn′dərd) *n.* Another term for **direct labor rate standard.**

rate variance (rāt′ vâr′ē əns) *n.* Another term for **direct labor rate variance.**

ratio (rā′shō *or* rā′shē ō′) *n., pl.* **ratios.** A numerical relationship between the amounts or sizes of two things: *The worker–manager ratio in the plant is 25 to 1.*

ratio analysis (rā′shō ə năl′ĭ sĭs) *n.* A technique of financial analysis in which meaningful relationships are shown between the components of the financial statements.

raw (rô) *adj.* **1.** In a natural condition; not processed: *raw materials.* **2.** Not cooked: *raw meat.*

Raw in Process Inventory (rô′ ĭn prŏs′ĕs ĭn′vən tôr′ē) *n.* An inventory account in the just-in-time operating environment that combines the Raw Materials Inventory and the Work in Process Inventory accounts.

raw material (rô′ mə tîr′ē əl) *n. (usually plural).* Something in its natural state that will be used in a manufacturing process: *the rising cost of raw materials.*

Raw Materials Inventory account (rô′ mə tîr′ē əlz ĭn′vən tôr′ē ə kount′) *n.* Another term for **Materials Inventory account.** Also called **Stores account** and **Materials Inventory Control account.**

real accounts (rē′əl ə kounts′) *pl.n.* Also called **permanent accounts.**

realizable value (rē′ə lī′zə bəl văl′yōō) *n.* The amount for which goods in inventory can be sold rather than the cost of replacing them. See also **market value.**

realization (rē′ə lĭ zā′shən) *n.* **1.** Conversion into cash, as happens in the sale of assets. **2.** The act of understanding sthg. completely: *our realization that we didn't have enough gas.* **3.** The result of making sthg. real: *the realization of his hopes.*

realize (rē′ə līz′) *tr.v.* **realized, realizing, realizes. 1.** To understand (sthg.) completely: *I think she realized her error.* **2.** To make (sthg.) real; fulfill: *He's only now realizing the benefits of his hard work.* **3.** To make (a gain or profit): *How much did you realize from the sale of your land?*

receipt (rĭ sēt′) *n.* **1.** A written or printed statement that a specified article or amount of money has been received: *Did you get a delivery receipt?* **2. receipts.** The amount received: *tax receipts.* Another term for **income. 3.** The act of receiving sthg.: *receipt of a package.*

receivable turnover (rĭ sē′və bəl tûrn′ō′vər) *n.* A ratio for measuring the relative size of a company's accounts receivable and the success of its credit and collection policies during an accounting period. This is found by dividing net sales by average net accounts receivable.

receive

receive (rĭ sēv′) *tr.v.* **received, receiving, receives. 1.** To get (sthg. given, offered, or sent): *She receives her mail at a post office box.* **2.** To hear or see (information, for example): *Has he received any news about the job offer?*

receiving (rĭ sē′vĭng) *n.* The department of a company responsible for accepting deliveries.

receiving report (rĭ sē′vĭng rĭ pôrt′) *n.* A form prepared by the receiving department of a company that describes the types, quantity, and condition of goods received.

recognition (rĕk′əg nĭsh′ən) *n.* **1.** The determination of when a business transaction should be recorded. **2.** The act of identifying sbdy./sthg.: *recognition of an old friend.* **3.** Acknowledgment or approval: *an award in recognition of superior sales performance.*

recognition issue (rĕk′əg nĭsh′ən ĭsh′ōō) *n.* The difficulty involved in deciding when a business transaction should be recorded.

recognition point (rĕk′əg nĭsh′ən point′) *n.* The predetermined time at which a transaction should be recorded; for example, the point at which title passes from the seller to the buyer.

recognize (rĕk′əg nīz′) *tr.v.* **recognized, recognizing, recognizes. 1.** To know or identify (sbdy./sthg.) from past experience or knowledge: *Do you recognize this man?* **2.** To accept (sthg.) as valid or real: *The bank will recognize my check.* —**recognizable** *adj.* —**recognizably** *adv.*

reconcile (rĕk′ən sīl′) *tr.v.* **reconciled, reconciling, reconciles. 1.** To resolve (a dispute): *reconcile the argument.* **2.** To bring (two or more things) into harmony or agreement: *reconcile a bank statement balance with a checkbook balance.* —**reconciliation** *n.*

recover (rĭ kŭv′ər) *tr.v.* **1.** To get (sthg.) back; regain: *The police recovered the stolen merchandise.* **2.** To make up for (sthg.); compensate for: *recover one's losses on the stock market.* —**recoverable** *adj.*

recovery (rĭ kŭv′ə rē) *n.* **1.** The receipt of money previously believed to be uncollectible. **2.** A return to a normal condition: *the economic recovery.*

recovery period (rĭ kŭv′ə rē pĭr′ē əd) *n.* The period of time required to collect money that is owed. The period of time from making a sale on account to the collection of cash on that account.

redeem (rĭ dēm′) *tr.v.* **1.** To turn in (sthg., coupons, for example); exchange: *That store redeems manufacturers' coupons.* **2.** To exchange (sthg., such as stocks or bonds) for cash. **3.** To buy back or repurchase bonds from bondholders.

redemption (rĭ dĕmp′shən) *n.* The act of exchanging sthg. for cash, especially coupons, stocks, or bonds.

reengineering (rē′ĕn jə nîr′ĭng) *n.* Another term for **downsizing**.

register (rĕj′ĭ stər) *n.* **1.** An official list: *a register of all imported materials.* **2.** A device that automatically records or displays a number or amount: *a cash register.* —*tr.v.* **1.** To record (sthg.) in a list: *register sales figures.* **2.** To record (sthg.) in writing: *register a complaint.*

registered bonds (rĕj′ĭ stərd bŏndz′) *pl.n.* Bonds for which the names and addresses of bondholders are recorded with the issuing company.

registered trademark (rĕj′ĭ stərd trād′märk′) *n.* *Symbol* ™. A federally registered word, phrase, symbol, or design that

replacement

identifies the source and quality of a particular good or service. Legal rights to a trademark exclude others from using the same trademark or one that is confusingly similar for an indefinite period of time. Also called **trademark**.

regulate (rĕg′yə lāt′) *tr.v.* **regulated, regulating, regulates.** **1.** To control or direct (sthg.) according to rules or laws: *power to regulate trade.* **2.** To adjust (sthg.) so that it functions properly: *regulate the flow of electricity.*

regulation (rĕg′yə lā′shən) *n.* **1.** The act of controlling sthg. by rules or laws: *the government regulation of corporations.* **2.** A rule, an order, or a law that controls or governs an activity: *regulations concerning waste disposal.*

regulatory agency (rĕg′yə lə tôr′ē ā′jən sē) *n.* A state or federal agency that controls specific activities.

reimburse (rē′ĭm bûrs′) *tr.v.* **reimbursed, reimbursing, reimburses.** To pay (sbdy.) back; compensate: *Have you been reimbursed for your travel expenses yet?* —**reimbursement** *n.*

relative sales value method (rĕl′ə tĭv sālz′ văl′yoō mĕth′əd) *n.* The use of revenue-producing ability (sales value) as the basis for allocating joint costs to specific products or services.

relevance (rĕl′ə vəns) *n.* The quality of being directly relevant to a specific issue or the outcome of a decision.

relevant (rĕl′ə vənt) *adj.* Related to a matter being discussed or considered: *Bring the relevant documents to the meeting.*

relevant decision information (rĕl′ə vənt dĭ sĭzh′ən ĭn′fər mā′shən) *n.* Information about future costs, revenues, and resource usage that relate to alternative courses of action being considered by decision makers.

relevant range (rĕl′ə vənt rānj′) *n.* The span of activity or volume in which a company's actual operations are likely to occur: *The relevant range of production for this company is between 5,000 and 6,000 units per year.*

reliability (rĭ lī′ə bĭl′ĭ tē) *n.* The quality of being faithful, verifiable, and neutral.

reliable (rĭ lī′ə bəl) *adj.* Able to be relied on; dependable: *a reliable source of information; a reliable car.*

rely (rĭ lī′) *intr.v.* **relied, relying, relies.** **1.** To be dependent on sbdy./sthg. for support or help: *Most people rely on a job for their living.* **2.** To have trust or confidence (in sbdy./sthg.): *Can we rely on you to finish the job on time?*

renew (rĭ noō′) *tr.v.* **1.** To make (sthg.) seem to be new again; restore: *renew an old section of town.* **2.** To take (sthg.) again; continue: *renew a contract.*

renewal (rĭ noō′əl) *n.* The act of restoring or continuing sthg.: *urban renewal; renewal of a contract.*

repair (rĭ pâr′) *tr.v.* To restore (sthg.) to a proper or useful condition after damage or injury: *repair a bicycle.* —*n.* **1.** The work, act, or process of restoring sthg. to working order: *make the necessary repairs on a truck.* **2.** The general condition of sthg.: *a building in good repair.*

replace (rĭ plās′) *tr.v.* **replaced, replacing, replaces.** **1.** To put (sthg.) back into its previous position: *Replace the chairs before you leave.* **2.** To take or fill the place of (sbdy./sthg.): *The belt on the motor should be replaced.*

replacement (rĭ plās′mənt) *n.* **1.** The act of putting sthg. back: *replacement of funds.* **2.** A person or thing that replaces: *our secretary's replacement.*

replacement value

replacement value (rĭ plās′mənt văl′yōō) *n.* The amount for which goods can be replaced; the cost of replacing goods. Also called **market value** (sense 2). See also **realizable value**.

report (rĭ pôrt′) *n.* An oral or written description of sthg., such as a book, event, or situation: *our CPA's report.* —*v.* —*tr.* **1.** To present an account of (sthg.): *The manager reported the latest sales figures.* **2.** To write or provide (information) for publication or broadcast: *report the news.* **3.** To notify sbdy. about (sthg.): *The manager reported the accounting error.* —*intr.* **1.** To provide information: *The treasurer will report on our financial situation.* **2.** To be present: *Did she report for work on time?* **3.** To be accountable (to sbdy., especially a superior): *He reports directly to the CEO.*

report format (rĭ pôrt′ fôr′măt) *n.* The form of the balance sheet in which assets are placed at the top and liabilities and owner's equity are placed below. See also **account format**.

reporting currency (rĭ pôr′tĭng kûr′ən sē) *n.* The currency in which consolidated financial statements are presented.

requisition (rĕk′wĭ zĭsh′ən) *n.* A formal written request for sthg. needed: *We need a requisition for the new computer system.* —*tr.v.* To request (sthg.) formally and in writing: *We've requisitioned more office supplies.*

research and development (rĭ sûrch′ ən dĭ vĕl′əp mənt) *n. Abbr.* **R&D** The planned search for new knowledge and the translation of that knowledge into a plan for a new product or process, or improvement to an existing product or process.

research and development costs (rĭ sûrch′ ən dĭ vĕl′əp mənt kôsts′) *pl.n.* The expense of funding research and development. These are treated as revenue costs and charged to expense in the period in which they are incurred.

reserve (rĭ zûrv′) *tr.v.* **reserved, reserving, reserves. 1.** To save (sthg.) for a specific purpose or later use: *reserve money to pay for research.* **2.** To order (sthg.) in advance for a specific time or date: *reserve a car at the airport.* —*n.* **1.** Something saved for a special purpose or future use: *a cash reserve.* **2. reserves.** Another term for **restriction on retained earnings**.

Reserve for Bad Debts account (rĭ zûrv′ fər băd′ dĕts′ ə-kount′) *n.* Another term for **Allowance for Uncollectible Accounts account**.

residual (rĭ zĭj′ōō əl) *adj.* Remaining as sthg. left over: *the residual effects of a strike.* —*n.* The amount left over at the end of a process: *store the residual.* —**residually** *adv.*

residual equity (rĭ zĭj′ōō əl ĕk′wĭ tē) *n.* The common stock of a corporation. Also called **net worth, owner's equity,** and **residual interest**.

residual value (rĭ zĭj′ōō əl văl′yōō) *n.* The estimated net scrap, salvage, or trade-in value of a tangible asset at the estimated date of disposal. Also called **salvage value** or **disposal value**.

responsibility (rĭ spŏn′sə bĭl′ĭ tē) *n., pl.* **responsibilities. 1.** The quality of being dependable and trustworthy: *The job carries with it a lot of responsibility.* **2.** Something that sbdy. must answer for: *There are many responsibilities connected with running a business.*

responsibility accounting (rĭ spŏn′sə bĭl′ĭ tē ə koun′tĭng) *n.* A system for reporting information that (1) classifies financial data according to areas of responsibility in an organization, and (2) reports each area's activities by including only the revenue and cost categories that the assigned manager can control. Also called **profitability accounting**.

retirement

responsibility center (rĭ spŏn′sə bĭl′ĭ tē sĕn′tər) *n.* In a responsibility accounting system, an organizational unit for which reports are generated, for example, a cost/expense center, a profit center, or an investment center.

restatement (rē stāt′mənt) *n.* **1.** The act of saying sthg. again or in a new form: *a restatement of the facts.* **2.** The stating of one currency in terms of another.

restrict (rĭ strĭkt′) *tr.v.* To keep or hold (sbdy./sthg.) within specific limits: *I try to restrict my time on the telephone.*

restriction (rĭ strĭk′shən) *n.* **1.** The act of limiting sbdy./sthg.: *a restriction on hiring.* **2.** Something that limits: *restrictions on using the Internet.*

restriction on retained earnings (rĭ strĭk′shən ŏn rĭ tānd′ ûr′nĭngz) *n.* The required or voluntary restriction of a portion of retained earnings that cannot be used to pay dividends. Also called **reserves** (sense 2).

restrictive (rĭ strĭk′tĭv) *adj.* Tending to limit: *a restrictive environment for business.*

restrictive endorsement (rĭ strĭk′tĭv ĕn dôrs′mənt) *n.* An endorsement, such as "Pay to the order of (name of bank), for deposit only," that restricts or limits any further negotiation of a check. It forces the check's deposit because the endorsement is not valid for any other purpose.

retail (rē′tāl′) *n.* The selling of goods or products to the public at a price greater than wholesale: *buy tires at retail.* —*adj.* Relating to the sale of goods at retail: *retail prices.* —*v.* —*tr.* To sell (things) to consumers for more money than their wholesale price: *This store retails garden tools.* —*intr.* To sell goods or be for sale at a retail price: *This camera retails for $400.*

retail business (rē′tāl bĭz′nĭs) *n.* Another term for **merchandising business**. See also **wholesale**.

retailing (rē′tā′lĭng) *n.* The business or occupation of selling goods for more money than their wholesale price: *He's been in retailing for more than 30 years.*

retail method (rē′tāl mĕth′əd) *n.* A way of estimating inventory, used in retail businesses. Under this method, inventory at retail value is reduced by the ratio of cost to retail price.

retain (rĭ tān′) *tr.v.* To keep possession of (sthg.); continue to have: *She retained her position.*

retained earnings (rĭ tānd′ ûr′nĭngz) *pl.n.* Stockholders' claims to assets arising from the earnings of the business; the accumulated earnings of a corporation from its inception, minus any losses, dividends, or transfers to contributed capital. Also called **earned capital**.

Retained Earnings account (rĭ tānd′ ûr′nĭngz ə kount′) *n.* The account that reflects the stockholders' claim to the assets earned from operations and reinvested in corporate operations.

retire (rĭ tīr′) *v.* **retired, retiring, retires.** —*tr.* **1.** To take (sthg.), such as a bond, out of circulation. **2.** To cause (sbdy.) to stop working at a certain age: *The company retires all workers at 65.* **3.** To take out of use or active service: *This year we'll have to retire our old computer system.* —*intr.* **1.** To leave a place in order to rest or be alone: *The judge retired.* **2.** To go to bed. *She retired at 9:00.*

retirement (rĭ tīr′mənt) *n.* **1.** An act of taking sthg., such as a bond issue, out of circulation. **2.** The act of leaving a job or an occupation, usually at a specific age. **3.** The state of having left a job or an occupation.

return

return (rĭ tûrn′) *v.* —*intr.* To go or come back, as to a former condition or place: *return to work.* —*tr.* **1.** To send, put, or carry (sthg.) back: *return the books to the library.* **2.** To take (sthg.) back, as in exchange for sthg. else: *return a suit to the store.* **3.** To produce (interest or profit) as a payment for labor or investment: *A restaurant does well to return 20 percent.* —*n.* **1.** The profit or interest earned on an investment: *This mutual fund earns only a modest return.* **2.** A formal declaration of income and taxes on the official form: *Did you mail your tax return on time?* **3.** The act of coming, going, bringing, or sending back: *the return of the inspector.* **4.** Something brought or sent back: *Merchandise returns are increasing.*

return on assets (rĭ tûrn′ ŏn ăs′ĕts) *n.* A measurement of a company's profitability or overall earning power, that is, how efficiently a company uses its assets to produce income. It is found by dividing net income by average total assets.

return on assets pricing (rĭ tûrn′ ŏn ăs′ĕts prī′sĭng) *n.* A way of pricing products or services in order to earn a profit equal to a specific rate of return on assets used in the operation.

return on equity (rĭ tûrn′ ŏn ĕk′wĭ tē) *n.* A measurement of profitability (how much income was earned on each dollar) that relates the amount earned by a business to the stockholders' investments in the business. It is found by dividing net income by average owner's equity.

return on investment (rĭ tûrn′ ŏn ĭn vĕst′mənt) *n.* A measurement of the earning power of an owner's investment in a business. Also called **yield.**

revenue (rĕv′ə noō) *n.* Increases in owner's equity that result from operating a business, such as selling goods (sales), performing services, or performing other business activities (rent and interest income). Such increases can be in the form of cash, credit card receipts, accounts receivable (charge accounts), or income from property or investments.

revenue and expense summary (rĕv′ə noō ənd ĭk spĕns′ sŭm′ə rē) *n.* Another term for **income summary.**

revenue expenditure (rĕv′ə noō ĭk spĕn′də chər) *n.* An expenditure for repairs, maintenance, or other services needed to maintain or operate a plant asset. It is recorded by a debit to an expense account.

revenue recognition (rĕv′ə noō rĕk′əg nĭsh′ən) *n.* In accrual accounting, the process of determining when a sale takes place.

reversing entries (rĭ vûr′sĭng ĕn′trēz) *pl.n.* Journal entries made on the first day of a new accounting period. These entries reverse certain adjusting entries and simplify the bookkeeping process for the next accounting period.

rework (rē wûrk′) *tr.v.* **1.** To change (sthg.); revise: *rework a letter.* **2.** To cause (sthg.) to go through a repeated or new process: *rework a product.* —*n.* The act of redoing sthg., such as a manufactured product: *Scrap and rework could be anticipated by traditional costing approaches.*

rightsizing (rīt′sī′zĭng) *n.* Another term for **downsizing.**

risk (rĭsk) *n.* **1.** The possibility of suffering harm or loss; danger: *Don't take unnecessary risks.* **2.** A person or thing thought of in relation to the possibility of loss or injury: *a good credit risk.* —*tr.v.* **1.** To put (sbdy./sthg.) in a dangerous situation: *He risked his savings on a foolish investment scheme.* **2.** To cause oneself to have the chance of (sthg.): *risk having an accident.* —**riskiness** *n.* —**risky** *adj.*

run time

round (round) *tr.v.* To express (a number) as a round number: *The number 3.45 can be rounded to 3 or 3.5.*

rounding (roun'dĭng) *n.* (of numbers) The process of making a number easier to deal with by making it the next highest or lowest whole number. There are three simple rules for doing this: (1) Round unit cost calculations to three decimal places where appropriate; (2) round cost summary data to the nearest dollar; (3) on the cost summary schedule, any difference caused by rounding should be added to or subtracted from the amount being transferred out of the department before the journal entry is prepared.

rule-of-thumb measure (rōōl'əv thŭm' mĕzh'ər) *n.* A method used by financial analysts, investors, and lenders to determine whether a financial ratio is considered acceptable or not, that is, whether it can be used as a benchmark. Also called **ideal measure.**

ruling method (rōō'lĭng mĕth'əd) *n.* A way of correcting accounting errors by drawing a single line through the incorrect entry and writing in the correct amount above it. Also called **correcting entry method.**

running balance (rŭn'ĭng băl'əns) *n., pl.* **running balances.** The process in which a balance is entered after each transaction is recorded; a continuously up-to-date balance: *maintain a running balance in one's checkbook.*

run time (rŭn' tīm') *n.* The actual total machine hours needed to produce sthg., less setup time.

Ss

salary (săl′ə rē) *n., pl.* **salaries.** A way of paying employees who receive wages at a fixed monthly or yearly rate.

salary allowance (săl′ə rē ə lou′əns) *n., pl.* **salary allowances.** A predetermined amount of pay that may be distributed to partners to compensate them for contributions to the firm. Distributions of income from the partnership go first to pay salary allowances, next to pay interest on partners' capital balances, and any remaining income (or loss) is distributed among the partners.

sales (sālz) *pl.n.* Another term for **net sales**.

sales budget (sālz′ bŭj′ĭt) *n.* A detailed plan, expressed in both units and dollars, that identifies the expected product (or service) sales for a future period.

sales discount (sālz′ dĭs′kount) *n.* A discount that is given to a buyer for early payment for a sale made on credit.

sales journal (sālz′ jûr′nəl) *n.* A type of special-purpose journal used to record credit sales.

sales mix analysis (sālz′ mĭks ə năl′ĭ sĭs) *n.* A special analysis that is prepared to determine the most profitable combination of product sales when a company produces more than one product or offers more than one service.

Sales Returns and Allowances account (sālz′ rĭ tûrnz′ and ə lou′ən sĭz ə kount′) *n.* A contra-revenue account used to accumulate cash refunds, credits on account, and other allowances that are made to customers who have received defective or otherwise unsatisfactory products.

sales tax (sālz′ tăks′) *n.* A tax that is levied by a state or city government on the retail sale of goods and services. The tax is paid by the consumer but is collected by the retailer.

sales tax payable (sālz′ tăks pā′ə bəl) *n.* The amount of sales tax collected by a merchant. It is a **current liability** until it is sent to the government.

sales ticket (sālz′ tĭk′ĭt) *n.* A prenumbered form that has two or more copies attached. At the time of a sale, the salesperson keeps one copy and gives the other one to the customer. It is a way of controlling cash receipts.

salvage (săl′vĭj) *n.* **1.** The act of saving endangered property from destruction: *They're in the business of salvage.* **2.** The goods or property saved from destruction or disaster: *We keep a special account for salvage.* —*tr.v.* **salvaged, salvaging, salvages. 1.** To save (sthg.) from loss or ruin: *We salvaged our photographs from the fire.* **2.** To save (discarded or damaged material) for future use: *The recycler salvages glass and aluminum cans.*

salvage value (săl′vĭj văl′yōō) *n.* The estimated net scrap, salvage, or trade-in value of a tangible asset at the estimated date of disposal. Also called **residual value** or **disposal value**.

scatter (skăt′ər) *tr. & intr.v.* To separate and spread or cause (sthg.) to separate and go in different, random directions: *scatter papers around the office. The children scattered when they saw the owner of the building.*

scatter diagram (skăt′ər dī′ə grăm′) *n.* A chart of plotted points that is used to analyze semivariable mixed costs. This diagram helps determine if a linear relationship exists between a cost item and its related activity measure.

Securities and Exchange Commission

schedule (skĕj′ōōl *or* skĕj′ōō əl *or* skĕj′əl) *n.* **1.** A form for entering and computing the units that are produced in a given accounting period. **2.** A list of future appointments, events, or times: *What's the factory's schedule for production?* **3.** A form for reporting one's taxable income. This form is supplied by a government. —*tr.v.* **scheduled, scheduling, schedules.** **1.** To put (sthg.) on a schedule: *schedule an interview.* **2.** To prepare a schedule for (sthg.): *schedule my workday.* **3.** To plan or provide a specific time for (sbdy./sthg.): *Schedule the trip for next week.*

schedule of equivalent production (skĕj′ōōl əv ĭ kwĭv′ə lənt prə dŭk′shən) *n.* A schedule that is used in process costing. For this schedule a period's equivalent units are computed for both materials costs and conversion costs.

scope (skōp) *n.* **1.** The range that is covered by an activity, a situation, or a subject: *Our company's aims are broad in scope.* **2.** The range of one's thoughts, actions, or abilities: *broaden one's scope by attending workshops.* **3.** Room or opportunity to function or perform: *Give full scope to your imagination on this project.*

scope section (skōp′ sĕk′shən) *n.* The part of the auditors' report that states that the examination of a company's financial statement was made in accordance with generally accepted auditing standards and provides a reasonable basis for an opinion.

scrap (skrăp) *n.* **1.** A small piece or bit of sthg.; fragment: *a scrap of paper.* **2.** Discarded waste material, especially metal that can be recycled and reused: *We sold our old car for scrap.* —*tr.v.* **scrapped, scrapping, scraps.** **1.** To break (sthg.) down into parts for disposal or salvage: *scrap an old stove.* **2.** To discard or abandon sthg. because it is useless: *We had to scrap the project.*

season (sē′zən) *n.* **1.** One of the four natural divisions of the year, spring, summer, fall, and winter. **2.** A period of the year marked by a specific activity or the appearance of sthg.: *the holiday season; tax season.*

seasonal cycle (sē′zə nəl sī′kəl) *n.* A predictable business cycle that is made up of recurring periods when sales are weak and other periods when sales are good.

SEC *Abbr.* An abbreviation of Securities and Exchange Commission.

secure (sĭ kyŏŏr′) *adj.* **1.** Free from danger, attack, or loss: *a secure building.* **2.** Free from fear, anxiety, or doubt; safe: *feeling secure in one's job.* —*tr.v.* **secured, securing, secures.** **1.** To guard (sbdy./sthg.) against danger or risk: *Police secured the building.* **2.** To cause (sthg.) to remain firmly in place or position: *Secure your seat belts.* **3.** To guarantee (sthg., such as repayment of a loan) by pledging an asset to be surrendered: *secure a car loan.* **4.** To acquire: *She is unable to secure another loan because she has so much debt already.*

secured bond (sĭ kyŏŏrd′ bŏnd′) *n.* A bond that gives the bondholders a pledge of certain company assets as a guarantee of repayment.

Securities and Exchange Commission (sĭ kyŏŏr′ĭ tēz ənd ĭks chānj′ kə mĭsh′ən) *n. Abbr.* **SEC** An agency of the federal government set up by the U.S. Congress to protect the public by regulating the issuing, buying, and selling of stocks and bonds. This agency has the legal power to set and enforce accounting practices for firms whose securities are sold to the general public.

security

security (sĭ kyōōr′ĭ tē) *n.* **securities.** Bonds, stock certificates, etc., given as evidence of a debt or of property. See also **marketable securities.**

segment (sĕg′mənt) *n.* **1.** A part into which sth. is or can be divided: *the segments of an orange; various segments of society.* **2.** A distinct part of a business operation, such as a line of business or a class of customer: *the production segment of the steel industry.*

segregation of duties (sĕg′rĭ gā′shən əv dōō′tēz) *n.* Another term for **separation of duties.**

sell (sĕl) *v.* **sold** (sōld), **selling, sells.** —*tr.* **1.** To give (sthg., such as a product) in exchange for money: *sell a car.* **2.** To offer (sthg.) to potential buyers: *This store sells books.* **3.** To promote (sthg.) to the public: *Advertising sold that car.* —*intr.* **1.** To engage in providing goods for sale: *He sells only at wholesale prices.* **2.** To be sold or to be on sale: *Strawberries sell well when they're in season.* **3.** To be very popular on the market: *This CD has sold well.* —*n.* (usually singular). A customer, spoken of in terms of his or her willingness to buy sthg.: *That client is a hard sell.*

selling cost budget (sĕl′ĭng kôst bŭj′ĭt) *n.* A schedule that is developed using information from the sales budget and the sales staff that details all anticipated costs related to the selling function of a business for a future period.

selling expenses (sĕl′ĭng ĭk spĕn′sĭz) *pl.n.* Expenses that are directly connected with the selling activity, such as salaries or sales staff, advertising expenses, and delivery expenses.

sell or process-further decision (sĕl′ ôr prŏs′ĕs fûr′thər dĭ sĭzh′ən) *n.* A decision analysis designed to help management determine whether to sell a joint product at the split-off point or process it further to increase its market price and the company's profits.

semivariable costs (sĕm′ē vâr′ē ə bəl kôsts′) *pl.n.* Costs that have both variable and fixed cost components. For example, telephone costs include long-distance calls (variable costs) and monthly service charges (fixed costs). See also **mixed costs.**

semiweekly (sĕm′ē wēk′lē) *adj.* Happening or published twice a week: *a semiweekly report.*

semiweekly deposit schedule rule (sĕm′ē wēk′lē dĭ pŏz′ĭt skĕj′ōōl rōōl′) *n.* An accounting rule pertaining to employers whose total amount of reported taxes for the four quarters in the **lookback** period is between $50,000 and $100,000.

separate (sĕp′ər ĭt *or* sĕp′rĭt) *adj.* Distinct from others; individual or independent: *We each made our separate decisions.*

separate entity (sĕp′ər ĭt ĕn′tĭ tē) *n.* A business that is treated as distinct from its creditors, customers, and owners. See also **economic entity.**

separate entity concept (sĕp′ər ĭt ĕn′tĭ tē kŏn′sĕpt) *n.* The concept according to which a business is treated as an independent economic or accounting entity separate from its owner, creditors, and customers.

separation of duties (sĕp′ə rā′shən əv dōō′tēz) *n.* A control procedure for safeguarding a company's assets in which different individuals or departments are responsible for custody of assets and the record keeping for the assets. Also called **segregation of duties** or **separation of incompatible functions.**

serial (sîr′ē əl) *adj.* **1.** Arranged in or forming a series: *serial publication.* **2.** Happening or presented in a series of installments: *a serial television program.*

significant

serial bonds (sîr′ē əl bŏndz′) *pl.n.* A bond issue with several different maturity dates. A certain portion matures each year. See also **term bonds**.

service (sûr′vĭs) *n.* **1.** Work or employment for another or others: *years of loyal service.* **2.** Work or duties done for another, such as a boss or a client: *require the services of a dentist.*

service business (sûr′vĭs bĭz′nĭs) *n.* A business that earns income by performing a service for fees or commissions.

service charge (sûr′vĭs chärj′) *n.* The fee a bank charges for handling checks, collections, and other items. It is in the form of a debit memorandum.

service overhead costs (sûr′vĭs ō′vər hĕd′ kôsts′) *pl.n.* A variety of costs (excluding direct labor costs) incurred specifically to develop and provide services.

service unit (sûr′vĭs yōō′nĭt) *n.* The length of time a tangible asset, such as a truck or machine, will remain useful. This may be expressed in terms of, for example, years, units produced, or miles driven.

SF *Abbr.* An abbreviation of sinking fund.

SFAS *Abbr.* An abbreviation of Statement of Financial Accounting Standards.

share (shâr) *n.* **1.** A part belonging to or contributed by sbdy. or a group: *You must accept your share of the blame. Here is your share of the money.* **2.** Any of the equal parts into which the capital stocks of a business are divided: *buy 100 shares of stock.* —*tr.v.* **shared, sharing, shares. 1.** To divide and distribute (sthg.): *share the proceeds.* **2.** To use or experience (sthg.) in common with other people: *share responsibility; share a computer.*

share of stock (shâr′ əv stŏk′) *n., pl.* **shares of stock.** A unit of ownership in a corporation.

shares outstanding (shârz′ out stăn′dĭng) *pl.n.* The number of shares in a company that have been issued and remain in circulation (in the hands of the shareholders). Also called **outstanding stock**.

short-term (shôrt′tûrm′) *adj.* **1.** Not lasting very long; temporary: *a way to account for short-term losses.* **2.** A period of time that is one year or less.

short-term investment (shôrt′tûrm ĭn vĕst′mənt) *n.* The temporary investment of excess cash, intended to be held until needed to pay current obligations. These investments are held three months to one year. Also called **marketable security**.

short-term liquid asset (shôrt′tûrm lĭk′wĭd ăs′ĕt) *n.* A financial asset that arises from cash transactions, the investment of cash for a period of one year or less, or the extension of credit up to one year. Accounts on the balance sheet that may be classified as short-term liquid assets include Cash, Short-term Investments, Accounts Receivable, and Notes Receivable.

signature (sĭg′nə chər) *n.* **1.** A person's name as he or she writes it: *What a messy signature!* **2.** The act of signing sthg.: *Your signature acknowledges receipt of the goods.*

signature card (sĭg′nə chər kärd′) *n.* The form depositors sign to give the bank a copy of the official signatures of any persons authorized to sign checks. The bank can use the form to verify the depositors' signatures on checks, on cash items that the depositors may endorse for deposit, and on other business papers that the depositors may present to the bank.

significant (sĭg nĭf′ĭ kənt) *adj.* **1.** Having a meaning; meaningful: *Is the amount of time significant?* **2.** Having or likely

significant influence

to have a major effect: *a significant change in our way of doing business.*

significant influence (sĭg nĭf′ĭ kənt ĭn′flōō əns) *n.* The ability of an investing company to affect the operating and financial policies of another company, even though it holds less than 50 percent of the voting stock.

simple (sĭm′pəl) *adj.* **simpler, simplest. 1.** Not complicated; easy: *a simple arithmetic problem.* **2.** Not showy or elaborate; plain: *simple words.*

simple capital structure (sĭm′pəl kăp′ĭ tl strŭk′chər) *n.* A capital structure of a company in which there are no preferred stocks, bonds, or stock options that can be converted into common stock. See also **complex capital structure.**

simple interest (sĭm′pəl ĭn′trĭst) *n.* The interest cost for one or more periods, under the assumption that the amount on which the interest is computed stays the same from period to period. See also **compound interest.**

single (sĭng′gəl) *adj.* **1.** Not with another or others; alone: *a single telephone line.* **2.** Made up of only one element, part, or section: *a single layer of cloth.* **3.** Separate from others; individual: *I've met every single one of the guests.*

single-step form (sĭng′gəl stĕp′ fôrm′) *n.* A condensed income statement that arrives at net income in a single step. See also **condensed financial statement, detailed income statement,** and **multistep form.**

sinking fund (sĭng′kĭng fŭnd′) *n. Abbr.* SF A special fund that accumulates the money needed to pay off a public or corporate debt.

slide (slīd) *v.* **slid** (slĭd), **sliding, slides.** —*intr.* **1.** To move smoothly over a surface while remaining in contact with it: *The car skidded and slid into a ditch.* **2.** To lose a safe footing; slip: *The woman slid on the polished floor.* **3.** To move downward or into a worse position: *Stocks slid after the President's speech.* —*tr.* To cause (sbdy./sthg.) to slip or slide: *Slide that file over here, please.* —*n.* **1.** An error in placing the decimal point in a number. For example, $163 entered as $1.63 is a slide. **2.** A sliding action or movement: *a graceful slide over the ice.* **3.** A fall of a mass of rock, earth, or snow down a slope; an avalanche or landslide: *That area is known for slides.*

Social Security (sō′shəl sĭ kyōor′ĭ tē) *n.* A U.S. government program that provides financial assistance in the form of retirement, disability, and medical benefits to people who are unemployed, disabled, or elderly. It is financed by payments from employers and employees. See also **Social Security tax.**

Social Security tax (sō′shəl sĭ kyōor′ĭ tē tăks′) *n.* A federal government tax levied on employees and employers, with the proceeds used for old-age pensions and disability benefits. Also called **FICA taxes.**

software (sôft′wâr′ *or* sŏft′wâr′) *n.* The programs in a computerized data processing system.

sole (sōl) *adj.* **1.** Being the only one; single: *the sole provider.* **2.** Relating only to one individual or group: *She has sole authority to make decisions.*

sole proprietorship (sōl′ prə prī′ə tər shĭp′) *n.* One of the three primary forms of business ownership; a one-owner business.

solvency (sŏl′vən sē *or* sōl′vən sē) *n.* The quality of being able to pay financial obligations: *Good credit depends on one's solvency.*

solvent (sŏl′vənt *or* sōl′vənt) *adj.* Capable of paying one's financial obligations: *Is that company still solvent?*

standard

source (sôrs) *n.* **1.** A place or thing from which sthg. comes; a point of origin: *a source of oil.* **2.** A person or a thing that provides information: *a confidential source on the committee.*

source document (sôrs′ dŏk′yə mənt) *n.* The written evidence, such as an invoice, a check, or a receipt, that supports the transactions for each major accounting function.

special (spĕsh′əl) *adj.* **1.** More than what is common or usual; unique: *a special talent.* **2.** Distinct among others of a kind: *That's his special chair.* **3.** Having a specific function or use: *receive special training.*

special order (spĕsh′əl ôr′dər) *n.* An order placed by a customer requiring that sthg. be produced, ordered, or prepared especially for him or her: *Your book is on special order.*

special-order (spĕsh′əl ôr′dər) *tr.v.* To place a special order for (sthg.): *We can special-order that camera for you.*

special order decision (spĕsh′əl ôr′dər dĭ sĭzh′ən) *n.* A decision about whether to accept or reject unexpected special product orders at prices below normal market prices.

special order decision analysis (spĕsh′əl ôr′dər dĭ sĭzh′ən ə năl′ĭ sĭs) *n.* A decision analysis designed to help management determine whether to accept or reject unexpected special product orders at prices below normal market prices.

special-purpose journal (spĕsh′əl pûr′pəs jûr′nəl) *n.* An input device in an accounting system that is used to record a single type of transaction.

specific (spĭ sĭf′ĭk) *adj.* **1.** Stated clearly and in detail: *specific instructions.* **2.** Special, distinctive, or unique: *known for a specific quality.*

specific identification method (spĭ sĭf′ĭk ī dĕn′tə fĭ kā′shən mĕth′əd) *n.* A way of pricing the cost of inventory by identifying the cost of each item in ending inventory as coming from a specific purchase.

split (splĭt) *v.* **split, splitting, splits.** —*tr.* To divide (sthg.) into parts; divide: *split a project. The issue split the group.* —*intr.* To become divided or separated into parts: *The group split over the issue.* —*n.* The act or result of being divided or separated: *a stock split.*

split off (splĭt′ ôf′) *tr. & intr.v.* To divide or be divided from sthg.; become distinct from sthg. else: *The businesses split off. Some liabilities can be split off from the larger ones for early payment.*

split-off point (splĭt′ôf′ point′) *n.* A point in the production or development process at which joint products or services separate and become identifiable.

spoil (spoil) *v.* —*tr.* To damage the value of (sthg.); ruin: *The news spoiled the meeting.* —*intr.* To decay or lose freshness: *vegetables spoiling in the refrigerator.* –*pl.n.* **spoils.** Goods, property, or advantage taken by sbdy. in a competition or war: *the spoils of victory.*

spoilage (spoi′lĭj) *n.* **1.** The loss of inventory as a result of decay: *Spoilage is a problem in many restaurants.* **2.** The process of decaying or losing freshness: *Refrigeration helps to stop spoilage of food.*

spreadsheet (sprĕd′shēt′) *n.* **1.** An accounting or bookkeeping program for use on a computer. **2.** The display, with multiple columns and rows, that such a program allows to be printed.

standard (stăn′dərd) *n.* **1.** A widely known and accepted measurement or weight used as a basis for a system of measurements: *a standard gallon of paint.* **2.** A rule or model used as a basis for

standard costs

judging quality, behavior, weight, or value: *high standards of behavior.* **3.** An acceptable level of quality: *an artist of standard talent.* –*adj.* **1.** Correct or acceptable in size, weight, or quality: *boards of standard length and width.* **2.** Ordinary; usual: *a standard performance.*

standard costs (stăn′dərd kôsts′) *pl.n.* Realistic costs for direct materials, direct labor, and factory overhead that have been determined before they occur.

standard direct labor cost (stăn′dərd dĭ rĕkt′ lā′bər kôst′) *n.* The standard hours of direct labor multiplied by the standard wage for direct labor.

standard direct materials cost (stăn′dərd dĭ rĕkt′ mə tîr′ē əlz kôst′) *n.* The standard price for direct materials multiplied by the standard quantity of direct materials.

standard factory overhead cost (stăn′dərd făk′tə rē ō′vər hĕd kôst′) *n.* The sum of the estimates of variable and fixed factory overhead in the next accounting period.

standard fixed overhead rate (stăn′dərd fĭkst′ ō′vər hĕd rāt′) *n.* The total budgeted fixed factory overhead costs divided by an expression of capacity. The rate can only be determined after a particular level of capacity is specified.

standard hours (stăn′dərd ourz′) *pl.n.* The fixed number of hours that a company or manufacturer allows for the performance of a specific task or process.

standard labor rate (stăn′dərd lā′bər rāt′) *n.* The usual amount of money paid to a worker for each hour worked. Employees performing the same task may have different wage rates, in which case a weighted average rate must be computed.

standard variable overhead rate (stăn′dərd vâr′ē ə bəl ō′vər hĕd rāt′) *n.* Total budgeted variable factory overhead costs divided by an expression of capacity, such as the expected number of standard machine hours or standard direct labor hours.

star network (stär nĕt′wûrk′) *n.* Another term for **home base network.**

stated (stā′tĭd) *adj.* Already declared or made public: *my stated intent.*

stated ratio (stā′tĭd rā′shō) *n.* A ratio used to distribute income and losses among the partners in a business. It is determined by each partner's contributions and investment.

stated value (stā′tĭd văl′yoō) *n.* A value assigned to no-par stock by the board of directors of a corporation.

statement (stāt′mənt) *n.* **1.** Something said or declared: *a statement of purpose.* **2.** A written or printed form that contains a summary of money paid, owed, or spent: *a monthly credit card statement; a bank statement.*

statement of cash flow (stāt′mənt əv kăsh′ flō) *n.* A primary financial statement that shows how a company's operating, investing, and financing activities have affected cash flow during an accounting period.

statement of changes in stockholders' equity (stāt′mənt əv chān′jĭz ĭn stŏk′hōl′dərz ĕk′wĭ tē) *n.* Another term for **statement of stockholders' equity.**

statement of cost of goods manufactured (stāt′mənt əv kôst′ əv goŏdz′ măn′yə făk′chərd) *n.* A formal statement summarizing the flow of all manufacturing costs incurred during an accounting period.

statement of financial position (stāt′mənt əv fə năn′shəl pə zĭsh′ən) *n.* Another term for **balance sheet.**

stock split

statement of owner's equity (stāt′mənt əv ō′nərz ĕk′wĭ tē) *n.* The financial statement that shows how and why an Owner's Equity, or Capital, account has changed over a specific financial period.

statement of stockholders' equity (stāt′mənt əv stŏk′hōl′dərz ĕk′wĭ tē) *n.* A financial statement that shows the same basic information as the statement of retained earnings but summarizes changes in the components of all accounts in the stockholders' equity section of the balance sheet. Also called **statement of changes in stockholders' equity.**

Statement of Financial Accounting Standards (stāt′mənt əv fə năn′shəl ə koun′tĭng stăn′dərdz) *pl.n. Abbr.* **SFAS** The rules governing accounting practice, developed and issued by the Financial Accounting Standards Board (FASB).

State Unemployment Tax (stāt′ ŭn′ĕm ploi′mənt tăks′) *n. Abbr.* **SUTA** A tax levied only on the employer in most states. Rates differ among the various states; however, they are generally 5.4 percent or higher of the first $7,000 of total earnings paid to each employee during the calendar year. The proceeds are used to pay minimum benefits to unemployed workers.

static budget (stăt′ĭk bŭj′ĭt) *n.* Another term for **fixed budget.**

statute of limitations (stăch′o͞ot əv lĭm′ĭ tā′shənz) *n.* A law that limits the period of time in which legal action may be taken. With regard to bad debts, such a law limits the period of time during which the courts may force a debtor to pay a debt, usually three years for charge accounts.

stock (stŏk) *n.* **1.a.** The money invested in a corporation by those who buy shares of ownership; each share gives the owner voting rights at meetings and often pays dividends: *The company's stock has increased in value.* **b.** A number of shares owned by a stockholder: *How much stock do you own now?* **2.** A supply saved for future use: *We have a stock of surplus wheat.* **3.** The total merchandise that is available for sale by a merchant or business: *a large stock of chairs and tables.*

stock certificate (stŏk′ sər tĭf′ĭ kĭt) *n.* A document issued to a stockholder indicating the number of shares of stock the stockholder owns.

stock dividend (stŏk′ dĭv′ĭ dĕnd) *n.* A proportional distribution of shares of a corporation's stock to its stockholders.

stockholder (stŏk′hōl′dər) *n.* A person who owns shares of stock in a company.

stockholders' equity (stŏk′hōl′dərz ĕk′wĭ tē) *n.* The owners' equity in a corporation. Stockholder's equity is made up of contributed capital and retained earnings. Also called **capital.**

stockholders' ledger (stŏk′hōl′dərz lĕj′ər) *n.* A record showing the name and address of each stockholder and the number of shares owned.

stock option (stŏk′ ŏp′shən) *n.* A right to purchase stock at the market price set at the time of the grant.

stock option plan (stŏk′ ŏp′shən plăn′) *n., pl.* **stock option plans.** A company's agreement to issue stock to employees according to specified terms, used as an incentive.

stock split (stŏk′ splĭt′) *n.* A method used to lower the market price of a company's stock by increasing the number of shares outstanding. In a 2-for-1 split, two new shares are exchanged for each original share, and the par value of each new share is one-half that of the original share. A stock split has no effect on the company's capital structure.

storage (stôr'ĭj) *n.* **1.** The act of storing sthg. or the state of being stored: *Our old records are kept in storage.* **2.** A space for storing things: *Our plant has a lot of storage.*

storage time (stôr'ĭj tīm') *n. (usually singular).* The length of time a product is in materials storage, work in process inventory, or finished goods inventory.

Stores account (stôrz' ə kount') *n.* An inventory account made up of the balances of materials, parts, and supplies on hand at a given time. Also called **Materials Inventory account** or **Raw Materials Inventory account.**

straight-line depreciation (strāt'līn' dĭ prē'shē ā'shən) *n.* Another term for **straight-line method** (sense 1).

straight-line method (strāt'līn' mĕth'əd) *n.* **1.** A way of depreciating assets in which it is assumed that depreciation depends only on the passage of time and allocates an equal amount of depreciation to each accounting period in an asset's useful life. **2.** A method of amortizing bond discounts or premiums. This method allocates a discount or premium equally over each interest period of the life of a bond.

straight-line percentage (strāt'līn' pər sĕn'tĭj) *n.* A percentage used to determine the amount of depreciation to be recorded each accounting period for the straight-line method. It is determined by dividing 1 by the number of accounting periods in the asset's useful life. The resulting percentage is multiplied by the asset's depreciable cost.

strategy (străt'ə jē) *n., pl.* **strategies.** A plan of action designed to accomplish some purpose or goal: *a strategy for making a better product.*

subsidiary (səb sĭd'ē ĕr'ē) *n., pl.* **subsidiaries.** An investee company in which another company owns a controlling interest. See also **controlling investment.**

subsidiary ledger (səb sĭd'ē ĕr'ē lĕj'ər) *n.* A ledger separate from the general ledger that contains a group of related accounts. The total of the balances in the subsidiary ledger accounts must equal the balance of a controlling account in the general ledger.

successful efforts accounting (sək sĕs'fəl ĕf'ərts ə koun'tĭng) *n.* A method of accounting for oil and gas resources in which the costs of successful exploration are recorded as assets and depleted over the estimated life of the resource and all unsuccessful efforts are immediately written off as losses. See also **full-costing.**

sum (sŭm) *n.* **1.** A number obtained by adding numbers: *The sum of 8 and 6 is 14.* **2.** The whole amount, quantity, or number: *the sum of my experience.* **3.** An amount of money: *He paid a large sum for it.*

summarize (sŭm'ə rīz') *tr.v.* To make a summary of (sthg.): *The researcher summarized the results for the manager.*

summarizing entry (sŭm'ə rī'zĭng ĕn'trē) *n., pl.* **entries.** An entry made to post the column totals of a special journal to the appropriate accounts in the general ledger. It is also used when individual sales invoices are posted directly to the accounts receivable ledger.

summary (sŭm'ə rē) *n., pl.* **summaries.** A brief statement that mentions only the main points of sthg.: *Have you read the accountant's summary?*

summary of significant accounting policies (sŭm'ə rē əv sĭg nĭf'ĭ kənt ə koun'tĭng pŏl'ĭ sēz) *n.* The section of a corporate annual report that discloses which generally accepted accounting principles the company has followed in preparing the financial statements.

systems analyst

sum-of-the-year's-digits method (sŭm'əv thə yîrz' dĭj'ĭts mĕth'əd) *n.* An accelerated method of depreciation in which the depreciable value of an asset (cost-salvage value) is multiplied by a decreasing fraction each year of the asset's useful life. The numerator of the fraction is the number of years of useful life remaining at the beginning of the year and the denominator is the sum of the years of useful life. For example, the fraction for the first year's depreciation for a three-year asset is 3/(1 + 2 + 3).

supplement (sŭp'lə mənt) *n.* Something added to complete sthg. or to make up for a weakness or lack: *a vitamin supplement.* —*tr.v.* To provide sthg. additional to (sthg.): *He supplements his income by working a night job.*

supplemental (sŭp'lə mĕn'tl) *adj.* Added to sthg.; additional: *supplemental income.*

supplemental information (sŭp'lə mĕn'tl ĭn'fər mā'shən) *n.* Additional information supplied with a company's financial statement. For example, the FASB and SEC have ruled that certain kinds of supplemental information must be presented with financial statements, such as **quarterly reports.**

supply (sə plī') *tr.v.* **supplied, supplying, supplies. 1.a.** To make (sthg.) available for use; provide: *supply computer paper.* **b.** To make sthg. available for the use of (sbdy.): *supply workers with uniforms.* —*n., pl.* **supplies.** Something, such as materials or other necessities, stored and used when needed: *office supplies.*

support (sə pôrt') *tr.v.* **1.** To hold or carry the weight of (sbdy./sthg.): *Beams support the roof. Can you support his weight?* **2.** To provide money or other necessities for (sbdy./sthg.): *She supported him while he finished law school. We supported our local food drive.* —*n.* The act of supporting sbdy./sthg. or the condition of being supported: *I appreciate your support in this matter. The candidate has a lot of support in this district.*

supporting service function (sə pôr'tĭng sûr'vĭs fŭngk'shən) *n.* An operating unit, activity, or department that supports the activities of a company's production facilities.

surplus (sûr'pləs *or* sûr'plŭs') *adj.* Not needed; extra: *surplus food.* —*n.* **1.** A credit or positive balance in the Retained Earnings account. **2.** An amount or a quantity that is more than what is needed: *We have a surplus of stocks on hand.*

SUTA (sōō'tə) *Abbr.* An abbreviation of State Unemployment Tax Act.

systems analyst (sĭs'təmz ăn'ə lĭst) *n.* The person who designs a computerized data processing system on the basis of an organization's information needs.

Tt

T account (tē′ ə kount′) *n.* The simplest form of an account, shaped like the letter T, in which increases and decreases in the account can be recorded. One side of the T is for entries on the debit (or left) side, and the other is for entries on the credit (or right) side.

take-home pay (tāk′hōm pā′) *n.* Another term for **net pay**.

takeover (tāk′ō′vər) *n.* The act or an instance of taking control of sthg., especially by force: *the recent takeover of a business by a multinational corporation.*

take over (tāk′ ō′vər) *tr.v.* **took** (tŏŏk) **over, taken** (tā′kən) **over, taking over, takes over.** To assume control or management of sthg., such as a nation or corporation: *The small company was taken over by a larger competitor.*

takt (täkt) *n. Japanese.* The baton used by a conductor to set the pace, or beat, of the music to be performed by a band or an orchestra.

***takt* time** (täkt′ tīm′) *n.* The pace that a factory must follow. This is computed by dividing time available by sold units, that is, those units that have actually been ordered. *A JIT cell with a* takt *time of five minutes must complete one unit every five minutes.*

tangible asset (tăn′jə bəl ăs′ĕt) *n.* A long-term asset that has physical substance. Also called **property, plant, and equipment.** See also **intangible asset.**

target (tär′gĭt) *n.* **1.** An object that is shot at in rifle and archery practice in order to test the accuracy of aim: *Set up the target over there.* **2.** Something aimed at or fired at: *use bottles for targets.* **3.** A desired goal or aim: *Increased efficiency is the target of the new program.* —*tr.v.* **targeted, targeting, targets. 1.** To make a target of (sbdy./sthg.): *He's been targeted for a promotion.* **2.** To aim at (sthg.): *This product targets the youth market.* **3.** To establish as a goal: *We're targeting $50,000 for our fund-raising campaign.*

target-costing (tär′gĭt kŏs′tĭng) *n.* A pricing method that (1) identifies the price at which a product will be competitive in the marketplace, (2) identifies the minimum desired profit to be made on the product, and (3) computes a target cost for the product by subtracting the desired profit from the competitive market price.

task (tăsk) *n.* **1.** A work element or operating step needed to perform and complete an activity: *How many tasks will be involved in the process?* **2.** An endeavor that is hard or tedious: *the task of ordering supplies.*

tax (tăks) *n., pl.* **taxes.** A fee levied by a government for its own support. It is required of people, groups, or businesses within that government's domain: *a new tax on imported cars.* —*tr.v.* **taxed, taxing, taxes. 1.** To place a tax on (property, income, or goods): *The city plans to tax all real estate sales.* **2.** To levy a tax on (sbdy.): *States tax truckers for road maintenance.* **3.** To make hard or excessive demands on (sbdy./sthg.): *That employee taxes my patience.*

taxable earnings (tăk′sə bəl ûr′nĭngz) *pl.n.* The amount of an employee's earnings subject to a tax (not the tax itself).

tax calendar (tăks′ kăl′ən dər) *n.* A chronological list of all the dates on which taxes, such as payroll and sales taxes,

114

total

must be paid. It is used to keep track of paying and reporting various taxes.

taxes payable (tăk′sĭz pā′ə bəl) *pl.n.* The amount of taxes owed to a government. This is recorded as a liability until it is paid.

tax table (tăks′ tā′bəl) *n.* One of the tables provided by a government agency that shows how much tax is owed on specific amounts of income and how to calculate the tax. The amount of tax to be paid is a percentage of the net income.

temporary account (tĕm′pə rĕr′ē ə kount′) *n.* Another term for **nominal account**.

term bonds (tûrm′ bŏndz′) *n.* A bond issue of which all the bonds will mature at the same time. See also **serial bonds**.

theft (thĕft) *n.* The act or an instance of stealing sthg.: *car theft*.

theoretical capacity (thē′ə rĕt′ĭ kəl kə păs′ĭ tē) *n.* Another term for **ideal capacity**.

throughput time (throō′pŏŏt′ tīm′) *n.* The time it takes to get a product through the entire production process.

tickler file (tĭk′lər fīl′) *n.* A file of unpaid vouchers, arranged by due date, used by the treasurer of a company to predict the amount of cash that will be needed to pay bills when they are due and to take advantage of cash discounts.

time and materials pricing (tīm′ ən mə tîr′ē əlz prī′sĭng) *n.* An approach to pricing used by service businesses. In this method, the total amount billed is composed of actual materials costs and actual labor costs plus a percentage markup of each to cover overhead costs and a profit factor.

time card (tīm′ kärd′) *n.* The basic record of time maintained for each employee. It shows the employee's daily starting and finishing times as recorded by the supervisor or a time clock.

time clock (tīm′ klŏk′) *n.* A clock in a workplace that is positioned so that employees can record the times of their arrivals and departures from work. Time clocks are usually used to calculate how many hours of work an employee must be paid for.

time standards (tīm′ stăn′dərdz) *pl.n.* The expected length of time that a specific process will take to complete. Meeting time standards is the responsibility of managers or supervisors.

time value of money (tīm′ văl′yōō əv mŭn′ē) *n.* The concept that cash flows of equal dollar amounts separated by a time interval have different present values because of the effect of compound interest.

title (tīt′l) *n.* **1.** The written evidence, such as a deed, that proves a legal right of possession or control: *hold title to property.* **2.** An identifying name given to a book, musical composition, play, film, or other work: *What's the title of the book you're reading?* **3.** A formal name attached to the name of a person that indicates rank, position, or responsibility: *Her title is Assistant Vice President.*

toll (tōl) *n.* A fixed charge or tax paid for the use of sthg., such as a highway or telephone network: *The state no longer collects tolls for using the old bridge.*

total (tōt′l) *n.* **1.** An amount obtained by addition; a sum: *The total of 5 and 7 is 12.* **2.** A whole amount: *The total of your bill comes to $25.* —*adj.* **1.** Relating to or being the whole: *the total cost.* **2.** Complete; absolute: *a total failure.* —*tr.v.* **totaled, totaling, totals** or **totalled, totalling, totals. 1.** To find (the sum of several numbers): *total a column of figures.* **2.** To equal (a total of); amount to: *Your bill totals $25.*

total cost curve

total cost curve (tōt′l kôst′ kûrv′) *n.* The line that represents the costs associated with making a product. The line curves upward on a graph, representing the fact that fixed costs of production, such as supervision and depreciation, will increase with increased production. See also **total revenue curve.**

total direct labor cost variance (tōt′l dī rĕkt′ lā′bər kôst vâr′ē əns) *n.* The difference between the actual labor costs incurred and the standard labor costs for the good units produced.

total direct materials cost variance (tōt′l dī rĕkt′ mə tîr′ē əlz kôst vâr′ē əns) *n.* The difference between the actual materials costs incurred and the standard costs of those items.

total inventory method (tōt′l ĭn′vən tôr′ē mĕth′əd) *n.* A lower-of-cost-or-market method of valuing inventory. In this method, the entire inventory is valued at both cost and market, and the lower price is used to value ending inventory. This is not an acceptable method for federal income tax purposes.

total manufacturing costs (tōt′l măn′yə făk′chər ĭng kôsts′) *pl.n.* The total costs of materials, direct labor, and factory overhead incurred and charged to production during an accounting period.

total overhead variance (tōt′l ō′vərhĕd vâr′ē əns) *n.* The difference between actual overhead costs incurred and the standard overhead costs applied to production using the standard variable and fixed overhead rates.

total quality management (tōt′l kwŏl′ĭ tē măn′ĭj mənt) *n. Abbr.* **TQM** An organizational environment in which all business functions work together to build quality into the firm's products or services.

total revenue curve (tōt′l rĕv′ə nōō kûrv′) *n.* A line on a graph that curves downward. This line represents the fact that, as one markets a product, price reductions and other factors involved in selling more of it will cause the rate of increase in revenue to decrease as more units are sold. See also **total cost curve.**

TQM *Abbr.* An abbreviation of total quality management.

trace (trās) *n.* A visible mark made or left by sbdy./sthg.: *The burglars left traces in the office.* —*tr.v.* **traced, tracing, traces.** **1.** To follow the course or trail of (sbdy./sthg.): *Can you trace the lost package?* **2.** To follow the history or development of (sthg.): *trace the history of the steam engine.*

traceable (trā′sə bəl) *adj.* Lending itself to or capable of being traced: *traceable documents.*

traceable fixed cost (trā′sə bəl fĭkst′ kôst′) *n.* A fixed cost that can be traced to a division, department, or other operating unit or product line.

trade (trād) *n.* **1.** The business of buying and selling goods: *international trade.* **2.** The people who work in a particular business or industry: *the building and construction trades.* **3.** An exchange of one thing for another: *I think we made a good trade.* **4.** An occupation, especially one that requires special skill with the hands; a craft: *She learned the woodworking trade from her father.* —*v.* **traded, trading, trades.** —*intr.* To buy, sell, or barter: *trade on the stock market.* **2.** To exchange one thing for another: *Let's trade.* **3.** To shop regularly: *We trade at the local market.* —*tr.* **1.** To exchange or swap (sthg.): *Let's trade places.* **2.** To buy and sell (sthg., such as stocks): *stocks traded on the open market.*

trade credit (trād′ krĕd′ĭt) *n.* Credit granted to customers by wholesalers or retailers.

transmittal

trade discount (trād′ dĭs′kount) *n.* A deduction (30 percent or more) off a list or catalog price.

trademark (trād′märk′) *n. Symbol* ™. Another term for **registered trademark**.

trade-in (trād′ĭn′) *n.* Something accepted as partial payment for a new purchase: *The dealer accepted our old car as a trade-in for the new one.* —*tr.v.* **trade in.** To use one thing as part of the purchase price of sthg. similar: *I traded in my old car for a new one.*

trade-in value (trād′ĭn văl′yōō) *n.* The actual value of sthg. traded in for a similar object, in contrast to its book value. Trade-in value is usually less than market value. Also called **trade-in allowance.**

trading on the equity (trā′dĭng ŏn thē ĕk′wĭ tē) *n.* Another term for **financial leverage.**

trading securities (trā′dĭng sĭ kyŏŏr′ĭ tēz) *pl.n.* Debt and equity securities bought and held principally for the purpose of being sold in the near future.

traffic (trăf′ĭk) *n.* **1.** The buying and selling of goods: *the traffic in pirated software in Asia.* **2.** The movement of people, vehicles, or messages along routes of transportation or communication: *Traffic on the Internet continues to increase.* —*intr.v.* **trafficked, trafficking, traffics.** To carry on trade or other dealings, especially illegally: *people who traffic in stolen goods.*

traffic-sensitive costs (trăf′ĭk sĕn′sĭ tĭv kôsts′) *pl.n. Abbr.* **TS** Costs that are related directly to the number of messages or the volume of traffic handled by a local or regional network. Such costs can be traced to one of three service categories: interstate toll, intrastate toll, or local service.

transact (trăn săkt′ *or* trăn zăkt′) *tr.v.* To do, carry out, or conduct (business or affairs): *transacted the sale of our house.*

transaction (trăn săk′shən *or* trăn zăk′shən) *n.* The act of transacting, especially a business agreement or exchange. See also **exchange of value** and **nonexchange transaction.**

transfer (trăns fûr′ *or* trăns′fər) *v.* **transferred, transferring, transfers.** —*tr.* **1.** To move or cause (sbdy./sthg.) to go from one place, person, or thing to another: *The employee has been transferred to another city.* **2.** To change the ownership of (property) to another person: *He transferred ownership of the business to his daughter.* —*intr.* To move oneself from one place or job to another: *I'm trying to transfer to another department.* —*n.* (trăns′fər) **1.** The moving of sbdy./sthg. from one place, person, or thing to another: *the transfer of property by will.* **2.** A person who changes location, for example, from one office or school to another: *college transfers; employee transfers.*

transfer price (trăns′fər prĭs′) *n.* The price at which goods and services are charged and exchanged between a company's divisions or segments.

transmission (trăns mĭsh′ən *or* trănz mĭsh′ən) *n.* **1.** The act or process of sending sthg.: *transmission of funds.* **2.** Something, such as a message, that is sent: *We received your transmission.*

transmit (trăns mĭt′ *or* trănz mĭt′) *tr.v.* **transmitted, transmitting, transmits.** **1.** To send or pass (sthg.) on from one person, place, or thing to another: *transmit an infection.* **2.** To send out (an electronic signal), as by wire or antenna: *The station transmits 24 hours a day.*

transmittal (trăns mĭt′l *or* trănz mĭt′l) *n.* The act or process of sending sthg. from one place to another: *transmittal of the required documents.*

Transmittal of Wage and Tax Statements

Transmittal of Wage and Tax Statements (trăns mĭt′l əv wāj′ ən tăks′ stāt′mənts) *n.* Another term for **Form W-3**.

transnational (trăns năsh′ə nəl *or* trănz năsh′ə nəl) *adj.* Reaching or happening beyond a nation's borders: *transnational trade*.

transnational corporation (trăns năsh′ə nəl kôr′pə rā′shən) *n.* Another term for **multinational corporation**.

transportation (trăns′pər tā′shən) *n.* **1.** The act or an instance of carrying sbdy./sthg. from one place to another: *the transportation of goods by rail.* **2.** A way of carrying sbdy./sthg. from one place to another: *Does she have transportation home?* **3.** The business of carrying (passengers or goods) from one place to another: *a company engaged in transportation.*

transportation in expense (trăns′pər tā′shən ĭn ĭk spĕns′) *n.* Another term for **freight in expense**.

transpose (trăns pōz′) *tr.v.* **transposed, transposing, transposes.** To reverse or transfer the order or place of (sthg.); interchange: *He accidentally transposed the numbers.*

transposition (trăns′pə zĭsh′ən) *n.* An error that involves interchanging, or switching around, digits during the recording of a number.

treas. *Abbr.* An abbreviation of: **1.** Treasurer. **2.** Treasury.

treasurer (trĕzh′ər ər) *n.* A person who is in charge of controlling a group's or an organization's money, especially the chief financial officer of a government, a corporation, or an association.

treasury (trĕzh′ə rē) *n., pl.* **treasuries. 1.** A place where private or public funds are controlled: *the club's treasury.* **2. Treasury.** The department of a government in charge of collecting, managing, and paying out public funds.

treasury stock (trĕzh′ə rē stŏk′) *n.* Capital stock, either common or preferred, that has been issued and reacquired by the issuing company but has not been resold or taken out of circulation.

trend (trĕnd) *n.* **1.** The general direction in which sthg. seems to be moving: *Before introducing a new product, we examined market trends for competitors' products.* **2.** A current style: *the trend toward organic food.*

trend analysis (trĕnd′ ə năl′ĭ sĭs) *n.* A type of horizontal analysis in which percentage changes are calculated for related items for several successive years instead of for two years. An **index number** is used to show charges in related items over a period of time.

trend percentages (trĕnd′ pər sĕn′tĭ jĭz) *pl.n.* Percentages calculated by dividing a specific item in an income statement by the corresponding item in the base year income statement.

trial (trī′əl *or* trīl) *n.* **1.** The examination of evidence, charges, and claims in a court of law: *a speedy trial.* **2.** The act or process of testing sbdy./sthg.: *the trial of a new drug; learn through trial and error.* —*adj.* **1.** Relating to or used in a trial: *trial evidence.* **2.** Tried or put forth on a provisional or experimental basis: *a trial period of employment.*

trial balance (trī′əl băl′əns) *n.* A comparison of the total of debit and credit balances in the ledger to check that they are equal.

true balance (trōō′ băl′əns) *n.* The amount of money in a bank account and a ledger after they have been reconciled. Another term for **adjusted balance**.

true interest rate (trōō′ ĭn′trĭst rāt′) *n.* Another term for **effective interest rate**.

TS *Abbr.* An abbreviation of traffic-sensitive (costs).

two-column general journal

turnover (tûrn′ō′vər) *n.* **1.a.** The number of times a particular product is sold and restocked during a fixed period of time: *Turnover on the new toy is very high.* **b.** The amount of business done in a fixed period of time: *Turnover in coats is good during the winter.* **c.** The number of shares of stock sold on the market in a fixed period of time: *Turnover on Wall Street was brisk today.* **2.** A sale made to a customer that is charged to his or her account and then paid off at a later date. **3.** The number of workers replaced with new hires by a business in a fixed period of time: *Turnover at the new plant is increasing.*

two-column general journal (tōō′kŏl′əm jĕn′ər əl jûr′nəl) *n.* A general journal in which there are two amount columns, one used for debit amounts and one used for credit amounts.

Uu

unappropriated (ŭn'ə prō'prē ā'tĭd) *adj.* **1.** Not intended or designated for a particular purpose: *Unappropriated funds can be spent on building maintenance.* **2.** Not owned by or formally assigned to a particular person or organization: *unappropriated land.*

unappropriated retained earnings (ŭn'ə prō'prē ā'tĭd rĭ-tānd' ûr'nĭngz) *pl.n.* The portion of Retained Earnings available for distribution as dividends to the stockholders.

uncollectible (ŭn'kə lĕk'tə bəl) *adj.* Not able to be collected; unpaid.

uncollectible accounts (ŭn'kə lĕk'tə bəl ə kounts') *pl.n.* Another term for **bad debts**.

understandable (ŭn'dər stăn'də bəl) *adj.* Capable of being understood: *an understandable message.*

understandability (ŭn'dər stăn'də bĭl'ĭ tē) *n.* The quality of being comprehensible.

underwriter (ŭn'dər rī'tər) *n.* A person or company that helps to issue stock or other securities for a fee.

unearned (ŭn ûrnd') *adj.* **1.** Not gained by work or service: *unearned praise.* **2.** Not yet earned: *unearned interest.*

unearned revenues (ŭn ûrnd' rĕv'ə nōoz) *pl.n.* Revenues received in advance for which the goods will not be delivered or the services performed during the current accounting period; a liability account.

unemployment insurance tax (ŭn'ĕm ploi'mənt ĭn shŏor'əns tăks') *pl.* A federal or state tax that an employer pays, intended to pay for programs to help unemployed workers. See also **Federal Unemployment Tax** and **State Unemployment Tax**.

unequal cash flows (ŭn ē'kwəl kăsh' flōz') *pl.n.* Cash flow from an asset that may vary from one year to the next. See also **equal cash flows**.

unit (yōo'nĭt) *n.* **1.** A thing, person, group, or structure regarded as one part of a whole: *How many units does this bookcase come with?* **2.** A single group regarded as a distinct part within a larger group: *a sales unit.* **3.** A mechanical part or piece of equipment: *an air-conditioning unit.* **4.** A precisely defined quantity used as a standard for measuring quantities of the same kind: *The mile is a unit of distance.* **5.** A product: *How many shampoo units do we sell?*

unit cost analysis schedule (yōo'nĭt kôst' ə năl'ĭ sĭs skĕj'-ōol) *n.* A statement used to (1) accumulate all costs charged to the Work in Process Inventory account of each department or production process and (2) compute cost per equivalent unit for materials costs and conversion costs.

units-of-production method (yōo'nĭts əv prə dŭk'shən mĕth'əd) *n.* A way of depreciating long-term assets. This method allocates depreciation based on an asset's estimated productive ability. It is found by subtracting trade-in value from cost and dividing the result by total estimated units of production and then multiplying that figure by the number of units produced during the accounting period.

Universal Product Code (yōo'nə vûr'səl prŏd'əkt kōd') *n. Abbr.* **UPC** A computer code made up of a series of vertical bars of different widths. The code is printed on a product package and scanned at the time of purchase. This code makes it easy to use a computer to monitor what is available for sale and what needs to be replaced. Also called **bar code**.

unlimited (ŭn lĭm′ĭ tĭd) *adj.* **1.** Having no restrictions or limitations: *an unlimited travel budget.* **2.** Without qualification or exception: absolute: *unlimited power.*

unlimited liability (ŭn lĭm′ĭ tĭd lī′ə bĭl′ĭ tē) *n.* The responsibility of all the partners in a company for its debt. Each partner in a partnership is personally liable for all the debts of the partnership.

unpaid (ŭn pād′) *adj.* **1.** Not yet paid: *unpaid bills.* **2.** Working without being paid: *unpaid research assistants.*

unprofitable (ŭn prŏf′ĭ tə bəl) *adj.* **1.** Making no money: *an unprofitable restaurant venture.* **2.** Having no useful purpose: *an unprofitable discussion.*

unprofitable segment decision analysis (ŭn prŏf′ĭ tə bəl sĕg′mənt dĭ sĭzh′ən ə năl′ĭ sĭs) *n.* A decision analysis designed to help management decide whether to continue operating a segment or to discontinue its operations.

unrealized (ŭn rē′ə līzd′) *adj.* Not made actual or real: *unrealized sales.*

Unrealized Loss or Gain on Long-Term Investments (ŭn rē′ə līzd′ lôs′ ôr gān′ ŏn lông′tûrm′ ĭn vĕst′mənts) *n.* A balance sheet account (or contra-stockholders' equity account) for entering increases or decreases in the value of long-term investments.

unrecorded (ŭn′rĭ kôr′dĭd) *adj.* Not having been written down or otherwise noted: *unrecorded data.*

unrecorded expense (ŭn′rĭ kôr′dĭd ĭk spĕns′) *n.* Another term for **accrued expense**.

unrecorded revenue (ŭn′rĭ kôr′dĭd rĕv′ə nōō) *n.* Another term for **accrued revenue**.

unsecured (ŭn′sĭ kyŏŏrd′) *adj.* Not requiring a tangible asset or available cash: *an unsecured loan.*

unsecured bond (ŭn′sĭ kyŏŏrd′ bŏnd′) *n.* A bond issued on the general credit of a company. This type of bond does not pledge specific company assets as a guarantee of repayment. Also called **debenture bond**.

UPC *Abbr.* An abbreviation of Universal Product Code.

useful (yōōs′fəl) *adj.* **1.** Capable of performing or serving a function well: *A knife is a useful tool.* **2.** Having practical usefulness: *a useful person to have around.*

useful life (yōōs′fəl līf′) *n.* The length of time a long-term asset, such as machinery, can be expected to perform its function.

usefulness (yōōs′fəl nĭs) *n.* The quality of being relevant and reliable.

Vv

val. *Abbr.* An abbreviation of valuation.

valuation (văl′yōō ā′shən) *n. Abbr.* **val.** The process of determining the present value of a bond based on the current market interest rate. If the market interest rate is higher than the stated rate the bond pays, the present value of the bond will be less than its face value.

valuation issue (văl′yōō ā′shən ĭsh′ōō) *n.* A controversial issue in accounting that concerns how one assigns a monetary value to a business transaction. **GAAP** requires assigning a value that is the original, or historical, cost because it is verifiable, instead of assigning a value in terms of worth, which can change over time.

value (văl′yōō) *n.* **1.** How much money sthg. is worth: *the value of a classic automobile.* **2.** The usefulness of sthg. compared to its cost: *That winter coat is a good value.* **3.** A belief or principle that sbdy. uses to make judgments: *Her values are uncompromising.* —*tr.v.* **valued, valuing, values.** To regard (sthg.) as important: *The manager values everyone in the department.*

value-adding activity (văl′yōō ăd′ĭng ăk tĭv′ĭ tē) *n.* A production- or service-related activity that adds cost to a product, but, from a customer's perspective, also increases its value.

value-adding cost (văl′yōō ăd′ĭng kôst′) *n.* The cost of an operating activity that increases the market value of a product or service.

value chain (văl′yōō chān′) *n.* All functions (and related activities) in the development path of a product or service that contribute to its value and marketability.

variable (vâr′ē ə bəl *or* văr′ē ə bəl) *adj.* **1.** Capable of or likely to change: *variable hours.* **2.** In mathematics, having more than one possible value: *a variable number.* —*n.* **1.** Something that changes or has the potential to change: *We need to consider all the variables before making a decision.* **2.** A mathematical quantity that has more than one possible value or a symbol representing such a quantity.

variable budget (vâr′ē ə bəl bŭj′ĭt) *n.* Another term for **flexible budget**.

variable costing (vâr′ē ə bəl kôs′tĭng) *n.* A costing method that uses only the variable manufacturing costs for product costing and inventory valuation purposes (as contrasted with absorption costing, which uses all product costs). Also called **direct costing**.

variable costs (vâr′ē ə bəl kôsts′) *pl.n.* Total costs that change in direct proportion to changes in productive output or any other measure of volume.

variable manufacturing costs (vâr′ē ə bəl măn′yə făk′chər ĭng kôsts′) *pl.n.* Costs that increase or decrease in direct proportion to the number of units produced.

variable overhead (vâr′ē ə bəl ō′vər hĕd′) *n.* The portion of mixed or semivariable overhead costs that changes proportionately with some measure of activity or output.

variance (vâr′ē əns *or* văr′ē əns) *n.* The difference between standard costs and actual costs.

variance analysis (vâr′ē əns ə năl′ĭ sĭs) *n.* The process of computing the amounts and isolating the causes of differences between standard costs and actual costs.

voucher system

vender or **vendor** (věn'dər) *n.* A person or company that sells sthg: *We are looking for a new vendor for paper.*

vertical analysis (vûr'tĭ kəl ə năl'ĭ sĭs) *n.* A technique for analyzing financial statements that uses percentages to show the relationships of each stated item to the total, which is 100 percent of the figure in a single statement.

volume (vŏl'yo͞om *or* vŏl'yəm) *n.* **1.** Amount; quantity: *We need to increase the volume of our sales.* **2.** The loudness of a sound: *Turn up the volume of the radio.* **3.** A book, sometimes in a series: *How many volumes have you published?*

voting stock (vō'tĭng stŏk') *n.* Common stock for which each share of stock has one vote in periodic (usually annual) elections for directors of a corporation. Also called **stock.**

voucher (vou'chər) *n.* A written authorization prepared for each business expenditure when it becomes a liability or an obligation to pay.

voucher check (vou'chər chěk') *n.* A form of check, used in a voucher system, that describes the reason for issuing the check.

voucher register (vou'chər rěj'ĭ stər) *n.* The book of original entry in which vouchers are recorded after they have been approved.

voucher system (vou'chər sĭs'təm) *n.* Any system that gives documentary proof of and written authorization for business transactions.

Ww Yy Zz

wage (wāj) *n.* **1.** Payment for services of employees at an hourly rate: *the minimum wage.* **2. wages.** The money paid to or earned by workers: *on strike for higher wages.*

Wage and Tax Statement (wāj′ ən tăks′ stāt′mənt) *n.* Another term for **Form W-2.**

wage bracket (wāj′ brăk′ĭt) *n.* The range of money earned during a calendar year. The wage bracket of an individual determines his or her economic class.

wage-bracket tax tables (wāj′ brăk′ĭt tăks′ tā′bəlz) *pl.n.* A chart providing the amounts to be withheld for income taxes based on amounts of earnings and numbers of exemptions claimed.

Wages and Hours Law (wā′jĭz ənd ourz′ lô′) *n.* Another term for **Fair Labor Standards Act.**

waste time (wāst′ tīm′) *n.* A period of time lost in productivity, for example, when a machine is not working and must be repaired before work can continue.

wasting asset (wā′stĭng ăs′ĕt) *n.* Another term for **natural resource.**

weighted-average-cost method (wā′tĭd ăv′ər ĭj kôst′ mĕth′əd) *n.* An average cost method procedure for determining the cost of ending inventory under the periodic system. It is found by multiplying the weighted-average cost per unit by the number of remaining units. See also **average-cost method** and **moving average method.**

wholesale (hōl′ sāl′) *n.* The sale of goods in large quantities, especially to a person or company that plans to sell them at retail: *It was bought at wholesale.* —*adj.* **1.** Relating to the sale of goods in large quantities for resale: *wholesale prices.* **2.** Sold in large quantities, usually at a cost below that of retail: *wholesale merchandise.*

whole unit (hōl′ yōō′nĭt) *n.* A product that has been completed in a given period of time.

withdraw (wĭth drô′ *or* wĭth drô′) *v.* **withdrew, withdrawn, withdrawing, withdraws.** —*tr.* **1.** To take (sthg.) back or away; remove: *withdraw money from the bank.* **2.** To remove (sbdy./sthg.) from participation or consideration: *She withdrew her application for the job.* —*intr.* To remove oneself from participation: *I withdrew from one of my classes.*

withdrawal (wĭth drô′əl) *n.* **1.** The act of removing sthg. that has been deposited: *a bank withdrawal.* **2.** The taking of cash or other assets out of a business by the owner for his or her own use. A withdrawal is treated as a temporary decrease in owner's equity because it is anticipated that it will be offset by net income. Also called **drawing.** **3.** An account to record an owner's removal of assets from a company. **4.** The physical and mental reactions to stopping the use of an addictive substance: *He's going through caffeine withdrawal.*

withhold (wĭth hōld′ *or* wĭth hōld′) *tr.v.* **withheld, withholding, withholds.** **1.** To keep from giving, granting, or allowing (sthg.): *withhold privileges.* **2.** To deduct (withholding tax) from an employee's wages or salary.

withholding allowance (wĭth hōl′dĭng ə lou′əns) *n.* An amount of an employee's annual earnings not subject to income tax. Another term for **exemption.**

124

zero coupon bonds

withholding (tax) (wĭth hōl′dĭng (tăks′)) *n.* The amount of an employee's wages or salary withheld by the employer as payment of the employee's income tax.

without recourse (wĭth out′ rē′kôrs) *adv.* (of sbdy. who buys a company's accounts receivable [**factor**]) Obligated to bear losses from uncollectible accounts.

with recourse (wĭth′ rē′kôrs) *adv.* (of sbdy. who buys a company's accounts receivable [**factor**]) Able to collect losses on uncollectible accounts from the seller.

work cell (wûrk′ sĕl′) *n.* An independent production line that can perform all required operations efficiently and continuously. Also called **work island**.

workers' compensation insurance (wûr′kərz kŏm′pən sā′shən ĭn shoor′əns) *n.* This insurance, primarily paid for by the employer, provides benefits for employees who are injured or killed on the job. The rates vary according to the degree of risk inherent in the job. The plans may be sponsored by states or by private firms. The employer pays the premium in advance at the beginning of the year, based on the estimated payroll. The rates are adjusted after the exact payroll is known. Also called **workers' comp**.

working capital (wûr′kĭng kăp′ĭ tl) *n.* A measure of liquidity equal to the current assets on hand that can be used to continue business operations; total current assets minus total current liabilities.

working papers (wûr′kĭng pā′pərz) *pl.n.* Documents used by accountants to organize their work and to report the information in the financial statements.

Work in Process Inventory Control account (wûrk′ ĭn prŏs′ĕs ĭn′vən tôr′ē kən trōl′ ə kount′) *n.* An inventory account in which all manufacturing costs incurred and assigned to products being produced are recorded.

work island (wûrk′ ī′lənd) *n.* Another term for **work cell**.

work sheet (wûrk′ shēt′) *n.* A type of working paper used as a preliminary step in the preparation of financial statements.

write off (rīt′ ôf′) *tr.v.* **wrote off, written off, writing off, writes off.** To consider (sbdy./sthg.) as a loss or failure: *I haven't written him off yet. We can write off the bad debts.*

write-off (rīt′ôf′) *n., pl.* **write-offs.** An income tax deduction: *The cost of professional travel is a write-off.*

yield (yēld) *n.* The money returned by an investment.

zero coupon bonds (zîr′ō koō′pŏn bŏndz′) *pl.n.* Bonds that do not pay periodic interest but that promise to pay a fixed amount on the maturity date.

Accounting Abbreviations

ABA	American Bankers Association
ABC	Activity-based costing
ABM	Activity-based management
A/C, a/c, acct.	Account
ACRS (ā′kərz)	Accelerated Cost Recovery System
adj.	Adjustment
AICPA	American Institute of Certified Public Accountants
AMHS	Automated material handling system
A/P	Accounts payable
appt.	Appointment
APR	Annual percentage rate
A/R	Accounts receivable
ATM	Automated teller machine
auto.	Automatic
av., ave., avg.	Average
b., B.	Base
bd.	Bond
B/E	Bill of exchange
BE	Breakeven
bus.	Business
CAD (kăd)	Computer-aided design
CAD/CAM (**kăd′**kăm′)	Computer-aided design/computer-aided manufacturing
c.h., C.H.	Clearing-house or clearinghouse
chg.	1. Change 2. Charge
CIM	Computer integrated manufacturing (system)
cl.	1. Classification 2. Clearance

Accounting Abbreviations

class.	1. Classification
	2. Classified
CMA	Certified management accountant
CMS	Cost management system
CNC	Computer numerically controlled (machine)
co, co., Co.	Company
comp., cpd.	Compound
cont.	1. Continued
	2. Continue
contrib.	Contribution
corp.	Corporation
cp.	Coupon
CPA	Certified public accountant
cr.	Credit
C-V-P	Cost-volume-profit (analysis)
denom.	Denomination
dep.	1. Department
	2. Deposit
dept., dpt., D.	Department
EFT	Electronic funds transfer
EIC	Earned income credit
EIN	Employer Identification Number
EPS	Earnings per share
ESOP (ē′sŏp)	Employee stock ownership plan
ex., exch.	Exchange
FASB	Financial Accounting Standards Board
FICA (fī′kə)	Federal Insurance Contributions Act
FIFO (fī′fō)	First-in, first-out inventory method
FMS	Flexible manufacturing system
FOB, F.O.B., f.o.b.	Free on board
FUTA (fyōō′tə)	Federal Unemployment Tax Act

Accounting Abbreviations

GAAP	Generally accepted accounting principles
G&A	General and administrative (expense budget)
GASB	Governmental Accounting Standards Board
IASC	International Accounting Standards Committee
IMA	Institute of Management Accountants
int.	**1.** Interest **2.** Interim
IPO	Initial public offering (of common stock)
IRS	Internal Revenue Service
JIT	Just-in-time operating environment
JIT/FMS	Just-in-time/flexible manufacturing system
Jrnl.	Journal
LCM	Lower-of-cost-or-market rule
LIFO (lī′fō)	Last-in, first-out inventory method
ltd., Ltd., Ld.	**1.** Limited (sense 1) **2.** A limited company
MACRS (mā′kərz)	Modified Accelerated Cost Recovery System
MICR	Magnetic ink character recognition
MIS	Management information system
n.s.f., N.S.F., NSF	Not sufficient funds
NTS	Nontraffic-sensitive
P/E	price/earnings (ratio)
PERC (pûrk)	Preferred equity redemption convertible (stock)
PIN (pĭn)	Personal identification number
Post. Ref.	Posting Reference (column)

Accounting Abbreviations

prin.	**1.** Principal
	2. Principle
PVA	Process value analysis
R&D	Research and Development
SEC	Securities and Exchange Commission
SF	Sinking fund
SFAS	Statement of Financial Accounting Standards
SUTA (**soo′**ta)	State Unemployment Tax Act
TQM	Total quality management
treas.	**1.** Treasurer
	2. Treasury
TS	Traffic-sensitive costs
UPC	Universal Product Code
val.	Valuation